BASIC IDEAS OF

National Socialist Economic Policy

Gottfried Feder

Published by Invisible Empire Publishing LLC © 2026
Hardcover ISBN: 978-1-963591-13-2
Original Published Year 2023
New Edition Published Year 2026
Printed in the United States of America

INVISIBLE EMPIRE
PUBLISHING

Trigger/Offensive Content Warning and General Disclaimer:

Gottfried Feder (1883–1941) was the chief economic theorist of early National Socialism, whose ideas were foundational to the movement's anti-capitalist, socialist agenda. Known for his 1919 Manifesto for Breaking the Thralldom of Interest and a pivotal speech that inspired Adolf Hitler's political entry, Feder's economic vision influenced the 25-point program of the National Socialist German Workers' Party. His seminal work, German State on the National Socialist Foundation, was praised by Hitler as:

"The catechism of the movement."

CONTENTS

CONTENTS

FORWARD

Publisher's Forward

This edition of Basic Ideas of National Socialist Economy offers an in-depth exploration of the foundational economic ideas that shaped Germany's early 20th-century policies. Central to this work is the pioneering thought of Gottfried Feder, whose vision for a self-sustaining, community-oriented economy laid the groundwork for National Socialist economic theory. Yet, Feder's contributions alone do not tell the full story. In response to modern interest, we have enriched this volume with passages from other significant thinkers and figures who influenced Germany's economic landscape. This expanded approach presents a broader historical context and reveals how a unified vision of economic and social goals evolved into a unique model with enduring impact.

Our intent in this new edition is to provide readers with a comprehensive, accessible entry into the principles that guided these policies. It is designed to illuminate not only the ideals and strategies of Feder but also the collaborative efforts of other contributors who shaped the political and economic narrative of the time. Readers will find here both foundational principles and detailed accounts of policy directives, each reflecting the distinct perspective of key figures whose ideas have shaped economic thought in varied ways.

Translator's Forward

Translating Basic Ideas of National Socialist Economy posed a unique challenge: preserving the original tone, accuracy, and intent while making the language accessible to today's readers. Feder's writing style, combined with the contributions of other influential National Socialists in this volume, represents a diverse array of perspectives and philosophical depths, each demanding careful handling in translation. This new edition honors their voices while providing clarity for those who wish to understand the origins and implications of these economic theories.

Our aim has been to capture the authenticity and rigor of the original texts, allowing readers to engage fully with the ideals and policies that defined this distinct economic model. By presenting Feder's ideas alongside those of his contemporaries, this translation seeks to offer a complete view of the economic principles that underpin the movement. It is our hope that this edition will serve as a valuable resource for both historical scholars and anyone interested in the ideological and economic constructs of this period.

PREFACE

At Weimar in 1926, the Council of the Party published a series of pamphlets, dealing in a concise form with the fundamental questions affecting every aspect of political life in Germany. Our intention was, and is, to present a consistent and complete picture of the attitude of National Socialism towards the various tasks of our public life, and of how it hopes to remove its errors and defects.

Our task is therefore to examine exhaustively how it stands, then to enquire scientifically whence it originated, and finally, with creative inspiration, to answer the fateful question, what then? The high aim of these pamphlets is to show new methods for the life of the State, for finance and economics; to set on high a 'rocher de bronze' during the chaos, to form a stock of apparent knowledge by close study, so that out of it all may emerge a united political will.

At the great meeting on August 31st, 1927, Adolf Hitler declared emphatically: "Questions of Program do not affect the Council of Administration; the Program is fixed, and I shall never suffer changes in the principles of the movement, as laid down in its Program." With this decisive pronouncement by our Führer, I associate myself whole-heartedly, for nothing is more dangerous to the life and striking force of a movement such as ours, than that, as time goes on, its fixed Program should be subjected to negative criticism.

No man who feels that he cannot go the whole way with us in the Jewish question, in our fight against high finance, the Dawes Pact and the pauperizing policy, or in questions in our Program, or is inclined to barter the liberty of the German nation through the League of Nations, the Locarno Pact, by compromise and cowardice, need apply to us; his place is outside the N.S.D.A.P. We utterly reject the 'superior private knowledge' which such as he is so ready to air in platform oratory and journalistic out-pouring.

A man who agrees with our principles might have scruples about a few minor details, for we cannot expect ever gone to agree absolutely on all questions, especially in an aggressive political movement.

It is, however, a different matter when political enemies make mincemeat of someone Point by odious misrepresentation quite beside the point, as has indeed happened. In such a case, an official commentary is necessary.

We refuse to vary our program for reasons of expediency, as other parties do, to suit so-called altered conditions. We intend to make conditions suit our program by mastering them.

Adolf Hitler has commissioned me to issue this series of pamphlets, which are to form the official literature of the Party.

I have included the official Manifesto of the Party on March 6th, 1930; also, my reply to ten questions set us by the Deutsche Tageszeitung, the leading organ of the Reichslandbund. That newspaper accepted my replies.

This is the best and most effective way to dispose of all the lies about our ill-disposition towards ownership and inheritance of landed property in Germany.

CHAPTER

1

GOTTFRIED FEDER

Gottfried Feder (***January 27th, 1883, Würzburg, Germany September 24th, 1941, Murnau***), was a German political activist who was the principal economic theoretician of the initial phase of German National Socialism.

Feder, a civil engineer, gained notoriety in 1919 for his book 'Manifesto for Breaking the Thralldom of Interest, and his speech before a German Workers' Party meeting at Munich in September of that year provided the immediate inspiration for Adolf Hitler's entry into politics. Feder's socialist and anti-capitalist ideas subsequently found expression in Hitler's 25-point program for the National Socialist German Workers' Party (***NSDAP***) in March 1920, as well as in Feder's own book, 'German State on the National Socialist Foundation', considered by Hitler to be "the catechism of the

(National Socialist) movement." Between 1924 and 1936 Feder sat in the German Reichstag and served as chairman of the N.S.D.A.P. economic council (*1931*), state secretary of the German Ministry of Economics (*1933*), and state housing commissioner (*1934*). With the general accommodation of National Socialist policy to the existing economic system, however, Feder's role in party affairs drastically diminished, and by 1936, he had been relegated to virtual obscurity.

The Program of the National Socialist German Worker's Party and its General Conceptions.

CHAPTER

2

A HISTORICAL ACCOUNT

The Rise of the N.S.D.A.P. with a Biographical Survey of the Career of Adolf Hitler.

Adolf Hitler was born on April 20th, 1889, at Braunau at the Inn, a village of the old Bavaria.

His father was the orphaned child of a poor peasant and worked his way up to be a Customs Official. His mother came from a German peasant family. When he was 13 years old, he lost his father, and four years later his mother. Adolf Hitler was then a scholar at the Realschuıe at Linz on the Danube, after leaving the National School. It had been his father's wish that he should become an official, but his desire was to be an artist. His mother's death obliged him without further delay earning his own living.

At 17 years old, Hitler went to Vienna, where he aimed to become an architect. He earned a living by his own efforts, first as a builder's laborer, mixing the mortar, then as an architect's draughtsman. At 18 years old, he was already taking an interest in politics; he became anti-Marxist, but so far took no leading part. From his earliest youth Hitler had been passionately nationalist, and he hoped to combine the social experiences of his working period with his nationalist convictions. For several years, he lived in Vienna in extreme poverty.

In 1912, he migrated to Munich, where he was a student. He had never known youthful enjoyments, but ever since the day when he left home with 50 kronen in his pocket, labor and privation had been his lot. In February 1914, he succeeded in getting free from the obligation to serve in the Austrian Army. Six months later, war broke out. He immediately volunteered for service in the German Army, and obtained, by a direct appeal to King Ludwig of Bavaria, permission to enter a Bavarian regiment as a volunteer for the war. On October 10th, 1914, the new regiment marched forth.

On December 2nd, 1914, the 25-year-old volunteer was awarded the Iron Cross, 2nd Class.

In recognition of his bravery in the attack on the 'Bayernwald' and in the other engagements near Wytschaete, he was ordered to take on duty as a dispatch-carrier, which demanded especial courage and reliability, for reports had often to be carried across open ground under heavy fire. This quickly made his name known throughout the regiment beyond the narrow circle of his comrades.

On October 7th, 1916, a shell splinter wound him. In March 1917, he returned to his regiment. He received several other distinctions, including a Regiments-Diploma for special bravery in the fights near Fontaines, and finally the Iron Cross, Class I.

On October 14th, 1918, he was severely injured along with many comrades in his regiment by the Mustard Gas, which the British were then using for the first time, and he was temporarily blinded. Whilst he was in hospital, the Revolution broke out. On this, Hitler resolved to become a politician. In 1919, he joined with a small party comprising 6 men and on it he founded the National Socialist German Workers' Party. He drew up in outline of the Program of the new movement and settled its character and aims.

CHAPTER 3

SEVEN MEN

In September 1919, Adolf Hitler made his first speech to seven men; he then addressed audiences of 11, 25, 47; in December 111; in January 1920, 270, and shortly afterwards 400. On November 14th, 1920, he spoke at a mass-meeting of 1700. He now organized the propaganda of the young Party, which after a year's work numbered 64 members. A year later 1920, it had already reached 3000. Hitler's propagandist activity in Munich was such that he was finally addressing mass-meetings three times a week, and on Mondays, he carried on a course of instruction. He attacked foremost the folly of Versailles, and denied the assertions of the Marxists, the Centre Party, etc. that it was possible to fulfill that Treaty. He attacked and ridiculed the slogan of these parties "Give up your arms, and the others will also disarm." He spoke on the assumption that after arms had been given up by us, the rest would continue to arm, if not with their own money, then with the millions wrung from the completely disarmed German nation. Whilst opposing the propaganda of the S.P.D. and Centre in favor of signing the Treaty, he prophesied the Ruhr would be occupied, whatever we signed.

1921

This year was marked by the foundation of the first local groups in Rosenheim and Landshut. Hitler organized the first body of men to protect the Party and began his fight against the Separatist movement in Bavaria. Our leader also addressed a meeting of over 5000 in the Circus in Munich.

He declared at his meetings that fulfillment of the Treaty would not help, as the S.P.D., Centre and Volkspartei asserted, to build up German prosperity in peace, but that the result of that foolish policy was bound to be inflation on a large scale, involving immense injury to German industry. Hitler's assertion that the black-red Government was planning to denationalize the State Railways was declared to be a 'bare-faced lie'. An attempt at a revolt within the Party was defeated. Hitler drafted the new Constitution of the Party, which gave him dictatorial powers.

Social Democracy, which could not continue to ignore the name of Hitler, now attempted to get rid of its bug bear by methods of terrorism. There were bloodshed and collisions at the meetings, in which our leader's iron nerves maintained the upper hand. We formed an invincible bodyguard during them, which thenceforward was named the 'Sturmabteilung'.

1922

Whilst the conquest of Munich was proceeding, the movement was spreading throughout the rest of Bavaria. Hitler rejected all overtures, through compromise, to join up with other parties. He gradually destroyed all similar 'nationalist' party formations and made the National Socialist movement supreme over them.

In October 1922, Hitler marched at the head of 800 men to Coburg, and in twice 24 hours for the first time utterly crushed the Red Terror in that town.

Adolf Hitler declared then publicly that we were rushing headlong toward inflation, which he had foreseen as the result of the policy of the black-red coalition. He became known as the most dangerous and best hated enemy of the system. Social Democracy and the Centre Party ceased defending themselves by argument and adopted a policy of defamation.

1923

In January 1923, the first great Party Conference was held, and the first banners of the Party were consecrated. The Sturmabteilung was formally incorporated.

The Party propaganda was exhaustively studied and improved, and the permanent principles of the organization were settled and established. Adherents gathered round Hitler in large numbers, most of whom are today his steadfast partners in the struggle. The attacks on him were, meanwhile, pursued with increasing determination; he found himself in prison for the first time on the charge of disturbing the meetings of his adversaries; he was constantly fined. He never, for one moment, ceased fighting against the system.

During the summer of 1923, Adolf Hitler broke down the Red Terror in most of the towns in Bavaria; Ratisbon, Hof, Bayreuth, Nürnberg, Fürth, Ingolstadt, Würzburg, Schweinfurt, often at the cost of bloodshed in street fights, in which he defeated the Social-democratic and Communist terrorist bands.

His struggle against the incompetent Government of the Reich was accompanied by bitter accusations. He prophesied the ill-success of the Government's feeble resistance in the matter of the Ruhr, and constantly attacked the stupid policy of an understanding with France, and that of fulfillment. He never failed to point out the necessity of an understanding with England and Italy.

In November 1923, Adolf Hitler made his attempt to overthrow the system. The rising failed, and Hitler was arrested.

1924

The great trial took place in Munich in March 1921. Though he was found guilty of the facts, our leader achieved overwhelming moral justification. Hitler's defense influenced the Court so much, and his assumption of sole and exclusive responsibility was so convincing that the speech of the counsel indicting him turned into a remarkable testimony to his honorable motives. The Judge, however, condemned him to a period of detention.

The National Socialist Party suffered by the loss of its leader. Its adversaries were convinced that the movement was done for, and took courage to sign the infamous Dawes Pact, thus deliberately starting the system of the plundering of Germany which was brought to a head in the Young Plan. What a triumph for the Social Democrats and the Centre! The aim of the enslavement of Germany was apparently achieved!

In vain, Hitler tried, through his associates, who were at liberty, to put up a fight against the Dawes Pact. In, vain he made them declare in public that the assurances of the Centre Party, the S.P.D. and the Volkspartei, that the foreign loans under the Plan would increase national prosperity that unemployment would cease, that wages would be raised, and taxes reduced, that agriculture would be saved, were merely a deception of the nation. In vain, he made them point out that the Dawes Pact was bound to increase poverty, since the interest on the loans would cripple industry, whilst the loans themselves merely served the purpose of fulfilling the financial obligations under the Plan; bankruptcy and unemployment would increase, wages would sink, prices and taxation would rise still further, and the farmers would face utter ruin and be forced to part with all they possessed.

On December 20th Hitler quitted the fortress.

1925

By February 27th, 1925, Adolf Hitler's call for the re-birth of the Party went forth, and he made his first speech after his imprisonment before an audience of 4000 people.

The National Socialist movement had been broken up after the events of November 9th, and all its property and money had been confiscated so that Adolf Hitler now started with nothing in hand to rebuild the Party from its foundations. Vorwärts and Germania in Berlin made fun of his efforts and mocked at the "fool whom imprisonment had made mad." The reconstruction of the Party proceeded with great rapidity under Hitler's leadership. The old leaders gathered faithfully round him once more. Hitler stimulated the Party press into fresh activity.

By December 1925, the Party numbered 27,000 members. The Centre and the Social Democrats in alarm decreed that the leader should not speak in public for two years.

1926

June of this year saw the first conference of the Party since Hitler's imprisonment.

The bourgeois world was still convinced that the policy of fulfillment would save Germany and that the Dawes Pact would revive industry. The Marxists were convinced that their domination was unshakable.

President von Hindenburg separated from his supporters and marched off with the Centre and S.P.D. The Party carried on the struggle; by the end of the year, it numbered 49,000 members.

1927

The order forbidding Hitler to speak in public was withdrawn, since it was found impossible to enforce it. He addressed numbers of mass meetings. Each month saw the Party more and more firmly consolidated.

Developments all round proved with greater and greater force that Hitler had been right. The Dawes Pact was unmasked, and its consequences were terrific. The Social Democrats and Centre Party attempted to save what might be saved through lies and abuse.

In August, Hitler summoned a Party Conference at Nürnberg, which proved a great success. By the end of the year, the Party numbered 72,000 members.

1928

Adolf Hitler led his party in an intensified assault on the existing system. National Socialism was now the inexorable enemy of the destroyers of Germany within and without. Hitler directed his attack especially against the senseless ruining of the farmers and middle classes. He prophesied the catastrophe which would fall upon the home markets. He declared at hundreds of meetings again and again that the policy of fulfillment was lunacy, and that its consequences would mean death and ruin to German industry. The Social Democrats and Centre mocked and jeered in their attempt to get their revenge. Their lies and abuse were directed at Hitler personally.

By the end of the year, the membership numbered 108,000, and 12 members of the Party sat in the Reichstag.

1929

Adolf Hitler continued his fight with the existing system with untiring energy. The Press of the Party was perfected. The Sturmabteilung increased, the Formations strengthened, and the propaganda intensified. The doctrines of National Socialism penetrated deeply into the national consciousness.

On August 4th, the second Party Conference took place at Nürnberg on a tremendous scale. Hitler attacked the black-red system with ever-increasing energy and stood forth without a rival as the most powerful leader against all that was meant by 'Democracy'. All attempts to oust him from the leadership of the Party were crushed.

By the end of the year, the Party numbered 178,000 members.

1930

The struggle against the Young Plan was in full swing. Hindenburg defended it with energy, asserting that by its Germany would be saved, that German industry would revive, that unemployment would be stemmed, that the farmers would breathe again, and that it would be possible to lighten taxation.

Adolf Hitler described such views as unreal and fatal; he prophesied the contrary. His Party enlightened the nation amidst severe fighting. The opponents replied with a stream of lies.

The Elections to the Reichstag took place on September 14th, 1930. The Party polled 6,5 million votes, and 107 members were elected. Its internal organization was stronger than ever. A few minor attempts at revolt, promoted from outside, were promptly crushed by Hitler, and expelled those who would not submit unconditionally.

The Centre Party, which had now delivered itself into the hands of the S.P.D. for good or ill, excited the Church against Hitler. Bishops and Priests, belonging to the Centre Party, started a fanatical attack against the National Socialist movement, excommunicated its adherents, and even refused them Christian burial. Hitler held unshakably to his conviction that the Centre spelt ruin for Germany and continued his fight against it with even greater determination than before. He sternly rejected any attempt to extort some modification of his opinions from him.

By the end of the year, the Party numbered 389,000 members.

1931

The fight against the Young Plan continued. The consequences foreseen by Hitler became a reality.

The Government administrated through emergency measures, thinking thus to save industry. Sharp disputes followed, in which Adolf Hitler again pointed out the fatal consequences of that policy. In a few months, a few weeks, even he was proved right.

Meanwhile, numbers of National Socialist newspapers had started into life, and the central publishing office of the Party had gradually grown to be a vast enterprise. The organization had become highly efficient, and the Sturmabteilung had, in course of time, reached a high stage of development.

Our opponents wallowed in lies and were allowing orders for goods to be placed in France.

By the end of the year 1931, the membership of the Hitler Party attained to 806,000, a month later to 862,000, and again a month later to 920,000. On the day of the Election there were something like a million members, and untold millions of supporters at the Polls.

The man who was once a poor worker and later a soldier at the front has thus in barely thirteen years-built op the greatest political organization which Germany has ever seen. The sole resources against this man which his opponents can employ are lies and defamation. And he has always won so far, despite all the lies, and this time he has come near to being elected President of the Reich.

Has anyone in the entire history of Germany ever accomplished a similar achievement in twelve years, in face of opposition from Party, high finance, Capital, Press, public opinion, bureaucracy, lies, terrorism, and persecution?

This was no sheltered child; from his earliest years, he has been a man in the highest sense of the word, relying solely on his own strength.

CHAPTER 4

POLICY & POSITION ON AGRICULTURE

Farming Class & Agriculture

The German nation derives a considerable portion of their food from importation of foreign foodstuffs. Before the world War we paid for these imports with our industrial exports, our trade, and our deposits of capital abroad. The outcome of the war put an end to this possibility.

Today we are paying for our imported food mostly with the help of foreign loans, which drive the German nation deeper and deeper in debt to the international financiers who provide credits. If things go on as they are, the German people will become more and more impoverished.

The only possibility of escaping from this thralldom lies in the ability of

Germany to produce essential foodstuffs at home. Increased production by German agriculture is therefore a question of life and death for the German nation.

A country population, economically sound and highly productive, is essential for our industry, which will in future have more and more to look for openings in the home market.

We also regard the country's population as the bearer of the inheritance of health, the source of the nation's youth, and as the backbone of its armed strength.

Maintenance of an efficient agricultural class, increasing in numbers as the general population increases, is an essential plank on the National Socialist platform, because our movement considers the welfare of all our people in the generations to come.

Neglected Farming Class & Agriculture

Agricultural production, which can be augmented, is being handicapped, because the increasing indebtedness of the farmers prevents their purchasing the necessities of cultivation, and because farming does not pay removes the inducement to increase production.

The reasons farming cannot give a sufficient return for the labor are to be sought:

1. In the existing fiscal policy, which lays undue burdens on agriculture. This is due to party considerations, and because the Jewish world money market which really controls parliamentary democracy in Germany wishes to destroy German agriculture, since this would place the German nation, and especially the working class, at its mercy;

2. in the competition of foreign agriculturists, who work under more favorable conditions, and who are not held in check by a policy of protection for German agriculture;

3. in the extravagant profits made by the large wholesale middlemen, who thrust themselves in between producer and consumer.

4. in the oppressive rates the farmer must pay for electric power and artificial manures to concerns mainly run by Jews.

The high taxation cannot be met out of the poor return for labor on the land. The farmer is forced to run into debt and to pay usurious interest for loans. He sinks deeper and deeper under this tyranny, and in the end forfeits all that he possesses to the Jew moneylender. The German farming class is being expropriated.

Land Shall Be Respected

There can be no hope of any sweeping improvement in the conditions of poverty of the country population, or of a revival of agriculture, if the German Government is in fact controlled by the international money-magnates, helped by the parliamentary-democratic system of government; for these desires to destroy Germany's strength, which is based on the land.

In the new and very different German State, to which we aspire, the farmers and agriculture will receive the consideration which is due to them because they are a crucial support of a truly national German State.

From this, emerge the following requirements:

1. The land of Germany, acquired and defended by the German nation, must be at the service of the German nation, as a home and as a means of livelihood. Those who occupy the land must administer it in this sense.
2. Only members of the German nation may possess land.
3. Land legally acquired by them shall be inheritable property. To the right to hold property, however, is attached the obligation to use it in the national interest. Special Courts shall be appointed to oversee this obligation; these shall comprise representatives from all departments of the land-holding class, and one representative of the State.
4. German land may not become an object of financial speculation, nor may it provide an unearned income for its owner. It may only be acquired by him who is prepared to cultivate it himself. Therefore, the State has a right of preemption on every sale of land. It is forbidden to pledge land to private lenders. The loans for cultivation on easy terms will be granted to farmers either by associations recognized by the State, or by the State itself.
5. Dues will be paid to the State for the use of land according to the extent and quality of the property. This tax on land will obviate any further taxation of landed property.

6. No hard and fast rule can be laid down as to the amount of cultivation. From the point of view of our population policy, we require large numbers of small and middle-sized farms. Farming on a large scale, however, has a very essential part to play, and, if it preserves a healthy relation towards the smaller businesses, it is justifiable.
7. A law of inheritance will be required to prevent sub-division of property and an accumulation of debt upon it.
8. The State shall have the right to appropriate land; suitable compensation being granted:

   A-8 | When not owned by a member of the nation;

   B-8 | When by a judgment of the Land Courts it is held that its owner, by bad farming, is not acting in the national interest;

   C-8 | For the purpose of settling independent farmers on it, when the owner is not cultivating it himself;

   D-8 | When it is required for special State purposes in the national interest (*e.g., communications, national defense*). Land acquired illegally (according to German law) may be confiscated without compensation.
9. It is the duty of the State to colonize land which has become available, by a scheme based on foremost considerations of a policy of population. The land shall be allotted to settlers as a hereditary possession under conditions which shall make a livelihood possible. Settlers shall be selected by examination as to their civic and professional suitability. Special favor shall be shown to sons of farmers who have not the right to inherit.

Colonization of the eastern frontiers is of extreme importance. Here, the mere establishment of farms will not be sufficient, but it will be necessary to set up market towns in connection with the new branch of industry. This is the only way to provide an opening for making the smaller farms a paying proposition.

It will be the duty of Germany's foreign policy to provide large spaces for the nourishment and settlement of the growing population of Germany.

Farming Class Economics & Education

1. The present poverty of the land population must be at once relieved by remissions of taxation and other emergency measures. Further indebtedness must be stemmed by reducing the rate of interest on loans to that of the pre-war period by law, and by summary action against extortion.

2. It must be the State's policy to see that farming will be made to pay. German agriculture must be protected by tariffs, State regulation of imports, and a scheme of national training.

   The settlement of prices for agricultural produce must be freed from market speculation, and a stop must be put to exploitation of the agricultural interest by the large middlemen, the transfer of whose business to agricultural associations must be encouraged by the State.

   It shall be such professional organizations to reduce the running expenses of farmers and increase production. (*Provision of implements, manures, seed, breeding stock on favorable conditions, improvements, war against vermin, free advice, chemical research, etc.*) The State shall provide full assistance to the organizations in carrying out their task. In particular, the State must insist on a considerable reduction in the cost to farmers of artificial manures and electric power.

3. The organizations must also establish the class of farm laborers as members of the farming community by contracts which are just in the social sense. Supervision and arbitration in these matters will be the function of the State. It must be made possible for good laborers to rise to the status of farm-owners. The much called for improvement in living conditions and wages of farm laborers will ensue as soon as the general farming situation improves. When these conditions take a turn for the better, it will be no longer necessary to employ foreign labor on the land, and this custom will in future be forbidden.

4. The national importance of the farming class requires that the State shall promote technical education in agriculture. (*Juvenile institutions, high schools for agriculture, with very favorable terms for youths with talent but no means.*)

National Socialist German Workers' Party Defends the Farming Class

Adolf Hitler:

The country's population is poor because the whole German nation is poor. It is an error to imagine that one single class of workers can escape sharing the fortunes of the German community, and a crime to make jealousies between town folk and country folk, who are bound together for good or ill.

Economic assistance under the present political system cannot produce a permanent improvement, for political slavery is at the root of our people's poverty, and political methods alone can remove that.

The old political parties, which were, and are, responsible for the national enslavement, cannot be the leaders on the road to freedom.

There are important economic tasks awaiting professional organizations in our future State; even now they can do much preparatory work in that direction; but for the political struggle of liberation, which is to lay the foundation of a new economic order, they are not suitable; for that struggle will have to be fought out from the point of view not of a single profession, but from that of the whole nation.

The movement which will carry through the political struggle for liberation to the end is the NSDAP.

CHAPTER 5

POLICY ON OWNERSHIP OF LAND & PROPERTY

The Deutsche Tageszeitung (No. 47) of January 25th, 1930, published several questions put to us by the leaders of the Brandenburg Landbund. Their main object was to obtain a definition of the attitude of the NSDAP towards private ownership of land, inheritance, raising of credits, tariffs, price regulation, profit-sharing, and towards questions of general social-political and election-tactical interest.

I.

To allay anxiety about any later arbitrary interpretation of Point 17 of the Party Program, the first question was put in the following words: "Is the NSDAP prepared to give a guarantee that it will not set its face against ownership of land?"

Answer: National Socialism recognizes private ownership as a principle and places it under State protection. It will seek to maintain a healthy combination of all businesses, small and great, in the economic life of the nation.

The spirit of the entire Program proves clearly that National Socialism, being a convinced and consistent opponent of Marxism, utterly rejects its ruinous central doctrine of general confiscation, and considers a permanent agricultural class to be the best and surest foundation for the national State.

But being also a determined opponent of the great capitalists whose aim it is to mobilize for themselves all agricultural values, and to oust the farmers through taxation and interest on loans, National Socialism demands State protection of the farmers against aggression by the big business interests.

We need a strong, healthy class of farmers, free from the thralldom of interest and the tyranny of taxation.

II.

The second question was addressed to me personally, as having been appointed by Hitler 'ultimate arbiter of all questions touching the Program'. "What is the attitude of National Socialism towards inheritance of property and succession duties?" Answer: Since it is the mainstay of the national idea, continuity of ownership, i.e., inheritance of the land, which a man's forefathers reclaimed and cultivated, is a natural consequence. National Socialism therefore recognizes the principle of inheritance, as it does that of ownership of land.

If property goes to distant relatives, the National Socialist State will levy a special tax, but in the case of nearer relationship this will be assessed at the rate prevailing now.

III.

This question was set owing to anxiety quite unfounded regarding the consequences of prohibiting loans from private capitalists on the security of the land. Answer: A State, which desires to make agricultural property free from debt, and to rescue the farmers from the claws of professional financiers so many farmers having been, as it is, driven from their homes by the Jews, a State, which desires to break down the money monopoly of capitalism and to abolish the thralldom of interest, is not likely to withhold the credits nor to charge extortionate interest; National Socialism intends to assist agriculture to the utmost.

IV.

"Breaking down the thralldom of interest." Abolition of unearned incomes. "What is the attitude of the National Socialist Party towards capital saved or inherited?" Answer: Has any farmer today an 'unearned income' out of demands for interest, or can any landowner live on money saved from his rents? This means that there is anxiety among certain landowners who still have a little capital left, or else there is intentional miscomprehension or ignorance of that most essential demand of the National Socialist Program.

N. B. We mean literally "breaking down the thralldom of interest." No one will describe small amounts of interest from savings or a mortgage or a government loan as the thralldom of interest. What we mean by it is when deliberate inflation has robbed us of all our savings, and the farmer must pay interest on fresh mortgages and short-term credits at rates which ruin him.

Those who favor of sticking to the present system of capitalism are against the true interests of the farmers, and in favor of allowing the banks and their agents to batten on agriculture. For the rest, I would refer readers to my pamphlets entitled Der Staat auf nationaler und sozialer Grundlage, and Das Programm der NSDAP (The German State on the National Socialist Foundation and the Program of the NSDAP).

V.

Our policy as regards taxation states clearly and consistently: To free the consumer from

the burden of indirect taxation, and the producer from taxes, which cramp his business.

"Does the Party intend to remove import duties?"

Answer: The Landbund ought to know that the National Socialist vote in the Reichstag went absolutely in favor of protective duties on agricultural produce, under its principal protection of the nation's work in town and country.

VI.

The question of Profit-sharing. It is impossible here to deal with this wide and difficult subject. In my weekly journal, Die Flamme, I have described our attitude in several articles.

The article in the Deutsche Tageszeitung is misleading, since it removes from their context the sentences which it quotes. I consider that profit-sharing in the general sense of the capitalist and Marxist schools of ideas is not the correct solution. On this subject, our program refers to workers in factories, and there is no point in attempting to clear up the question in a pamphlet dealing with agriculture.

VII.

Extension of Old Age Insurance Benefits.

"How is it proposed to raise the funds for this purpose?"

Answer: There is provision now for Old Age Insurance, but it is in many cases insufficient, and is regarded as pauperization. Once the burden of taxation is removed, and those who are now unemployed but able to work are restored to the economic sphere, there will be a sufficient means for providing ample Old-Age benefits for those who are past work.

VIII, IX, X.

These are merely questions to do with party tactics, and not with any principle. Opposing a coalition which has brought unhappiness to Germany, we have naturally now and again to vote with the Communists (although a entire world divides us from them), just as the German National and the Christian National Farmers do. We allow no one to dictate to us where we get our adherents from, but we turn to all workers, bourgeois and farmers who have a good German heart in their bodies' and are men of good will, and desire to see an end of Parliamentary misgovernment and the wretched policy of fulfillment (of the Peace Treaties). We do not consider that 'social communication' with other parties is a proper method of freeing the German nation from Marxism and Parliamentarianism, for that leads to political bargaining. Nothing but dictatorial action and determined exercise of power can pull Germany out of the mud.

The nation wants not fine words, but forcefulness; not bargaining, but solid work for our poor, down-trodden nation.

A full and clear account of the foregoing is given in No. 19 of the National Socialist collection Unser täglich Brot: Basic Questions of German Agriculture; by Hermann Schneider, Eckersdorf, Kreis Namslau, regarding the whole policy of National Socialism with respect to agriculture. It contains well-conceived proposals for re-establishing the suffering farming class of Germany.

No. 16, by Dr. Buchner, contains an excellent essay on the meaning and spirit of our economic policy.

No. 12, by Colonel Hierl, describes our policy of national defense.

We shall conclude with a few remarks on certain questions which our political enemies misrepresent spitefully and untruthfully hoping to do us an injury.

Our attitude towards the permanent official class is surely a worthy one. We should not be such whole-hearted admirers of the great King of Prussia if we were against this class. What the Army was abroad, a pure, incorruptible official class, was for the State at home. Honor and duty must once again become essential qualities in our officials. The officials, who are at the beck and call of the Reds and the Blacks, will disappear in the coming State; such party wirepullers have no use for honor and duty.

The suggestion that the National Socialists are against the officials and intend to reduce their pay and do away with pensions, is a political lie, which has been circulated by the Press of our opponents. We desire to grant to all members of the nation who have served Germany faithfully all of their lifelong pensions of honor, which will relieve them of cares in their old age. It is only thus that social assistance will be freed from the stigma of making a person or group very poor 'Impoverished'.

We must also refer to the extension of the pension idea to the independent trades and handworkers. There is no need to worry about how we are to raise funds for the purpose. When we cease paying thousands of millions abroad each year, and still more to our own banking houses, a fraction of those sums will pay for Old Age Pensions.

Unemployment Assistance & Insurance

It is not the affair of the State to support with State funds by men who are able to work. Our attitude towards the present system of assistance for those who cannot earn a living has never altered; we have always pressed in Parliament for better conditions for the unemployed. This we do, not because we think it a right state of things, but because a government like the present one, whose idiotic foreign and domestic policy has carried labor, food production and all commerce to the edge of the abyss, is in duty bound to let its policy go by the board.

A State which cannot reinstate millions of men who can work in this economic world deserves to be swept away; so, if it fails financially, to meet the problem of assistance to unemployment, we merely shrug our shoulders.

The various attacks on the system of the dole, even if justified when they refer to cases of abuse of this social assistance, fail to turn us from the principle we believe in. Granted that, amongst nearly 3,000,000 unemployed there may be 2 or 300,000 notorious slackers who would readily return to work if the dole were removed, we must not forget that there remain at least 2,5 million good workers, employees, engineers, technicians, foremen, clerks, etc. seeking desperately for work and unable to find it. It is owing to the failure of our thoroughly unsound State policy that it is impossible to make any change in the miserable unemployed dole.

Attacks on Religion and the Clergy

We cannot declare too often that the NSDAP is not dreaming of attacking the Christian religion and its worthy servants.

It is the corrupting policy of the Centre and the Bavarian People's Party which we attack; these lose no opportunity of crying "Church in Danger" except when they are making common cause with the atheist, God-denying Social Democracy.

It is because we have so high and holy an ideal of man's relation to-wards his God that we hate to see religion besmirched with the dirt of political conflict.

CHAPTER

6

THE 25 POINTS

The National Socialist German Workers' Party at a great mass-meeting on February 25th, 1920, in the Hofbräuhaus-Festsaal in Munich, announced their Program to the world.

In section 2 of the Constitution of our Party, this Program is declared to be inalterable.

The Program

The Program of the German Workers' Party is limited as to period the leaders have no intention, once the aims announced in it have been achieved, of setting up fresh ones, merely to increase the discontent of the masses artificially, and so ensure the continued existence of the Party.

1. We demand the union of ail Germans to form a Great Germany based on the right of the self-determination enjoyed by nations.
2. We demand equality of rights for the German People in its dealings with other nations, and abolition of the Peace Treaties of Versailles and St. Germain.
3. We demand land and territory (colonies) for the nourishment of our people and for settling our superfluous population.
4. None but members of the nation may be citizens of the State. None but those of German blood, whatever their creed, may be members of the nation. No Jew, therefore, may be a member of the nation.
5. Anyone who is not a citizen of the State may live in Germany only as a guest and must be regarded as being subject to foreign laws.
6. The right of voting on the State's government and legislation is to be enjoyed by the citizen of the State alone. We demand therefore that all official appointments, of whatever kind, whether in the Reich, in the country, or in the smaller localities, shall be granted to citizens of the State alone. We oppose the corrupting custom of Parliament of filling posts merely with a view to party considerations, and without reference to character or capability.
7. We demand that the State shall make it its first duty to promote the industry and livelihood of citizens of the State. If it is not possible to nourish the entire population of the State, foreign nationals (non-citizens of the State) must be excluded from the Reich.
8. All non-German immigration must be prevented. We demand that all non-Germans, who entered Germany after August 2nd, 1914, shall be required forthwith to depart from the Reich.
9. All citizens of the State shall be equal in regards rights and duties.
10. It must be the first duty of each citizen of the State to work with his mind or with his body. The activities of the individual may not clash with the interests of the whole but must proceed within the frame of the community and be for the general good.

We demand therefore:

11. Abolition of incomes unearned by work. Abolition of the Thralldom of Interest.
12. In view of the enormous sacrifice of life and property demanded of a nation by every war, personal enrichment due to a war must be

regarded as a crime against the nation. We demand therefore ruthless confiscation of all war gains.

13. We demand nationalization of all businesses which have been up to the present formed into companies (Trusts).
14. We demand that the profits from wholesale trade shall be shared out.
15. We demand extensive development of provision for old age.
16. We demand creation and maintenance of a healthy middle class, immediate communalization of wholesale business premises, and their lease at a cheap rate to small traders, and that extreme consideration shall be shown to all small purveyors to the State, district authorities and smaller localities.
17. We demand land-reform suitable to our national requirements, passing of a law for confiscation without compensation of land for communal purposes; abolition of interest on land loans, and prevention of all speculation in land.[1]
18. We demand ruthless prosecution of those whose activities are injurious to the common interest. Sordid criminals against the nation, usurers, profiteers, etc. must be punished with death, whatever their creed or race.
19. We demand that the Roman Law, which serves the materialistic world order, shall be replaced by a legal system for all Germany.
20. With the aim of opening to every capable and industrious German the possibility of higher education and of thus obtaining advancement, the State must consider a thorough re-construction of our national system of education. The curriculum of all educational establishments must be brought into line with the requirements of practical life. Comprehension of the State idea (State sociology) must be the school objective, beginning with the first dawn of intelligence in the pupil. We demand development of the gifted children of poor parents, whatever their class or occupation, at the expense of the State.
21. The State must see to raising the standard of health in the nation by protecting mothers and infants, prohibiting child labor, increasing bodily efficiency by obligatory gymnastics and sports laid down by law, and by extensive support of clubs engaged in the bodily development of the young.

22. We demand abolition of a paid army and formation of a national army.
23. We demand legal warfare against conscious political lying and its dissemination in the Press.

    To facilitate creation of a German national Press we demand:

    A. That all editors of newspapers and their assistants, employing the German language, must be members of the nation;

    B. That special permission from the State shall be necessary before non-German newspapers may appear. These are not necessarily printed in the German language;

    C. That non-Germans shall be prohibited by law from participation financially in or influencing German newspapers, and that the penalty for contravention of the law shall be suppression of any such newspaper, and immediate deportation of the non-German concerned in it. It must be forbidden to publish papers which do not conduce to the national welfare. We demand legal prosecution of all tendencies in art and literature of a kind likely to disintegrate our life as a nation, and the suppression of institutions which militate against the requirements above-mentioned.
24. We demand liberty for all religion's denominations in the State, so far as they are not a danger to it and do not militate against the moral feelings of the German race.

    The Party, as such, stands for positive Christianity, but does not bind itself in the matter of creed to any confession. It combats the Jewish-materialist spirit within us and without us, and is convinced that our nation can only achieve permanent health from within on the principle:

The Common Interest before Self.

25. That all the foregoing may be realized we demand the creation of a strong central power of the State. Unquestioned authority of the politically centralized Parliament over the entire Reich and its organization and formation of Chambers for classes and occupations for the purpose of carrying out the general laws promulgated by the Reich in the various States of the confederation.

The leaders of the Party swear to go straight forward if necessary to sacrifice their lives in securing fulfillment of the foregoing Points. Munich, February 24th, 1920.

After full discussion at the General Meeting of members on May 22nd, 1920, it was resolved that "This Program is unalterable." This does not imply that every word must stand unchanged, nor that anything done to deepen or develop the Program is to be prohibited, but it implies with absolute decision and unswerving clarity that the principles and leading ideas contained in it may not be tampered with.

There can be no bending or twisting from considerations of expediency, no hidden interference with very important and for the present-day arrangements in politics, society and economics, very unwelcome points in the Program, no deviation of sentiment.

Adolf Hitler prints its two main points in leaded type: The Common Interest before Self, the spirit of the Program. Abolition of the Thralldom of Interest is at the core of National Socialism. Once these two points are achieved, it means a victory of the approaching universalist ordering of society in the 'true State' over the present-day separation of State, nation, and economics under the corrupting influence of the individualist theory of society as now constructed. The sham State of today, oppressing the working classes and protecting the pirated grains of bankers and Stock Exchange speculators, is the arena for reckless private enrichment and for the lowest political profiteering; it gives no thought to its people and provides no high moral bond of union. The power of money, most ruthless of all powers, holds absolute control, and exercises corrupting, destroying influence on State, nation, society, morals, drama, literature, and on all matters of morality, less easy to estimate.

There must, of course, be no wavering, no drawing back in this giant struggle; it is either victory or defeat. The somewhat varied view of the same basic principle, which 1 gave in my book, Der deutsche Staat auf nationaler und sozialer Grundlage, (F. Eher Nachf.) is not an alteration, but a series of points which belong together, collected, and arranged according to various political, economic, financial, cultural, aspects of life.

If those views of mine (See p. 22) could be looked on as varying from or opposed to the 25 Points, Hitler would never have described my book in his brief preface as the "catechism of our movement." Anyone is free to choose either of the views according to his taste, but if he compares them together, he will not find them mutually contradictory.

To insure for the future absolute agreement in our demands as expressed in our Program, and to guard the movement against the shocks likely to injure any movement, the 'suggestions for improvement' offered by professional and amateur critics, grumblers and know it all's, Adolf Hitler, at a conference of all district organizers held at Bamberg on February 11th , 1926, formally appointed Gottfried Feder to be the final judge of all questions connected with the Program.

CHAPTER

7

THE BASIC IDEA

It is our intention in this pamphlet to expose the essential principles of the National Socialist conception of the State as briefly and simply as possible. We shall in a later one deal in more detail with the sociological, theoretic, and spiritual aspects of that conception.

We shall also not attempt to describe the various other political aspirations nor those who represent them in the different parties and associations this is a task by itself, but we set down here merely the essential points of our demands.

The world arose out of chaos, order out of disorder, organization out of wild confusion.

Today chaos is a rampart in the world, confusion, struggle, hatred, oppression, robbery, cruelty, self-seeking. Brother is estranged from brother. Members of the same nation attack each other, stab a man to death simply because he wears a Swastika Cross. They all suffer under the same burdens, the same privations; yet who ever during these last months, has heard of Marxist workers attacking or killing their employers, or their party leaders, or any of the bankers and Stock Exchange bloodsuckers, or any of the wholesale profiteers? The sole sacrifice to chaos is the good, simple worker. The Marxists have lost their heads and are crowding to join up with the plunderers of their own class, whilst they turn savagely against those who stand ready to rescue it.

The Nationalist and other parties are in the Government or are fighting to get into it with those who have destroyed their national ideals and lose both honor and character. The defense associations are striving to penetrate 'into the State' the State of Severing and Grzesinsky, pacifists, internationalists, and Jews, with whom they believe they can run the government

They have gone off their heads! The so-called Rechtskreise fails to see that eagles and snakes, wolves and lambs, mankind, and the cholera bacillus, cannot join in co-operation. They are putting forth all their strength to give an appearance of 'order' to disorder, political chaos, political effeteness. But they set their faces against the National Socialists, those 'fanatics', being filled with crazy fears that the latter might deprive them of some of their former privileges and positions, forgetting that they lost all through the very people from whom they now demand 'a share in the political loaves and fishes.

The industrials, great or small, have but one end in view profits, only one longing credits, only one protest taxation; they fear and respect only one thing the banks; they shrug their shoulders over the National Socialist demand for breaking down the thralldom of interest.

Their one desire is to 'make debts'. The vast tribute extracted from loans by the banks, without trouble or labor, they regard as perfect in order. They found parties of economy and vote for the Dawes Laws, which are the main cause of the heavy taxation.

Honor has departed from business, which is all in the hands of powerful companies. The producers have surrendered to high finance, their greatest enemy. The employers in the factories and offices, deep in debt, must be content with the barest pittance, for all the profits of labor go into the pockets of the impersonal money power in the form of interest and dividends.

The people in control are totally unable to stem the chaos. Crushed from above by taxation and interest payment, menaced from below by the grumblings of the submerged workers, they have bound themselves blindly to a State controlled by capitalism, whilst the exploiters of the present chaos suffer them to remain in power merely as slavedrivers over the laboring masses. Their fury is directed not against the lunacy of Marxism, but against the wearers of the Hooked Cross. They forget that we and we alone saw the tragedy of German economics approaching, perceived, and showed how, if taken in time, Germany by her own strength could restore the balance.

Associations under every kind of name, reasonable in their basic ideas hopeless in the present chaos of public life, are seeking how to produce order. It is all in vain, for they are not in touch with the nation as a great social whole. All are merely intent on snatching small advantages for their own caste; bare of any political or economic principle, they apply to each political party in turn. They bow to the existing system and kowtow to the so-called supreme authority.

They cost the German nation untold sums in payments to numberless organizers, directors, and wirepullers, but no one of them does the least good. Inflation a criminal measure robbed all classes, the thrifty, members of associations, artisans of their savings. Some new tax, straight from the green table, destroys the hopes based on years of work. An advantage gained after numberless meetings, discussions, deputations to the Government, is usually annulled by to a rise in the cost of living, a rise, or a fall in prices.

Chaos and lunacy! How can a farmer live under such persecution? How can the worker buy with prices rising all the time? What good is it to raise the pay of officials and employees when the index of the cost of living continues to rise? They look in their credulity for help from the State, the State which has caused all the impoverishment and suppression, which is not the 'Father of the Nation', but the tyrant and tax collector of the money despotism.

So, they turn again and again to the old Parties, say they don't care for politics and belong to no Party, and at the same time let the wretched Party squabbles go on as before.

The great task which National Socialism has set before it is a determination to restore form, to dispel the chaos, to set the world, which has departed from the old dispensations, in order again, and to guard that order in the highest Platonic sense.

It should be stated here that we regard as 'Order' neither the apparent order of a policed State, nor the robbery of finance hallowed by custom and permitted by law, nor the conspiracies of syndicates, trusts, and other organized measures of national betrayal, however well they 'function'. Even a band of robbers has 'order', prisons have their 'regulations'. But in the nation, taken as an organic whole, every aspect of our public life shows pain, bondage, suppression, insincerity, and presents a chaotic picture of a struggle of all against all.

Government against people, Party against Party, at the same time concluding most unnatural alliances, employer against employee, merchant against producer and consumer, landlord against tenant, laborer against farmer, officials against the public, worker against 'bourgeoisie', Church against State, each blindly fitting out at his adversary and thinking only of his own selfish interests, his advancement, and his moneybags. No one reflects that the other has a right to live, or that pursuit of his own selfish ends means that someone else must pay for it. No one thinks of his neighbors' welfare, or of his higher duties to the community. A breathless pursuit after personal gain. Elbow your neighbor to get on, tramp on his body if you will get anything by it why care? That is modern business.

Let us not deceive ourselves. We are during a great world change, and it is natural that simple souls, poor wandering spirits, see no way out of the chaos, seek relief in suicide, or think the world is coming to an end and join in the race after the golden calf and rush blindly into the whirlpool. "Enjoy while you can after us the deluge."

So terrible a blow to the morale of a nation is only possible and explicable when the whole intellectual foundation of society is shaken or else false, and in fact we see that Marxism, Capitalism, and the leaders of our public life all worship the same god Individualism. Personal interest is the sole incentive, obtaining advantages for one's own narrow class in life.

Later, a further contribution to this series will appear, devoted to a careful sociological study of the construction of society.

Here I shall only attempt shortly to show a comparative picture of the difference between the organic errors in the State and political economy of today and the essence of a National Socialist State. The present-day doctrine is Society is the sum of the individuals the State at its best a convenient aggregation of individuals or associations.

We may compare this doctrine of the construction of society to a heap of stones. The only real thing about it is the individual pieces of stone. Its shape is a matter of chance; whether a stone is on top, or underneath is indifferent. The result is neither more nor less than a heap of stones.

By the same simile, the State which answers to our National Socialist doctrine of society and philosophy of the State is the house. Speaking mechanically, the house also consists of so many individual bricks sand, cement, joists, windows, doors, floors, etc. But anyone can see that a house, a room, is a higher entity, something new and peculiar and complete, more than a mere sum total of bricks heaped together. Anyone can understand that a house does not come into being by piling several single parts in a heap, but only by assembling these parts according to a deliberate plan.

Thus, it is with a nation. Not until chaos has been organically, by a deliberate plan, brought into order and gives place to form, not until a reasoned whole has been assembled out of the mass of parts, can the true Sate appear. Only then will the component parts assume a purposeful shape. Othmar Spann, formerly Rector of Vienna University, has explained admirably in his book, Der wahre Staat, and in his Gesellschaftslehre the sociological bases of the present-day individualistic State as opposed to the high ideal of universal order in a State founded on scientific principles.

We National Socialists coined the phrase, which all men can comprehend:

The Community before the individual.

It is only by serving the general interest as a member of the national community that the individual awakes to a higher life, each one in his own place. Only so will each one attains to the genuine Socialism, the communal feeling, the true life, win consciousness of security, and realize that only under the domination of -this idea can an organic, national government arise from tile present day system of robbery, and be of profit to the community, and to each member of the community.

Today, the individual is a helpless victim of the forces fighting for the mastery; his associations are powerless to help him. It is not clearly realized who is the real enemy the idle profiteer and exploiter. Despite the Marxist cry against capitalism, the pious pronouncements of the Centre, the complaints of the business world about the burden of taxation and interest, no one realizes the world enemy, the finance which overshadows the world, and its representative, the Jewish magnate.

All classes have felt the lash of interest; the tax collector bears heavy on every section of the population, but who dares oppose the power of bank and Stock Exchange? Capital proclaims its character by growing, contrary to all -experience elsewhere on earth, as it was outside itself without pains or labor, by means of interest and dividends, and by waxing greater and more powerful each minute. The devilish principle of lies has bested the decency of creative labor.

Break down the thralldom of interest is our war-cry.

I know that this demand, which underlies every other, is not properly understood in its full vast significance, even' in our own ranks. Very few of our speakers, for instance, dare to attack this basic question, though most of them feel how important it is; for one of our Party slogans is "Fight capital and the Stock Exchange." But what the 'thralldom of interest' really is, how it bears on the life of the nation and the individual, how 'finance' has enslaved the population, and what the right and practical methods are which must be adopted to break-it, and what the results of breaking it would be for the whole population is sufficiently clear to very few to enable them to explain it in their own words.

In his great work, Mein Kampf, (Vol. I, pp. 224 225) Adolf Hitler has indicated the vast importance of this question as follows: "As I listened to Gottfried Feder's first lecture on breaking down the thralldom of interest in June 1919, I knew at once that this was a theoretic truth immensely important for the future of the German nation ... The fight against international capital and finance has become the chief point in the Program for the German nation's struggle for independence and liberty."

All serious National Socialists share this conviction, for the solution of this question implies the solution of the Jewish question and much more than that.

Anti-Semitism is in a way the foundation of the feeling underlying our whole movement. Every National Socialist is an Anti-Semite, but every antisemite need not be a National Socialist. Anti-Semitism is negative; the Anti-Semite recognizes the carrier of the national plague-germ, but this knowledge usually turns into hatred of the individual Jew and the success of the Jews in the life of business. Then in the best event, Anti-Semitism rises to help in driving the Jew out of our State and economic life. The Anti-Semite does not worry his head about how and what next.

If, even after the Jew was driven out, there still remained the principle of present-day Jewish domination self-interest before general interest and the Jewish banking and credit system, there would still be enough bastard Jews, or even 'normal Germans' of mixed race as ready to step into the Jews' shoes and rage against their own race as are the Jews today, and we should perhaps see plenty of ' Anti-Semites' sitting where the Jews once sat.

Now, National Socialism, with its main demand, breaking down the Thralldom of Interest, is essentially constructive. It bites deeper, and the consequences are far more all-embracing.

In my essay, Das Herzstück unseres Programms, (Nat.Soc. Jahrbuch, 1927) I pointed to the peculiar position that demand gives us among all other parties and associations. In all our other demands, we find similar and parallel aspirations in the Parties of the Right and Left. No other party, but ours can show any counterpart of this one demand.

We all know that neither the Left, with their false cry of "Down with Capitalism", nor the Right with their phrases about the Fatherland, are capable of starting a new world epoch, for neither the Marxists nor the reactionaries could alter anything in our economy but would only destroy as the Communists in Russia do. They are incapable of construction like the Communists in Russia.

What do we mean by Thralldom of Interest?

The condition of peoples under the money domination of the finance of the world Jewry.

The landowner is under this thralldom, who must raise loans to finance his farming operations, loans at such high interest as almost to eat up the results of his labor, or who is forced to make debts and to drag the mortgages after him like so much weight of lead.

So is the worker, producing in shops and factories for a pittance, whilst the shareholder draws dividends and bonuses which he has not worked for.

So is the earning middle class, whose work goes almost entirely to pay the interest on bank overdrafts.

So are all who must earn their bread by mental or bodily work, whilst a comparatively small proportion, without labor or trouble, pocket huge profits out of their dividends, speculations, and bank shares. We do not refer to the thrifty savers and small capitalists though they too owe, or owed, their winnings to a false system, but all their lives long many of times the amount of their little interest was taken from them in the form of taxes, so that we can easily afford to repay them in their old age a part of their full earnings, which were taken away. I shall have more to say about this later.

So is the industrial, who has laboriously built up his business, and turned it in course of time into a company. He is no longer a free agent but must satisfy the greedy board of directors and his shareholders as well if he does not wish to be squeezed out.

So are all nations that cover their deficits by means of loans.

This thralldom spell ruin for any nation that hands over to the money power, the bankers, its sovereign rights at home, the control of its finances, of its railways, and of taxation and customs, as Germany has done by accepting the Dawes Law.

Creative labor is under the same thralldom if it thinks of money before all else. Today, money, the 'servant of business', has become the master, in fact, the brutal tyrant of labor.

Thralldom of interest is the real expression for the antagonisms, capital versus Labor, blood versus money, creative work versus exploitation.

The necessity of breaking this thralldom is of such vast importance for our nation and our race, that on it alone depends on our nation's hope of rising from its shame and slavery; in fact, the hope of recovering happiness, prosperity and civilization throughout the world.

"It is the pivot on which everything turns; it is far more than a mere necessity of financial policy. Whilst its principles and consequences bite deep into political and economic life, it is a leading question for economic study, and thus affects every single individual and demands a decision from each one: Service to the nation or unlimited private enrichment. It means a solution to the Social Question."

All 'world-questions' are capable of being described in one word, which rises like a flame out of chaos; at the same time, countless prophets and books cannot exhaust all the questions which arise out of that word.

We can say no more at present on this vast basic principle of National Socialism. I have already thrown light on every essential side of the problem in my pamphlets: Das Manifest zur Brechung der Zinsknechtschaft Munich, 1926 (now out of print); Der Staatsbankrott, Die Rettung Jos. C. Huber, Diessen, 1919; Der kommende Steuerstreik Diessen, 1921; and Der Deutsche Staat auf nationaler und sozialer Grundlage Frz. Eher Nachf., Munich, (all obtainable through the library of our Party in Munich, Thierschstr. 11).

Intensive study is required to master the details of this problem, for the practical economics of the last 50 years have followed the capitalistic idea so closely, that all who have grown up with it need a complete change of orientation to get free from it.

A pamphlet on the subject is soon to appear, which will give our members an explanation for this highly important task of the coming nationalist State.

In addition to the two quite novel basic principles of our Program given above, we must mention certain others in connection with the general policy of the State. The principle underlying our policy of the State is shortly as follows: The German Reich is the home of the Germans. It is the great principle for our whole foreign policy, and includes Germany's political liberation, all the requirements of our racial policy, and the conditions of membership of the State.

Our economic principle is: The duty of the national economy is to provide the necessities of life and not to secure the highest possible profits for capital. This principle of economic policy embraces a fundamental attitude of National Socialism towards private property, and with regard to the various forms of business, from the very small to the very great Syndicates, Trusts and also to the great moral questions which must be a living force in business, if the 'national economics are not to sink to being mere exploitation of the nation and to being run simply for profit!

Our principle as regards finance is as follows:

Finance shall exist for the benefit of the State; the financial magnates shall not form a State within the State.

This principle involves a seismic change. It concerns the practical measures which will have to be taken to break the Thralldom of Interest, nationalization of finance, control of the system of credit, and the banking system.

Every one of these tasks is of the greatest importance from the point of view of our Program. They involve all tax legislation, with the ultimate and seemingly impossible aim of a State without taxation.

Our principle as regards social subjects is as follows:

The general welfare is the highest law of all.

This principle of ours is in direct opposition to present day practice, according to which every class, every profession, tries to win advantages for its own group in social policy without regard to the general interest. We wish to make it possible for all to find a dwelling and for all to make a living, and to institute a general system of care for the aged.

As regards educational and moral progress, it is our unchangeable principle: that all work in that direction is to be done from the sole point of view of German nationality. It cannot be by order or by force that the moral and intellectual forces of our nation may introduce a new Renaissance, a new classic epoch in the arts. A stop will have to be put to the injuries suffered by our German artistic and intellectual life at the hands of the Jewish dictatorship, especially through the poisoning of the press.

Apart from this important domain of public life, there are, of course, plenty of other improvements to be considered.

Our system of Law will have to be modified to meet the variety of fresh institutions; that the scandal of election to Parliament by the democratic vote will have to be removed, and that, following the transitional period of a Dictatorship, we shall have to decide on the outward visible form of the State and the internal functions of the federal States.

Already, however, we can see in this brief outline the vast dimensions of these questions when set face to face with the tremendous fundamental principles of our Program.

It is not fundamental in fact it is indifferent to us whether it is to be a monarchy or a republic, whether we are to have a federation of 5 or 25 States, provided only they are all German States combined under a strong central government, when face to face with the foreigner, and provided only the citizens of the German State at home may live happy and contented.

CHAPTER 8

THE PROGRAM REQUIREMENT DETAILS

It will make for clarity, when enlisting new members, to make use of the Program in the form which follows. The minor clauses are ranged under the more important headings, corresponding to the principles enunciated in the preceding chapter.

The Political & Economic Program

Our aim is Germany's re-birth to German liberty in the German spirit. The means to this aim are:

1. **The Political Principle:** The German Reich is the home of the Germans.

A-1| *In foreign policy:*

i. Formation of a homogenous national State, embracing all German race.
ii. Energetic representation of German interests abroad.

B-1| *In racial policy:*

i. Formation of a homogenous national State, embracing all German race.
ii. Energetic representation of German interests abroad.

C-1| *In internal policy:*

i. None but Germans who profess entire community with the spirit and destiny of Germany may exercise the rights of a citizen of the State.
ii. He who is not a German may only live in the German State as a guest and is under foreign law.
iii. The rights of Germans shall have the preference over those of citizens of foreign nations.

2. **Our Economic Principle:** The duty of the State is to provide the necessaries of life and not to secure the highest possible profits for capital.

A-2| National Socialism recognizes private property as a principle and protects it by law.

B-2| The national welfare, however, demands that a limit shall be set to the amassing of wealth in the hands of individuals.

C-2| All Germans form a community for the promotion of the general welfare and culture.

D-2| Within the limits of the obligation of every German to work, the sanctity of private property being respected, every German is free to earn and to dispose of the results of his labor.

E-2| The healthy combination of all forms of business, small and large, in every domain of economic life, including agriculture, shall be encouraged.

F-2| All existing businesses which until now have been in the form of companies shall be nationalized.

G-2| Usury and profiteering and personal enrichment at the expense and to the injury of the nation shall be punished with death.

H-2| Introduction of a year's obligation to work (for the State), incumbent on every German.

3. **Our Financial Principle:** Finance shall exist for the benefit of the State; the financial magnates shall not form a State within the State. Hence, our aim is to break the thralldom of interest.

A-3| Relief of the State, and hence of the nation, from its indebtedness to the great financial houses which lend on interest.

B-3| Nationalization of the Reichsbank and the issuing houses.

C-3| Provision of money for all great public objects (waterpower, railroads, etc.), not by means of loans, but by granting noninterest bearing State bonds or without using ready money.

D-3| Introduction of a fixed standard of currency on a secured basis.

E-3| Creation of a national bank of business development (currency reform) for granting non-interest-bearing loans.

F-3| Fundamental re-modeling of the system of taxation on social-economic principles. Relief of the consumer from the burden of indirect taxation, and of the producer from crippling taxation (fiscal reform and relief from taxation).

4. **Our Social-Political Principle:** The general welfare is the highest law of all.

A-4| Development on a large scale of Old Age Insurance by nationalizing the system of annuities. Every member of the German State shall be assured of enough to live upon on attaining a certain age, or, if permanently disabled, before that age.

B-4| Participation by all engaged in productive enterprises in the profits according to efficiency and age. Responsibility will also be shared in fulfilling the task from a national point of view.

C-4| Seizure for social purposes of all profits made from the War and the Revolution, not due (o honest work, and of the fortunes of usurers and money-grabbers.

D-4| Relief of the shortage of dwellings by extensive fresh construction throughout the Reich by the means suggested in No. 20 (a new national bank).

5. **Our Cultural Aim:** is that all the sciences and fine arts shall flourish based on a politically free, economically healthy State. The means of achieving this will be:

A-5| Training the young up to be healthy in body and free in mind, after the great traditions of German culture.

B-5| Complete liberty of creed and conscience.

C-5| Special protection for the Christian denominations.

D-5| Discouragement of dogmas, which are opposed to German moral instincts and contain matter injurious to the State and the nation.

E-5| Discouragement of all evil influences in the press, in literature, the stage, the arts and the picture theatres.

F-5| Liberty of instruction in the German secondary schools; formation of a ruling class of high-minded men.

6. **Military Affairs:**

A-6| To make the nation efficient by permitting every free German to serve and bear arms.

B-6| Abolition of the paid Army.

C-6| Creation of a national army for national defense under the command of a highly trained corps of professional officers.

7. **Other Recommendations:**

A-7| Press reform. Suppression of all journals which militate against the national good. Strict responsibility for all untrue and intentionally falsified intelligence.

B-7| Modification of the franchise laws to cut out the demoralizing methods of election contests, and the immunity of those elected.

C-7| Formation of special Chambers for trades and professions.

D-7| Judicial reform as regards the Land Laws' recognition of the rights of property in land as a principle; no right to borrow from private sources on the security of the land; the State to have the right of pre-emption, especially in the case of foreigners and Jews; the State to be empowered to administer estates in the event of bad management on the part of the owner. Civil Law greatly increased protection for personal honor, health, as opposed to the one-sided legal protection of the rights of property, which predominates at the present day.

8. **State Law Reform:**

A-8| The form of State most suitable to the German character is sovereign control united in a central personal power. The nation must decide later whether this central personal power shall be wielded by an elected monarch or a president.

i. Federal character of the Reich.

ii. The constitution of the German nation out of several countries closely bound together by race and history makes it necessary that each one of the States shall be very extensively independent in internal affairs.

iii. It is the affair of the Reich to represent the German nation abroad, and to provide for passports, customs, also for the Army and Navy.

There are three main obstacles to carrying out this national Program of National Socialism: Marxism, the Parliamentary system, and the capitalist magnates.

1. **Our Anti-Marxist Campaign** is directed against the disruptive doctrines of the Jew, Karl Marx that of the class-war which splits up the nation, that of abolishing of private property which makes business impossible and against the whole economic, materialistic view of history.
2. **Our Campaign Against Parliaments** is directed against the lack of responsibility of the so-called representatives of the people who being immune can never be summoned in practice to answer for the results of their decisions; also, against all the evils which arise out of the system (moral corruption, nepotism, venality), all resulting in the final evil a government which is dependent on such a parliament.
3. **Our Campaign Against Mammon**, which ranks above the other two, is directed against the world-embracing power of money, i.e., the perpetual exploitation of our nation by the great lending houses.

It is also a tremendous struggle against the soul-killing, materialist spirit of greed and rapacity with all its disruptive accompaniments throughout our public, commercial, and cultural life.

The main battle is one between two world-theories, represented by two essentially differing structures the spirit which has created and is creative and the unquiet, grasping spirit. The creative spirit, deep-rooted, but superior to the rest of the world in spiritual experience, is carried; mainly by the Aryan race; The grabbing spirit, without roots anywhere, aiming only at material things, commercial, is chiefly represented by the Jews.

National Socialism, like Anti-Semitism, regards the Jewish-materialistic spirit as the chief cause of the evil; it knows, however, that this greatest struggle in history must not stop short at merely destroying the Semitic spirit; which is why the great Program of National Socialism goes far beyond the anti-Semitic desire to destroy, for it offers a positive constructive picture, showing how the National Socialist State of labor and achievement ought to appear when completed.

Once this high aim is achieved, the National Socialist Party will dissolve automatically; for National Socialism will then be the entire life of the whole German nation. The N.S.D.A.P. is not a political Party in the ordinary sense of the word, but is that section of the nation, which is confident, and sure of the future, which has gathered round strong and determined leaders to deliver Germany from shame and impotence abroad and from demoralization at home, and to make her once again strong and respected abroad, and morally and economically healthy at home.

"The German Reich is the home of the German people."

Every word of this principle of State policy is a cut with a lash when we consider the miserable state of things today.

The 'German Reich' where is there a German Reich today? Can Germany lay claim to be called an independent State? No! Not even the most complacent pundits in State Law could describe a country, such as Germany is now, as one in full enjoyment of all its rights of sovereignty.

The five most important rights of a State are: sovereignty over its territory, its army, its finances, its internal administration arid communications, and lastly its justice.

You have only to put the matter in this way to any layman without further explanation of a nation's rights under International Law, and compare it with Germany's position today, and it becomes clear that it is impossible to maintain that a sovereign 'German Reich' exists any longer.

Our control of our territory is a mockery, for whenever France chooses, she can seize upon German land without asking leave and without suffering opposition. Czechs, Poles, Danes can venture on any inroad into a German territory without fear of hindrance. The 'accursed old regime' put a very different interpretation on the slightest breach of frontier. A military inroad into German territory then implied a "state of war."

To protect its territorial sovereignty, a nation needs an armed force capable of repelling any attack on its land, and therefore on the lives and happiness of its nationals. A free state cannot permit a foreign Power to scrutinize its actions, or to have the right of deciding the strength, equipment, armaments, garrisons of its Army; if i! does, it is certainly not 'sovereign'; it cannot command its means of power; it has given up control of its military forces. Germany has done this by giving in to the enemy Commissions for Disarmament and Control.

Germany had already suffered this humiliation under the Armistice conditions and had lost her international rights.

Nevertheless, she might have retained some part of her internal control; but as soon as the military control was destroyed, the financial magnates seized the opportunity for limitless exploitation of German labor.

First, the muddy torrent of revolution burst forth over Germany; then the usurers and profiteers, the Social-democratic traitors, sons of chaos, deserters, jailbirds shared the power with the Democrats and Centre, and behind and over all the financiers, the Jews, did their business. Soon the Free Masons of the so-called National Parties, especially Brother Stresemann, were called in. The final blow was soon to come. The experts with their Dawes Law robbed Germany of control of her finances, which were bartered away to a handful of Jews, the German and foreign financial magnates. The Reichstag let the railways go, and with them all control of communications, also a great part of the control of taxation and customs, by handing them over to the Reparations Commissioner.

Control of justice hardly exists anymore. The occupied districts are under foreign military law; special regulations govern the rest of Germany, such as those for the defense of the Republic; insecurity of rights, organized public robbery through the so-called Aufwertungsgesetze, forcing the Courts to declare that wrong is right.

Germany is no longer a sovereign state. She is a colony of slaves. Germans are oppressed, thrown into prison, denied free speech simply because they are still 'German' and desire to end their slavery.

Yes, we want to have Germany free again, and this coming German Reich shall be the home of the Germans, not merely a machine for keeping order, not merely a 'State', an 'authority', a 'government', a sinecure for a handful of reigning houses, but a Home, that word of charm love of home, lovely, sunny, beloved. The smell of the home earth rises the wanderer thrills with joy at feeling the home soil beneath his feet; he is bound to it by blood ties. The home feeling is the feeling of security, and from that blossom is the fine flower of love of home. The State and nation can have no finer aim than this.

It is greater than a cautious social policy, than unemployment insurance, than housing schemes, though indeed having one's own home is one of the Strongest incentives for love of home.

Home is more than an 'Imperial State', which one serves, whether from enthusiasm or under compulsion.

It is more than an administration, more than the defense of one's own interests, more than a crib for cattle, or protection for person and property. All these public objects must serve the conception of home. Just as the idea of home has a special charm of the children in a properly organized family, as one's own room arouses very different feelings from a room in a hotel or a prison cell; home is something unspeakably tender and yet powerful, superior to the idea of an association for a purpose, which is the Liberal parliamentary democratic conception of the social State.

Policy of the State

Principle: The German Reich shall be a home for the Germans not for Jews, Russians (Communists), Social Democrats, who have no fatherland called Germany (Crispien), nor for all the foreigners who make a longer or shorter stay on German soil.

We are in sharp and fundamental opposition to the Weimar Constitution, which speaks only of 'German nationals', but ignores the conception of 'German' in the national, or rather racial, sense.

Point A - Foreign Policy:

1. Creation of a solid national State, embracing all branches of the German race.

   All German blood, whether living under French, Danish, Polish, Czech or Italian sovereignty, shall be united in a German Reich. We demand neither less nor more than what was demanded of our enemies the right of Germans to decide to belong to their motherland, the German State.

   We claim all Germans in Sudeten Germany, Alsace-Lorraine. Poland, the League colony of Austria, and the States which succeeded in the old Austria. This demand, however, expressly excludes any tendency towards imperialism; it is the simple and natural demand, which any strong nationality puts forward as its natural requirement.

2. Strong representation of German interests abroad is a further and necessary corollary of Point A.

   It is usually the best, most industrious and venturesome engineers, explorers, professors, merchants, doctors who go into foreign lands, carrying German Culture with them. They are members of the great German national family, to which they must never be lost. They have a right to expect protection from home when they are abroad. They should be not merely disseminators of culture, but the conscious advance guard of the Germanic idea in the world; not 'apostles of humanity', but bearers of the Nordic idea.

   Those who represent Germany abroad should not acquire foreign notions but stick to their superior German character. Our Foreign Office must be swept clean with an iron besom. We must finish with the obsequiousness towards the foreigner after the manner of Erzberger and Stresemann, and it will be seen that strong representation of German interests will be quite otherwise respected, and attention to German desires in place of contempt will be the result.

Point B - Racial Policy:

1. Exclusion of Jews and all non-Germans from all responsible positions in public life.

   This demand is so natural to us National Socialists that no further explanation is needed; but it is not possible to give convincing arguments in brief to those who fail to take on the principles of our racial doctrine.

   Anyone who looks on a Jew as a 'citizen of the State of the Jewish religion and not as a heterogeneous, segregated people, parasitic in character, will fail to appreciate the essentialness of this demand. If a man were to say or think that a cabbage which had grown by chance in the middle of a strawberry plant was a strawberry plant, and that good strawberries could be got from it, he would be as wrong as if he thought that a lion cub which had got in among a flock of sheep thereby became a sheep. A German would not be good as a government official in China or India, and we should not like to have a Chinaman or a Hottentot as a Treasury official or mayor of a German town.

   And yet it would be better to have an Enver Pasha or a Chang Kai Chek in control in Germany than to have a Jew with free play for his disintegrating racial characteristics. What is certain is that the Revolution loosened the bands of order in the State, and that the long-established Jewish bankers, as well as the Jews from the East who have recently immigrated into Germany, have enriched themselves by impoverishing Germany. We have all seen and had experience with this; it has always been going on, this disintegration of Nordic institutions. "There is but one way open for these crafty people it has nothing to hope for so long as order is maintained." (Goethe at the fair at Plundersweilen)

Therefore, we demand:

2. That the immigration of Eastern Jews and other parasitic aliens shall be stopped, and that undesirable aliens and Jews shall be deported.

   At the time of the great inflation, Jews from Galicia and Poland flocked like vermin into the towns of Germany. Though there was a great dearth of houses, they soon were very well housed, whilst Germans had to creep into holes. They started their dirty business, buying up everything pearls, Persian carpets, diamonds, gold, silver, platinum,

War Loan, thousand-mark notes, copper, lead, literature, theatres, grain (the Evaporator Company). They quickly became visibly rich and took rank as Germans in the eyes of 'normal Germans'.

Compromise is utterly inadmissible in meeting the case. We must have administrators whose racial beliefs are clear and unbending. The health of the race must be restored by practical application of the Anti-Semitic treatment, and our nation must be turned Northward in the sense of the Nordic idea.

This question does not perhaps belong properly to the 'provisional Program' of the N.S.D.A.P.; but we must all clearly understand that not much can be done with the German nation until it has been 'debastardized'.

But we can state here and now that the terrible racial decadence has only, at any rate in theory, been stemmed, because of the remarkable interest aroused generally by questions of race and by there being several books on the subject; nothing however, but solid and continuous work, can allow us to make real progress.

Point C - As Regards State Citizenship:

We demand:

1. That none but Germans, who believe in German Culture and the common destiny of all Germans, shall enjoy the rights of a citizen of the State.

   Even here, limits must be drawn. People, who, even though German born, act consciously in a way injurious to the nation and the State, and receive and obey orders from abroad i.e., do not accept a share in the common destiny, may not be allowed the rights of citizenship; there are plenty to whom we shall have to deny the high honor of enjoying these rights.

2. non-Germans may only dwell in the German State as guests and shall be regarded as being subject to foreign law.

   This is a necessary principle, calculated to put an end forever to the eternal obsequiousness towards the foreigner. But it does not mean that we shall not welcome citizens of a foreign country warmly and treat them well as guests so long as they conduct themselves properly; but

3. The rights and interests of Germans shall have preference over those of the subjects of a foreign nation.

Our further requirements need not be included in our Program in detail. For instance, the form assumed by the laws affecting foreigners will come on for settlement later, also the methods for excluding the Jews. A Program of principles cannot be expected to be a Program of action, giving tactical details of how supremacy is to be secured, etc. I am opposed altogether to fixing our Program too rigidly, for in this great struggle we must first determine the principles from which we shall never drawback, and not imitate the vote catching methods of the bourgeois and Socialist Parties.

Economic Policy

It is the duty of the National Government to provide the necessaries of life and not to secure the highest possible profits for Capital.

It may occur to simple, plain-thinking men that to announce this obvious fact as a principle is superfluous. It is a commonplace to the producer, the farmer, the artisan, the manufacturer, that what he makes is either used or consumed, by himself or, as an article of commerce, by others.

In his eyes, business which is not concerned with production or consumption is ridiculous, impossible, against common sense.

This brings us to one of the great intellectual difficulties in our recruiting work. Our fellow-countrymen are bound to say: Of course, your natural sentiment in thinking of the meanings and aims of labor and economics is quite correct, but unfortunately our so-called political economy of today in no way answers to this natural claim. If you look closer, you will discover the terrible characteristics which are utterly opposed to the obvious duty of all national political economy.

For what about the moneylenders and profiteers? Do these universal plunderers give a thought to providing the necessaries of life? No! Are they engaged in creating values, do they produce anything? No! They are robbers and traitors in the economic sense, and merely amass wealth for themselves.

What about the banks? They circulate money and give 'credit'. Yes, but the Post Office does this, and cheaper, quicker, and better; and to whom do the banks give credit? To the needy, the laboring masses, who have no home of their own, or for building houses, for supplying the crying need of dwellings? No! Or to the farmers, or to those who run businesses and who produce and distribute the economic necessaries? Not freely, and only if security is offered, over and above the natural engagement to repay; moreover, they charge interest. Do the banks care whether the producers' customers are served well, cheaply, and promptly, or whether economic necessaries are supplied quickly, cheaply and with due attention? No! Their one thought is for making their profit out of the interest, commission, or whatever the banking process of tapping the supply of money is called. What do the banks produce? Nothing! What do they earn? Vast sums.

Thus moneylenders, profiteers, banks, financiers supply no necessity, but instead they draw huge profits from the prevailing capitalist system in fact they tyrannize over and exploit the anti-social, economic system of to-day. The main task of economics is to see that the interest on loans is secure, i.e., the workers are forced to give up part of their earnings to the 'City'. What does the factory -owner, or as the workers call him, the 'exploiter' and 'bloodsucker' do? By paying the lowest possible wages, by using inferior material, by mass-production, averaging, and high retail prices, he tries to make the largest possible profit for himself.

He gives no thought to his employees' poverty; he does not care if his wares must be quickly thrown away as rubbish all the better, since it means more work and more profits for him. The silly people rush again and again after cheap rubbish, if only it is displayed attractively.

The return on his capital comes first with him, supplying necessaries of life comes a bad second. He does, however, do something. He supplies work.

The true factory-owner is something quite different, he who is conscious of his high task as an economic leader. He must possess high moral worth in the economic sense, at least. His task is to discover the real economic needs of the people if he is also an inventor, he does this pioneer work himself. He must keep his costs as low as he can and lay them out to the best advantage, keep prices down as low as possible to get his goods on to the market; keep up both quality and quantity of production, pay his employees well, so that they may be able to purchase goods freely, must always be thinking of improvements and renewals of plant and trading methods.

If he puts all this first in his business, he is 'supplying the necessaries of life' in the best and highest sense," and profits will come of themselves without his making them his first object. 'The finest and most universally known example of this kind of manufacturer is Henry Ford. There are other names in our own heavy industries which stand equally high Krupp, Kirdorf, Abbe, Mannesmann, Siemens, and numerous others.

The character of such businesses is altogether different when they are not personally controlled by men of high moral qualities who look after the interests of their workers but are handed over to impersonal limited companies.

So long as the founder of a business is also the chief shareholder and can maintain the standard of excellence of his products, all may be well; but as soon as conversion takes place, it is overwhelmed by the interests of the capitalist shareholders. The former owners, the managers, now depend on the Board, representing the shareholders, for improvements in business methods and working conditions, and the shareholders have no-interest (beyond that of the slavedriver) in the welfare of the workers and the excellence of the work, so long as the dividends coming out of it are good large ones. The introduction of proprietary shares has had a most devastating influence, for any chance speculator can corner the shares and become owner of large industrial works without knowing anything about them. To the Stock Exchange, stocks and shares are merely so much paper for them to play with. They are not interested in conditions of production and labor, most of them could not say what the products or the conditions of marketing, labor, wages, and maintenance are in the business of which they are the owners by law. (!) And owners they are, just because they happen to have cornered the shares of this or that factory in the market.

Let us now examine this situation in the light of its effect on political economy, to realize the corrupt character of the capitalist system.

Today, business merely looks for a return on capital.The large retail stores follow different methods. They cultivate 'attraction', 'bluff', 'averaging', 'luxury articles', and arouse a desire for non-necessaries, as shown above.

Great palaces, built with all the arts of refinement, invite to purchase apparently cheap, but mostly quite useless articles, and by offering easy conditions of payment, they entice their customers to spend all manner of sums on pure luxury. Restrooms are provided to enable people to spend a long time in the stores, which thus become mere hot beds for extravagance, for let no one imagine he gets anything as a present. Really well-off people don't buy in large stores; they know what the poorer one doesn't know he who buys cheap buys dear. Do the crowds who buy in those palaces imagine that they were built otherwise than with their saved-up pennies? Do they think they get off paying for the escalators, the lifts, the restrooms, the fairy-like illumination?

Realize, also, that the large stores spell ruin to the small shopkeepers, that they exploit home-labor and their staffs most cruelly, that what is manufactured is mostly rubbish. The better articles are usually dearer than in respectable specialized shops, a fact which justifies our fight against the large stores. We regard them as a special form of the capitalistic idea in practical operation, which does not provide necessaries of life, but is merely there for the purpose of producing huge profits for the shareholders.

Given this leading conception of provision of the necessaries of life (which, we should observe, has nothing to do with the Communist scheme of economics), the question ranks first in importance in our attitude towards private property.

National Socialism recognizes private ownership of property as a principle and protects it by law, given that it is acquired and employed honorably. We cannot discuss it here, but anyone who rightly comprehends the term 'work' will quickly see that the product of 'work' must be the property of him who works. A producer will fail to understand why his work, or its value, should be the property of a vague 'community', nor will he readily admit that the fruits of his labor should go to an individual, the capitalist. Hence, a right understanding of the meaning of 'work' leads naturally to recognition of private ownership.

There is finally a further subject the conception of the home. The Home is not a reality unless it really is a man's own property, and his own home shelters his own family. A man's own fruit and vegetables out of his own garden taste better than a meal eaten in a crowded eating house.

Anyone who does not know the longing for possessions, nor the joy of possession will fail to understand the importance of recognizing private ownership. Such a man has no roots anywhere. It is curious that the preying type of man is always envious, always seeking something fresh to possess, whilst the Nordic man, the solid man of the soil, is modest in his ideas.

He wants no more than he can get by his work. A workman does not wish to have a fine villa which he could never earn; he wants a nice little house of his own, not a hired one for which during his life he would be paying three or four times much as the house cost to build. But the Jew, the capitalist he does not want to be tied to any plot of land; his ideal is a big safe stuffed with scrip, mortgage deeds and promissory notes.

Wealth, not in property but in other people's mortgaged property, is his aim. He does not work, but he rests not till he has amassed bundles of bonds giving him the whip hand over all those to whom he has lent money. The next demand of our Program is framed to put a stop to this.

The welfare of the nation demands that a limit shall be set to the amassing of wealth in the hands of individuals.

Wealth is not injurious in itself; on the contrary, possessions well administered do good to all who relate to them. But again, it is the capitalist system of loans which has turned wealth from a blessing into a curse; it is robbery. The great mass of possession less workers 40 and the indebted middle class are getting further and further separated from the rich; countless small owners are distraint upon for debt, and the power of the financiers, who know no fatherland, no homeland, waxes ever more sinister, as they sit in their modern robber-baron castles, the banks. To meet this, the National State shall see to it that:

All Germans shall be formed into a community of work for the furtherance of the common welfare and culture. This idea of a community of work implies the economic overthrow of the universalist conception of society. All work and production must be included within the higher idea of service to the community. It is in no way opposed to personal effort and industry, but it means that individual progress shall not be at the expense of one's fellow men. The following point gives expression to this demand.

Within the frame of the general duty of work attaching to every German, and with recognition of private ownership as a principle, every German shall be free to earn in whatever manner he chooses, and free to dispose of the results of his labor.

The foregoing expressly rejects the socializing schemes of Marxism and high finance. The State shall include the greatest possible number of free existences linked by the social idea of service. It is of course out of the question to run mines, blast-furnaces, rolling mills, shipyards on a small scale, but a hundred thousand free and independent master-shoemakers are better than five monster shoe factories.

The great landed estates in the North and East of Germany are more productive by being run on a large scale than if managed by small freehold farmers. Small freeholds do best if within easy reach of towns and villages. Our next point demands that:

A healthy combination of businesses of all kinds, large and small, including farming, shall be maintained.

Great businesses (syndicates, trusts) are nationalized. This demand is consistent with our general struggle against the capitalistic idea. The first aim of syndicates and trusts in any branch of production is to unite with other similar businesses for the purpose of dictating prices. They are governed by no desire to distribute good wares at a cheap price. Such 'rings' are especially attracted by new businesses which are doing well. New firms in the same line of business are bought up and put out of the way, often at a very large price by way of compensation. Supply is regulated by pooling, by which means they can regulate prices in accordance with an apparently genuine 'supply and demand'. That is what concerns the shareholders, who have no desire to see prices kept low by competition. New ideas and inventions are viewed with a hostile eye and preferably suppressed if their adoption would endanger the paying capacity of older plants. Such businesses, run as huge trusts from a big central office, are clearly 'ripe for socialization', i.e., they have ceased to fulfill any of the services If to the community which individual competition performs. They are paralyzed from the start and only serve the greed for capitalism.

Usurers and profiteers, and ruthless self-enrichment at the expense of the nation, shall be punished with death.

The Law, as it is now, gives special protection to individual property. Small thefts are punished inhumanly, whereas the Law supplies no way of catching large scale swindlers, who rob an entire nation by "capitalistic methods." We refer especially to those who promoted and profited by the inflation. It was the first time in history that an entire industrious nation was robbed of the whole of its savings by a crime of inflation on the vast scale as happened in Germany.

The greed of the banks after the stabilization was worse than highway robbery. More Germans fell victims to the practices of the 'war companies' than to any organized robber band.

When the time comes, we shall deal with these things more in detail and shall have to find a legal formula for them. But everyone will agree that 'organized fraud against the nation' must be punished as, and even more severely than small thefts of money, or fraud.

Introduction of an obligation year of labor or service for every German.

The obligation to serve by working will be the visible expression to the public of the duty of service. It is meant to be educational, and to place before each German an example of the whole community working as one man together. It will show to each German the blessing of the strict fulfillment of duty in working for the service of the nation.

Financial Policy

Breaking the thralldom of interest.

Our principles on this subject have been so fully set down in the second chapter that we shall only describe here the measures suitable for achieving our objective in practice.

Liberation of the State, and so of the nation, from its indebtedness and from the obligation to pay interest to the great financial houses. The State may make no debts for it has no necessity to do so. There is no comparison between the State and the private person who now and then requires loans and is forced to make debts. The State controls the Mint; it can thus make money, which the private person cannot do! It did this in a lunatic fashion during the inflation. It did the same with the Rentenmark, and the same after resigning its control to the so-called Reichsbank with the so-called Reichsmark.The State could make far better use of this right to make money, without the danger of inflation being involved.

But only if first:

The Reichsbank and all the issuing banks are nationalized, and if there is a provision of money for all great public objects (waterpower, railroads, etc.) not by means of loans, but by granting non-interest-bearing State bonds, or without using ready money.

In other words:

Wanton printing of bank notes, without creating new values, means inflation. We all lived through it. But the correct conclusion is that an issue of non-interest-bearing bonds by the State cannot produce inflation if new values are at the same time created.

The fact that to-day great economic enterprises cannot be set on foot without recourse to loans is sheer lunacy. Here is where reasonable use of the State's right to produce money which might produce most beneficial results.

It must be clear to anyone that, for instance, a great electrical plant using waterpower might well be erected in the following unexceptional manner:

> The Government introduces a Bill in the legislative Council for exploiting the waterpower of Bavaria, Saxony, etc., by satisfying all economic requirements. The local Diet, or other body, decides on construction, empowers the finance minister or the State Bank to issue a series of bank notes, marked specially to show that they are fully covered by the new works under contemplation. These notes are supported by the combined credit of the State or the Reich. No one can show any objection on the score of inflation. Construction takes place on the additional credit granted by the Council representing the nation, and the notes become legal tender like the rest.
>
> When the work is completed, nitrates or electricity are supplied to customers against this money, and in a few years the issue can be recalled and destroyed.
>
> Result: The State, the nation, has instituted a new work, which secures to them a great new source of revenue, and the nation is the richer by it.

To prove the folly of the present system, let us compare the foregoing with what goes on now:

> A loan is taken up.
>
> A few capitalists do what the whole nation, even though Parliament may vote in favor of it, cannot do; they allow the State to borrow money from them. Instead of using its direct authority for the benefit of the nation, the State engages to pay permanent interest for the sum required to complete certain work, thereby hanging a millstone round its neck.
>
> And what is most costly of all, it issues bonds, thus creating 'fresh purchasing capacity. On the balance sheet, it makes no difference whether the new work is represented by new paper money or new bonds. But the community suffers injury because the bonds imply that the new work is mortgaged to capital, which naturally makes itself quite secure, dictates prices, and takes the profits.

> Thus, it is really the financiers who are the richer by the development of the nation's waterpower; they are indifferent about repayment; they like to have to such monopolies as permanent milking cows. The population is forced to pay dear for electric current or nitrates, and once again a part of the national property is converted in the interests of the financiers.

I must refer the reader to my earlier writings, especially Der deutsche Staat, which treats these questions in more detail than is possible in this pamphlet. Several numbers in this series, moreover, deal with various special aspects of the coming State's novel methods of creating money.

We demand introduction of a fixed standard of coinage. That we admittedly have now, but the robbery remains the same as before. We National Socialists had everything ready, once we were in power, for bringing the inflation swindle to an end forthwith, and for introducing a new guaranteed standard of coinage.

Establishment of a New National Bank For Development & Economy

This demand is exhaustively explained in Pamphlet 8 of the National Socialist Library: ***Die Wohnungsnot und die Sociale Bau-und Wirtschaftsbank als Retterin aus Wohnungselend, Wirtschaftskrise und Erwerbs1osene1end.*** It is remarkable that this demand of ours for a financial policy has penetrated deeply into other political circles besides our own.

In 1921, I submitted this demand to the Bavarian Government in the form of a fully worked out Bill. There was at first much sympathy with the idea: but once the 'experts' banking fraternity were drawn into consultation, the Government rejected 'Feder's Utopia'.

After the successful Election in Thuringia in February 1921, our Party in the Landtag there worked hard for establishing such a bank and found von Kluchtzner, the finance minister, prepared to co-operate; the bourgeois section also was in sympathy. By a majority vote in the Landtag, the Government was empowered to establish a Social Bank for development and economy. Whereupon the Government of the Reich, under pressure from the Reichsbank, forbade the will of the people being carried out.

I had meanwhile managed to have a Bill in outline introduced in the

Reichstag, providing for similar banks in the different states; in the short Session of the Dawes year (1924) however, it was cautiously postponed by the Government Parties until the dissolution in the autumn of that year.

A Bill for a bank was before the Landtag of Mechlenberg. The Resolution was made ineffective by the vacillation of the German nationalist Finance Minister, also owing to the obstacles which the Reichsbank was expected to place in the way.

The idea underlying the bank for development is no less simple than the plan explained above for creating money for great public purposes.

A combined economic corporation, such as the bank for economic development, should be given the right to issue money for development (Baumark-Scheinen) covered by the value of the newly built houses. These could then be erected free from the huge burden of interest, which alone to-day makes it impossible to build in sufficient quantities

Every German with a home of his own. A free people on unencumbered land.

Complete re-modeling of the system of taxation on social-political economic principles. Delivery of the consumer from the burden of indirect taxation, and the producer from taxes which cramp his activities.

Social Policy

Social policy is the favorite motto of our present political cure-alls. It sounds so nice, makes them popular, and attracts votes for the Party which promises to make everything right.

When every Party promises the official, for instance, an increase of pay, they call that Social Policy.

It is the same when they promise to grant the wishes of the clerks and workers; or when they do a little to relieve people with small incomes, or war sufferers, or young teachers, or Germans abroad.

And all the people run after these political ratcatchers when they play on their 'social' flute.

It must first be made clear that Social Policy denotes the public welfare of the highest law, and that, as now understood, social policy is really one of self-interest having no regard to the general welfare. All sorts of careless promises are made, and those who make them must know from the start that it is impossible to fulfill them.

Now that Germany is so powerless politically, economically, and financially, which finds expression first in the Dawes Laws and now in the Young Law, and in the so-called policy of fulfillment which has laid burdens on our nation, making life almost impossible it is both false and ridiculous to talk about 'Social Policy'. Now that German life is so cramped, when each man is treading on his neighbor and trying to get ahead of him and to shove him aside, when the different classes of the population are at variance, promises to favor one group at the expense of another are not 'Social Policy for the general good', but one of inciting one class against another. They know very well that a momentary 'improvement' is annulled by a higher cost of living and higher taxation.

Social policy means something very different a determination to solve the social problem.

The out-of-luck, the exploited working classes believe that they're just wages, their proper position in the social order is being withheld from them hence class war.

It is clear to all that our economic life is suffering from deep injuries, bitter injustice. And yet the conclusions drawn by Marxism with its 'class war' and its 'social and economic demands' of 'expropriating the expropriator' and 'socialization' are utterly false, for that strikes at all the true requirements of a genuine social policy, whose highest law is the general welfare.

The leading principle of class war as a principle of policy is hatred. 'Expropriation of the expropriator' makes of envy a principle of economics, and 'socialization' means striking down personality in leadership, and setting up materialism, the mass, in the place of intellect and efficiency.

Nothing further is needed to prove the utter break-down of the Marxist doctrines, seeing the complete bankruptcy of the Communist system of economics and the miserable failure of the German Revolution of 1918.

I would call my readers' particular attention to the fact that this pseudo-socialism, born of Marxism, is not founded on common sense nor on any 'social' idea, is not constructive, but remains sunk in the lowest depths of political thought, that it rests on the same general principle of crass and chaotic individualism as we have always known it to do. It is believed merely by several individuals, united by feelings of hatred and envy, not by any constructive purpose against the other half of the nation. Can we be surprised that the social question is not, and cannot be, solved by this means, and that their sole solution is hatred and the desire for loot that a living State could not result from the Marxist Stock Exchange revolt, but only a heap of ruins.

Once again, National Socialism finds the right word:

Stock Exchange revolt.

Marxism is an expression of capitalistic treason. Capitalistic, because when a society founded on individualism has fallen into chaos, it of necessity falls under the sway of the great financial magnate.

The social-political theories, which pretend to be 'anti-capitalistic' (Marxism, the war between classes) Social policy as understood to-day are necessarily capitalistic, for they share the same intellectual principle. They have not the wish to construct organically member by member, to interlock with painful care the different classes working under the high conception of national unity, but their aspirations are purely selfish, **their wish is to better their own position without regard to others.**

Capitalism and Marxism are one and the same!

They grow on the same intellectual stem. There is a whole world of difference between them and us, their bitterest opponents. Our whole conception of the construction of society differs widely from theirs. It is neither a class-struggle nor class-selfishness, but our chief law is the general welfare.

Great developments in Old Age Insurance by nationalizing life-annuities. Every member of the German nation shall be assured of enough to live upon on attaining a certain age, and before that age, if permanently disabled.

That is the solution to the social problem.

It is not so much direct discontent with wages, salaries and incomes which cause social tension, as uncertainty, a man's anxiety about his later years, lest he may be flung on the streets. It is this gnawing anxiety which drives the various occupations to join in sham-social organizations of the Marxist and capitalist types and embitters the animosity between employer and employee. It releases the basest instincts on both sides, and mutual animosity is the result. The worker's proper aim in life fades away in the struggle for a momentary increase of wages, and he never realizes what the great aim of social policy should be the proper provision for old age.

We note once again how the State discovered a good and commendable solution in the case of the official class, by providing for them after retirement. It is the proper and happy solution of the capitalist ideal of income, namely, to convert it into the true State's ideal of provision, based on personal labor and efficiency.

It will be the highest and noblest aim of National Socialism to realize this standard of general welfare.

Profit-Sharing for All

The NSDAP identifies itself with this demand. It is in fact a purely socialist demand in the proper sense of the word; nevertheless, it comes to us as an attractive but corrupting present from capitalism.

Sharing of profits arising out of the work of others' comes under the head of the unearned income, which is most sharply attacked by National Socialism. Sharing of the profits from a man's own work is a demand so natural and social so just that nothing can be advanced against it as a principle.

It is in the carrying of it out that the difficulty arises, that is, in limiting the amount of the share due to the production, skill and industry of the worker, and of that due to the brainwork of the inventor, the accountant, the merchant, the management, and other circumstances connected with the business.

It is, of course, highly important that the parties who increase the value of a product should not be left out of consideration. Even under the present system, some part of the booty which capital hopes to get out of a business could be recovered for the worker.

We shall not discuss here the question of how later the National Socialist State will solve the problem. I personally considered that a general lowering of prices, at the same time maintaining wages at the present level, would be the better and more practical way to fulfill the demand for sharing out the profits of the whole of our national production.

It is, however, possible that the National Socialist State will solve the problem in a far more comprehensive manner than is conceived to-day by brains with a Marxist and capitalistic tendency. The present demand for profit-sharing springs either from a desire for profits (essentially capitalistic), or from envy (essentially Marxist).

In the ideal State alone, as we conceive it, is it justified, because, when we come to solve it, we must avoid the capitalistic method of granting a small share in the business, the sole object of which is to secure for the larger shareholders their right to their dividends, and the Marxist idea of envy, for that debases the personal factor and injures the public.

We give a few examples for the sake of clarity.

It does no good to the 'profit-sharing' workers in a shoe factory to get a few shares in the business or a small bonus or a pair of shoes at cost price, if they must pay just as dear for their shirts, suits, socks, food, and drink, because the tailors, bakers and brewers cover the greed of the clothiers, bakeries, and breweries by their own 'profit-sharing'.

Lowering of prices is the charm which must give every member of the nation a share in the profits of national production.

It will not satisfy the feeling of social justice of a genuine National Socialist it the street-sweepers, day-laborers, railway men, postmen, transport-workers, hospital-workers to name only a few, agricultural laborers, miners, builders, laborers, are to be excluded from profit-sharing, simply because these classes do not contribute to increase values. Also, of agriculture, (in which not merely the details of farming must be considered, but also the millions engaged in other businesses connected with it) it must be said that it 'pays' in years when the harvest is good; in the heavy industries also, the mines only yield a bare profit owing the pressure of world competition.

Can we assert that these millions of workers and employees, who are often engaged in most important branches of industry, but who, owing to the circumstances, cannot hope for a direct share in the profits, are to get less consideration than the numerous classes, who work perhaps as washers-up or porters in a nightclub or a Turkish bath, or in an optical or chemical factory enjoying a monopoly and supplying the whole world? Are the latter to share the profits and dividends on luxury production, are they to make it more and more impossible for most of the nation to attain to these advantages?

We like to contemplate a shower of dividends, bonuses, Christmas presents of money poured out upon workers and officials who have done splendid work for a business for years. Such aspirations of a social-political nature need not be discussed and argued in this treatise on general principles. The demand, as things are now, is an important demand, and one which should attract adherents. 'Profits' depend mainly on the general business situation and on the technical skill and salesmanship of the management; failure may come through faulty construction or a mistake in calculations. However skilled the workers may be, however industrious, they can have little or no influence on the results of the year's work, or on the gains or losses. Their efficiency justifies them in demanding a proper and sufficient wage, but there are no moral or economic grounds for their claiming a share in the profits. They would quite rightly resist the suggestion that they should cover any losses of the business year out of their savings; they would rightly resist being expected to make up, by a lowering of wages, for bad management or extravagant living on the part of the directors. But 'profit-sharing' is only justifiable if there is ability and readiness to share risks and losses, or if special efficiency merits it."

Here is one aspect of general profit-sharing.

Why, for instance, should the great dye-works of Germany, with their predominant position of monopoly, continue to be but a capitalistic milking cow for the shareholders of the I. G. Farbenindustrie, and at the best, by raising prices, give a share of profits to their workers and officials?

It will be the task of the National Socialist State to see that huge monopolist profits shall be placed at the general disposal by a most generous lowering of prices.

It is obvious that the problem is not a question of social policy but is closely bound up with the present-day capitalistic social order (shareholders' claims). We wish to apply these shortly expressed principles; and to be guided by them in our aim of realizing profit-sharing as widely as possible in all businesses in which the profits go only into the pockets of professional financiers.

Expropriation of all profits not made by honest work, but through the war, the Revolution and further the stabilization and revaluation of the mark; also, the property of moneylenders and grabbers. This is a measure of punishment and justice, requiring no explanation under any principle.

Removal of the dearth of housing by extensive building throughout the Reich with the means provided under No. 20 (the bank for development). This closes the list of social-political demands. On the technical, financial question not, much can be said in this pamphlet, for it is a very large special subject, and one which, it would seem, only financial minds understand, and which will have to be carried out by them. Pamphlet 8 of the N. S. library deals fully with the subject.

Religion & Art

It is not possible to state on this subject more than a very few leading principles in the space of a Program. That has already been done. For the rest, it must be our principle not to drag questions of religion into statements on general politics, although we may well treat the corrupting influence of the secret doctrines of Judaism as an object for public statements and attacks.

The same applies to all the stupid attacks on Christianity. Expressions such as "Christianity has only done harm" merely show that the man who says them has neither human nor political intelligence.

One may well blame the Church for meddling in politics, and all good Christians will disapprove the cruelties practiced in the name of the Cross by the Inquisition and trials for witchcraft, but it is wrong to abuse in general terms the greatest phenomenon in human history for the mistakes and depravities of individuals. The Christian religion has raised and edified millions and millions and brought them to God by the way of suffering.

The culture of the Middle Ages stood up in the sign of the Cross; achievement, sacrifice, courageous faiths have their roots in Christianity. Thus, we must be careful to distinguish the inner spiritual kernel of Christianity from the various forms of excrescence which have appeared upon it in its passage through history.

Our Party stands upon the basis of positive Christianity. (This view drastically changes after 1936 where many decrees are signed into law in hopes to remove Christianity slowly from the German minds (Hitler Jugend). Thus, ushering in a new German Spiritual Age with out influence from the faiths and churchs of Abraham. A faith in a God was still an important aspect of German life). This is not the place to discuss all the problems, hopes and desires, whether the German nation may at some time discover some new form for its religious beliefs and experiences; these are matters quite beyond the limits of a Program such as that of National Socialism.

It is of urgent importance to set our face against all the disruptive influences which are doing harm to our nation in the domain of art, literature, science, the stage, the moving pictures, and above all throughout the entire

Press. Our Program of principles the 25 Points goes far enough into detail for it to be unnecessary to say any more on this subject.

Military & Other Reforms

The national Army, the Chambers of trades and professions, reform of the franchise and the law, are such vast questions affecting public life that they cannot be dismissed in a few sentences. The leading ideas are set out in the Program itself, but the task of thinking and working them out and, above all, of grafting them on to the historical past will be the great problem of the coming years, when we hope that political power will be ours, and when we shall have to be equipped with the force and knowledge necessary for taking over the business of the State.

Here we have a rich field for research under National Socialism.

The significance of National Socialism is shown by the fact that it leaves no domain of the national life untouched; for it provides an entirely new foundation on which we shall have to build up that life.

CHAPTER 9

WHAT WE DO NOT DESIRE

To strengthen the positive side of our Program it will be well to state shortly what we do not desire.

We do not desire the wheels of history to turn backwards nor to restore to life dynasties which faded away, leaving hardly a trace of themselves through their own fault. Nor do we desire to set the classes that have been dethroned up again in their former privileged positions. The officer class and the officials are no higher or better than any other professional class, in so far as they genuinely work in with our idea of serving the nation first.

It is not uniform or gold lace, but performance, which makes a man.

We do not desire one-sided preference or artificial elevation for the working class, nor any kind of proletarian dictatorship. No man may talk himself" into believing that any class may, simply from having been oppressed in the past, assume a claim to be given power. Such aspirations, when translated into realities, unfailingly lead to terrible consequences, such as those which accompanied the Stock Exchange revolt of November 1918. So far it is not the 'oppressed' section of the population, which is on top, but a crowd of political swindlers, greedy adventurers, profiteers, jabberers, and fools who have got possession of the political machine and the administration. The promised dictatorship of the) proletariat has turned into the dictatorship of the 'Proletariat'.

Even a new ordering of the State under National Socialism could have no hope of success unless it had at its disposal a thoroughly trained staff of resolute men completely imbued with the principles of our Program, serious men of energy and experience. Even with us, too many pure demagogues would elbow their way in and reap advantage under the new order.

It is much easier to criticize the faults of a collapsing social order than to do constructive work on it.

We require not merely a new Party, slowly obtaining a footing in Parliament and administration, and then perhaps accepting a post or two in a coalition Ministry, only to get its back broken in the end, for then our part in history would be played out, just as to-day Social Democracy is finished as a political and intellectual force in Germany. The same applies to the German Nationalists, who have already gone back on their main principles to get seats in the Government.

We do not want Ministers who take office purely for the sake of the position or for power, but we shall consider any such position as a stage towards our great objective. Between us and the rest, there is always the flaming sword of our world theory.

On the one side of the State, or rather the sham State, of the Liberal-democratic parliamentary stamp, forced by necessity to mask the tyranny of the financiers, and at its feet a seething mob of Jew camp-followers and place-hunters, fighting to make a living out of the system.

On our side, the fight for the liberation and purification of our people, till we achieve the true State of social justice and national liberty.

Conclusion

The task of this first pamphlet of the N. S. Library is to teach the National Socialist what he should know about the Party Program. We have seen again and again the single main principle which is drawn through all our arguments like a scarlet thread: National Socialism is a theory of the world, standing in sharp opposition to the present-day world of capitalism and its Marxist and bourgeois satellites.

Our life is a struggle in the service of this mighty idea, a struggle for a new Germany.

We National Socialists wave our storm-banner before the world. Ever young, shining and glittering in the sun, rises the Hooked Cross, the symbol of re-awakening life.

CHAPTER 10

ABOLITION OF INTEREST

Mammonism is the heavy, all-encompassing, and overwhelming sickness from which our contemporary cultural sphere, and indeed all mankind, suffers. It is like a devastating illness, like a devouring poison that has gripped the peoples of the world.

By Mammonism is to be understood:

On the one hand, the overwhelming international money-powers, the supra governmental financial power enthroned above any right of self-determination of peoples, international big capital, the purely Gold International; on the other hand, a mindset that has taken hold of the broadest circle of peoples; the insatiable lust for gain, the purely worldly oriented conception of life that has already led to a frightening decline of all moral concepts and can only lead to more.

This mindset is embodied and reaches its acme in international plutocracy.

The chief source of power for Mammonism is the effortless and endless income that is produced through interest.

From the thoroughly immoral idea of interest on loans the Gold International was born. The mental and moral constitution grown from the lust for interest and profiteering of every kind has led to the frightening corruption of a part of the bourgeoisie.

The idea of interest on loans is the diabolical invention of big loan-capital; it alone makes possible the lazy drone's life of a minority of tycoons at the expense of the productive peoples and their work-potential; it has led to profound, irreconcilable differences, to class-hatred, from which war among citizens and brothers was born.

The only cure, the radical means to heal suffering humanity, is the abolition of thralldom of interest.

The abolition of enslavement to interest on money signifies the only possible and conclusive liberation of productive labor from the hidden coercive money-powers.

The abolition of enslavement to interest signifies the restoration of the free 7 personality, the redemption of man from slavery, from the curse whereby Mammonism has bound his soul. Whoever wishes to fight capitalism must abolish enslavement to interest.

Where must the abolition of enslavement to interest begin? With loan-capital!

Why?

Because loan-capital, compared to all industrial big capital, is so overpowering that the great money-powers can only be fought effectively through the abolition of interest-slavery.

20:1 is the proportion of loan-capital to industrial big capital. The German people must annually raise more than 12 billion in interest for loan capital in the form of direct and indirect taxes, rent, and the rising cost of living, while even in the boom-years of the war the sum-total of all dividends distributed by the German joint-stock companies amounted to only 1 billion.

The avalanche-like growth of loan-capital surpasses all human capacity for calculation, through eternal, endless, and effortless income from interest, and from interest on interest.

What blessing does the abolition of enslavement to interest bring for the laboring folk of Germany, for the proletarians of all countries of the Earth?

The abolition of enslavement to interest gives us the possibility of pursuing the repeal of all direct and indirect taxes. Hear this, you value-producing men of all lands, all states, and continents: all state revenues flowing from direct and indirect sources pour constantly into the pockets of big loan-capital.

The profits of state-owned businesses, including the postal service, telegraph, telephone, railroad, mines, forests, and so on, suffice entirely for the funding of all essential state commitments for schools, universities, courts, administrative agencies, and social welfare.

Thus, no true socialism will bring any blessing to humanity if the profits from public enterprises remain tributary to big loan-capital.

Therefore, we demand as a fundamental law of the state, first for the German peoples, then as a fundamental law for all those kindred peoples that wish to enter with us into the cultural community of a league of nations, the following:

1. War-bonds, along with all other debt-instruments of the German Reich, along with all other debt-instruments of the German federal states, especially railroad-bonds, as well as debenture-bonds of all local governments, are declared, under cancellation of the obligation for interest, to be legal tender for the face-value (or rather are to be converted into bank-credit).

2. With all other fixed-interest papers, covered bonds, industrial bonds, mortgages, etc., the obligation for interest is replaced by the obligation to repay the principal; thus after 20 or 25 years, depending on the interest rate, the lent capital is repaid, and the debt retired.

3. All real-estate debts, mortgages, etc., are to be paid off on installments of the same amount as the payments required hitherto, in keeping

with the charges recorded in the land-register. The property in houses and land freed from debt in this manner becomes partly the property of the state or of the local government. In this way the state becomes better situated to control and to lower rents.

4. The entire monetary system should be under the state's central bank. All private banks likewise; postal-check banks, savings banks, and credit unions all become affiliated as branch-operations.

5. All credit for real estate is awarded only through the state's bank. Personal credit and commercial credit are mandated to private bankers under a concession from the state. This concession is granted based on consideration of need, with a ban on the establishment of branches for certain districts. The scale of charges is fixed by the state.

6. Equity-securities are paid off in the same manner as fixed-interest papers at the annual rate of 5%. Excess profits are paid out in part to the stockholders as compensation for "risked" capital (in contrast to fixed interest and coin-backed papers), while the remaining surplus, by the sovereign right of labor, is either socially distributed or applied for the reduction of the prices of products.

7. For all persons who for physical reasons (advanced age, illness, physical or mental work-disability, extreme youth) are not able to earn their livelihood, the interest-incomes from present capital assets continue to be paid as a pension at the same, and eventually even increased levels, in return for delivery of securities.

8. In the interest of a reduction of the current inflation of paper money, a universal, strongly graduated tax on war-bond certificates and other debt instruments of the Reich and of states is enacted. These papers are to be pulped.

9. Through intensive enlightenment of the people, it is to be made clear to the people that money is and should be nothing other than a voucher for completed labor; that while every highly developed economy of course has need of money as a medium of exchange, the function of money also ends with that, and in no case should money be lent a supra-mundane power to grow of itself by means of interest, at the expense of productive labor.

Why have we not already done all this, which is so self-evident, which must be regarded as the Egg of Columbus for the social question?

Because in our Mammonistic blindness we have unlearned how to see clearly that the doctrine of the sanctity of interest is a monstrous self-deception, that the gospel of the loan-interest that alone makes one blessed has entangled our entire thinking in the golden web of international plutocracy. Because we have forgotten and are deliberately kept in confusion by the omnipotent money-powers about the fact that except in the case of a few rich people the interest that seems so lovely, and is so beloved of the thoughtless, is completely offset by taxes. All our tax-legislation is and remains, so long as we do not have liberation from enslavement to interest, only a tribute-obligation to big capital, and not, as we would imagine, a voluntary sacrifice for the accomplishment of labor for the community.

Therefore, liberation from enslavement to interest on money is the clear motto for the global revolution, for the liberation of productive labor from the chains of the supra-governmental money-powers.

Implementation & Rationality

We stand during one of the most grievous crises that our impoverished folk have had to endure in its painful history. Seriously ill is our folk; seriously ill is the entire world. Helplessly, the nation's stammer; a passionate longing, a cry for redemption passes through the gloomy masses. With laughter and dancing, with cinema and pageantry, the folk seeks to forget its own lamentable destiny to forget about its disillusioned hopes, about the deep inner pain, about the terrible disappointment over what one would so gladly call "gains of the revolution." But how did we imagine it all differently? How did all the fine promises run differently? All that we hoped to gain in the dark of night, in the darkness of our military collapse, seemed to be glistening gold, but now, when the gray day illuminates the find, it is all rotten bits of wood. Now we stand here at a loss. For the sake of these rotten bits of wood that shone so finely in the night, we have thrown away everything that hitherto was dear and valuable to us and have stuffed all our pockets with this lamentable trove. No wonder that the rage of despair grips precisely the poorest of the poor, and that they rage in senseless wrath against their own brothers, and in their deep longing for redemption seek to destroy all that stands in the way. This condition must lead to utter madness if conscience lessness and stupidity goad the people further.

And where this madness leads is evident in Bolshevik Russia, where nationalization—there called 'socialization'—has proven a failure, as even the unperturbed Lenin admits. The economy is destroyed, the buying-power of money is down to nothing, the intelligentsia killed, the laborer without bread. Despair in the entire people; only bloody terror based on Chinese and Latvian mercenaries can protect the red dictators from the vengeance of the betrayed folk. Among us too, the development will follow this course, if international speculators, obsessed party fanatics, representatives of the most grievously burdened bourgeoisie, and members of a race most deeply alien in nature to the German folk, continue to be allowed in the government.

What indeed were those pretty-pretty words that one whispered into our ear? Negotiated peace, League of Nations, parliamentarianism, sovereignty of the people, democracy, dictatorship of the proletariat, socialism, destruction of capitalism, liberation from militarism, and other such pretty slogans. A new free people were supposed to arise, which should determine its own destiny. None of that has come true, was able to come true, or ever could come true, if we do not with the highest moral seriousness investigate all these apparitions, all these slogans if we do not conscientiously test the symptoms of the illness like an intelligent, concerned physician, and painstakingly diagnose the present condition of the sick person, sparing no effort to ascertain whence this serious critical illness arises.

The sickness of our age is called Mammonism.

What is Mammonism?

Mammonism is the sinister, invisible, mysterious reign of the great international money-powers. Mammonism is, however, also a mindset; it is the worship of these money-powers on the part of all those who are infected with the Mammonistic poison. Mammonism is the unlimited hypertrophy of the healthy human drive for acquisition. Mammonism is the lust for money grown into a madness, which knows no higher goal than to pile money on top of money, which seeks with unequaled brutality to coerce all forces of the world into its service, and must lead to the economic enslavement, to the exploitation of the work potential of all peoples of the world. Mammonism is the mindset that has led to a decline of all moral concepts. Mammonism, considered as a worldwide phenomenon, is to be equated with brutal, ruthless egoism in man. Mammonism is the spirit of greed, of boundless desire to rule, of the mentality entirely focused on seizing the goods and treasures of the world; it is at its core the religion of the purely worldly oriented human type.

Mammonism is the direct opposite of socialism. Socialism, conceived as the highest moral idea, as the idea that man is not in the world only for himself alone, that every man has duties toward the community, toward all humanity, and that he is not only responsible for the momentary wellbeing of his family, of the members of his tribe, of his folk, but that he also has unshakable moral obligations toward the future of his children and his folk.

More concretely, we must see Mammonism as the conscious collusion of the power-hungry big capitalists of all peoples. Noteworthy in this has always been the hidden arrival of Mammonism.

The big tycoons lurk indeed as the ultimate driving force behind world encompassing Anglo-American imperialism; nothing else. The great money-powers indeed financed the terrifying mass-homicides of the World War. The great money-powers have indeed, as owners of all great newspapers, woven the world into a web of lies. They have with satisfaction whipped up all lower passions, have diligently fostered the growth of present tendencies, and have through clever press-propaganda brought French revanchism to a boil. They carefully nurtured the Pan-Slavic idea, the Serbian conceit of being a great power, and the need of these states for money, to the point that the world conflagration must ignite.

Even among us in Germany the spirit of Mammonism that wanted to know only more export-figures, national wealth, expansion, big bank projects, and international finance deals, led to a rout of public morality, to the decline of our ruling circle into materialism and hedonism, to a superficiality in our national life, all factors that share blame for the terrifying collapse.

With astonishment we must ask ourselves whence Mammonism, whence international big capital derives its irresistible power.

It is not to be overlooked that the international collaboration of the great money powers represents a completely new phenomenon. We have no parallel to this in history. International obligations of a monetary nature were practically unknown. Only with the rising global economy, with general global commerce, did the idea of international interest-economy establish itself, and here we touch the deepest root, here we have hit upon the innermost source of strength from which the Golden International draws its irresistible power.

Interest, the effortless and endless influx of goods based on the mere ownership of money without any addition of labor, has caused the great money-powers to grow. Loan-interest is the diabolical principle from which the Gold International was born. Loan-capital has firmly attached to its blood-funnel everywhere. Like the arms of an anemone, big loan capital has ensnared all states, all peoples of the world.

Government loans, government bonds, railroad bonds, war bonds, mortgages, covered-bond obligations in short loan-instruments of every kind have in a manner ensnared our entire economic life, so that henceforth all the peoples of the world wriggle helplessly in the golden webs. For the sake of the interest principle, in keeping with a thoroughly mad political delusion that every kind of possession carries an entitlement to earnings, we have submitted to enslavement to interest on money. Not a single real, valid moral reason can be given as to why mere possession of money should bring an entitlement to perpetual interest payments.

This inner opposition to interest, and to income of every kind without any occurrence of productive labor, extends through the soul-life of all peoples and times. But never has this deep inner resistance to the power of money become so conscious for the nations as in our time.

Never has Mammonism been prepared in such a world-encompassing manner to begin world-domination. Never yet has it placed in its service all baseness, lust for power, lust for revenge, greed, envy, and falsehood in such a cleverly concealed and yet brutally pushy manner as now. The World War is at its inmost core one of the biggest decisions in the evolutionary process of humanity in the struggle to decide whether in the future the Mammonisticmaterialistic worldview or the socialistic-aristocratic worldview should determine the fate of the world.

On the surface, the Mammonistic Anglo-American coalition has, without a doubt, been initially victorious. As a reaction against it, Bolshevism arose in the East, and if one wishes to see a great idea in Bolshevism, it is without a doubt the position was diametrically opposed to the Mammonistic worldview. The methods that Bolshevism seeks to employ for this, however, are the botched cures of a Dr. Eisenbarth. They are the attempt to help someone sick from internal poisoning with a scalpel by amputating his head, arm, and legs.

Against this rampage of Bolshevism, against this senseless overturning, we must present a workable new idea that with unifying force unites all laboring classes, to drive out the poison that has made the world sick.

I see this means in the abolition of enslavement to interest on money.

There are three factors that make interest in loan-capital conspicuous as the authentic and true cause of our financial misery.

First, the monstrous disproportion of fixed-interest loan-capital, thus of capital that grows of its own accord without application of creative labor, and indeed grows on forever. Among us in Germany, this loan-capital has already reached a level that we do not consider too high at 250 billion. In contrast to this enormous sum, the industrial working capital of our entire German industry stands at only 11.8 billion. In addition, there is the 3.5 billion in capital of the 16,000 industrial limited-liability companies (G.m.b.H), so that altogether we have only about 15 billion in industrial capital to tabulate. 20:1 is the first fundamental finding.[3]

This appraisal means that in financial problems of the largest importance, all measures concerned with loan-capital must prove 20 times as effective as measures directed at industrial big capital.

Second: the interest-payment on the loan-capital above, estimated at 250 billion, considered in its totality for all times, amounts to about 12½ billion annually. By contrast, the Sum-total of all industrial dividends distributed in the year 1916 mounted in the year 1915 to about one billion marks. In the preceding decades, this number was, on the average, about 600 million. In the last two years of the war (1914-1918) it may very well have gone up considerably but will record an all the-greater crash for the current year (1919).

The average profitability of all German stock-corporations (A.G.) was 8.21%; thus, only about 3½% higher than the average return on fixed-interest loan-values.

Thus, I recapitulate, in the future the German people will have to pay about 12.5 billion (annually) for the various eternal interest-charges of big loan-capital, while the yield from industrial capital in the greatest boom-year was 1 billion, and in times of undisturbed prosperity only 0.6 billion. Thus, we see again here a proportion of the orders of magnitude of 20:1 to 12:1.

The third and most dangerous factor is the enormous growth beyond comprehension of big loan-capital through interest and through interest in interest. I must here digress a bit more and hope through a small excursion into higher mathematics to explain the problem. First some examples.

The charming story of the invention of the game of chess is well known.

The rich Indian king Shihram granted to the inventor, as thanks to the invention of the royal game, the fulfillment of a wish. The wish of the wise man was that the king should give him one grain of wheat on the first square of the chess-game, two on the second, four on the third, and thus always on each square twice as many as on the one before. The king smiled at the seemingly modest wish of the wise man and ordered that a sack of wheat be brought so that, for every square, the grains of wheat could be apportioned. As we all know, the fulfillment of this wish was impossible, even for the richest prince in the world. All the world's harvests in a thousand years would not suffice to fill the 64 squares of the chessboard.

One more example: many will still remember from their schooldays the torture of calculating compound interest; how the penny invested at the time of the birth of Christ multiplies at compound interest so that it doubles every 15 years. In the year 15 after the birth of Christ, the penny has grown into 2 pennies. In the year 30AD to 4 pennies, in the year 45AD to 8 pennies and so on. Very few will remember what value this penny would represent today: a volume of gold equivalent to the volume of the Earth, the Sun, and all the planets combined would not be adequate to represent the value of this penny invested in compound interest.

A third example: the fortune of the House of Rothschild, the oldest international plutocracy, is valued today at about 40 billion. It is well known that in Frankfurt around the year 1800, old Mayer Amschel Rothschild, without wealth of his own worth mentioning, laid the foundation for the gigantic fortune of his house through fractional-reserve lending of the millions that Count Wilhelm I of Hesse had entrusted to him for safekeeping.

Had the accretion of money through interest and interest on interest with Rothschild succeeded only at the modest rate of the penny, the curve would not have climbed so steeply as it had. But if the Rothschilds' collective wealth increased only at the rate of the penny, the Rothschilds' fortune in the year 1935 would be 80 billion, in 1950 160 billion, in 1965 320 billion, and with that it would already exceed by far the total German national wealth.

From these three examples, a mathematical law can be derived. The curve that represents the rise of the Rothschild fortune, the curve that can be derived from the number of wheat-grains for the chessboard, and the number that the multiplication of the penny produces at compound interest, are simple mathematical curves. All these curves have the same character. After initially modest and gradual increase, the curve becomes ever steeper and soon practically approaches being almost tangential to infinity.

Altogether differently, however, does the growth-curve of industrial capital proceed. Likewise sprung mostly from small beginnings, soon a strong escalation of the curves appears, until a certain saturation of capital is reached. Then the curves run flatter, and in certain industries will perhaps even decline slightly, if new inventions have led to the devaluation of existing factories, machines, and so on. I would like to select only one example here; the development of the Krupp works. In 1826, old man Krupp died almost without assets. In 1855, Alfred Krupp received his first order for 36 cannons on behalf of the Egyptian government. In 1873, Krupp had already employed 12,000 workers. In 1903, Frau Berta Krupp sold the entire works and property to the Alfred Krupp joint-stock company for 160 million. Today, the total value of the stock-capital amounts to 250 million. What does the name Krupp connote for us Germans? The acme of our industrial development. The world's first maker of (steel) cannons. A vast sum of the most tenacious, purposeful, intensive productivity. For hundreds of thousands of our folk-comrades, the Krupp endeavor has meant bread and work. For our nation, weapons, and defense –and yet it is a dwarf compared to the Rothschild billions. What significance does the growth of the Krupp fortune during a century have compared to the growth of the Rothschild fortune through effortless and endless accretion from interest and interest in interest?

The two curves drawn in bold lines represent loan-interest and indeed the upper curve shows the development of the Rothschild fortune and the lower curve, at first flat and then rapidly rising, shows in a very general way the characteristic development of all such curves, in which a small advance on the horizontal axis can produce a doubling of the value on the vertical axis. The hatched line shows the development-curve of our total industry in the last 40-50 years. The differently hatched fine lines show the development of several randomly selected big industrial enterprises from which the general character of the hatched curve of industrial capital is derived.

It must be expressly remarked that the curves of loan-capital are shown strongly compressed. Thus, for example, the curve of the Rothschild fortune must be set 80 times so high as the Krupp curve. The purpose of showing the curves, of course, is only to demonstrate the fundamentally different character of the two types of capital. The curves of loan-capital show at first and quite gradually rising development; the development then goes faster until, ever wilder and dragging everything with it, it raises itself far beyond human concepts and strives toward infinity.

The curve of industrial capital, by contrast, remains in the finite! However strong the divergences that a trace may show in detail, overall, the fundamental character of industrial development will always be such that after strong initial development of a certain period of maturity, of saturation, follows, after which sooner or later the decline ensues.

Nothing shows us more clearly the deep essential difference between loan-capital and industrial capital. Nothing can make the difference clearer for us between the devastating effects of loan-capital and the business-profits (dividends) of business capital put up and risked in large industrial enterprises than this comparison.

It cannot be emphasized enough that the recognition of the mathematical laws that loan-capital and industrial capital follow alone shows us the clear path where the lever is to be applied for setting aright our wrecked finance-economy. We recognize clearly that not the capitalistic economic order, not capital and as such, is the scourge of humanity. The insatiable interest-need of big loan-capital is the curse of all laboring humanity!

Capital must be! Labor must be! Labor alone can do little. Capital alone can do nothing!

Capital without labor can only be sterile! Therefore, the most important demand, the most noble task of the revolution, the most sensible meaning of a world revolution, is the abolition of enslavement to interest on money.

The House of Rothschild today is valued at 40 billion. The billionaires of American high finance, Misters Cahn, Loeb, Schiff, Speyer, Morgan, Vanderbilt, and Astor are valued together at 60-70 billion at the least. At an interest-rate of only 5% this means an income for these eight families of 5-6 billion, which, according to the research of Karl Helfferich, is roughly 75% of the annual income that all taxpayers in Prussia had in the year 1912. (There were at that time around 21,000,000 taxpayers, 75% of that would be about 15,000,000. For every taxpayer, there are, on the average 1.56 relatives; hence, 23 million relatives.)

Around 38,000,000 Germans thus have had to live on what the afore-mentioned billionaires have as a yearly income. Certainly, the American billionaires are not pure loan-capitalists in the same sense as the House of Rothschild and so on. I do not care at all to argue about whether the American billionaires are really "100-million-dollar millionaires" or "1000million-mark billionaires"; in the former case, one would just have to reckon in one or two dozen additional Croesuses. Or let us simply accept Rathenau's "300"; then our inventory will certainly be in order. Here, it is not important to give an exact number, but the acknowledged ratio of 300 to 38,000,000 opens our eyes to the brutal reign of international loan-capital.

Therefore, let us cast off these terrible chains that can only strangle all energetic labor; let us tear away from money the power to bear interest, and ever again to bear interest until all humanity has become entirely obligated for interest to international loan-capital.

Thus, it is these three points that make clear to us for the first time where alone the lever may be effectively applied for the alleviation of our internal financial distress.

For another thing, we recognize that the assault of the entire socialist world of ideas against industrial capital has been completely off the mark, because even an intended complete regulation or socialization of all entrepreneurial profit assuming an unweakened economy would yield a laughably meager sum, compared to the enormous financial burdens of the budgets of our Reich and our State.

Through the abolition of enslavement to interest on money, the entire financial malaise can be eliminated with one blow. At once we feel solid ground under our feet again; at once, it must and will become clear to us we have only deceived ourselves in the most grotesque manner with this wretched bond-economy.

For what else is loan-capital, but debts? Loan-capital is debts! One cannot repeat that often enough. What form of madness is it when the German people in its totality have borrowed 150 billion for its war? When it has even promised itself for this a quantity of 7½ billion in interest and now feels itself shifted into the awkward situation, inevitable from the start, of trying to collect this 7½ billion from itself in the form of entirely fanciful taxes?

The tragic thing about this self-deception meanwhile is less the stupidity of this whole war-bond economy, of which we have always made so much better use than the rest of the world, than the fact that only a relatively small number of big capitalists derives enormous benefit from it, while the entire laboring folk, including the medium-sized and smaller capitalists, as well as business, trade, and industry, must pay the interest. And here the political side of the whole idea comes to light. Here they can recognize that in fact big loan-capital and only this (i.e., not industrial capital) is the curse of all laboring humanity. One may twist and turn the thing as one wishes, but always the mass of all hard-working people must in the end bear the cost of interest-payments on loan-capital. The middle-sized and smaller capitalists have nothing to show for their lovely interest-payments; can have nothing to show, for the sums of interest must be entirely taxed away. Whether in the form of direct taxes or indirectly in the way of indirect taxes, stamps, tariffs, or other burdens on commerce, the hard-working folk are always the sucker and big capital the beneficiary. It is now quite astonishing to see how the socialist idea-world of Marx and Engel.

It is now quite astonishing to see how the socialist idea-world of Marx and Engels, from the Communist Manifesto to the Erfurt Program (especially Kautsky), and even the current socialist leaders, spare the interests of loan-capital as if on command. The sanctity of interest is taboo; interest is the holy of holies; no one has yet dared to call it into question. While property, nobility, security of person and possessions, the laws of the Crown, privileges and religious conviction, honor of officers, fatherland, and freedom are outlawed, interest is holy and unassailable. Confiscation of wealth and socialization, thus outright violations of the law that are only somewhat sugarcoated, insofar as they are committed ostensibly in the name of the totality of individuals, are the order of the day: all of that is permitted, but interest is the "noli me tangere," the "touch-me-not."

The interest payment on the Reich's debt is the alpha and omega of the state budget. Its gigantic weight drags the ship of state into the abyss and yet... it is all a big swindle... a monstrous self-deception, fostered only and solely for the benefit of the great money-powers.

Here I would like to touch briefly now upon the objections relating to small pensioners, to be discussed later, so that one does not get hung up thinking about them. In the consideration of the very big questions these are not considered, but it goes without saying that these compensations will be provided through the broadest expansion of social-welfare services.

Swindle, I said! Interest-swindle! A strong word. But if this word has justification, which during the war was perhaps the most used word in the field and at home, it has the most justification regarding the interest-swindle.

But what about the war-bonds? With the first 5 billion, the Reich took out of the pockets of the people's savings that existed. The money flowed back again. Then came the new loan to suck up the money again, and with that, the last residual savings. And again, came the pump and sucked up the billions, and again they ebbed back again, until merrily, after this charming game was repeated nine times, the Reich had incurred 100 billion in debt.

In exchange, the people of course held in their hands 100 billion in finely printed paper at first, we imagined that we had become so much richer, but then comes the state and says, "I am facing bankruptcy."

Yes, but why? I certainly cannot go bankrupt, even if I occasionally take a hundred-mark note from the right upper pocket and put it into the left. Certainly, it would be the biggest folly of all if we continued the folly of our war-bond economy by declaring bankruptcy.

Let us break the enslavement to interest on money! Let us declare the war-bond certificates to be legal tender with interest canceled, and the nightmare of state bankruptcy will melt away from us like March snow under the Sun. People say to me; the cancellation of interest-payments is a disguised state bankruptcy. No, that is not true! The specter of state bankruptcy is only a fairytale, and a bogeyman invented by the Mammonist forces.

The book by Franz Röhr, Was jeder vom Staatsbankerott wissen muß (What Everyone ought to know about State Bankruptcy), is completely stuck in Mammonistic ways of thinking. Although the author in general quite clearly recognizes the economic problems that threaten us through socialization, and although he advises emphatically and correctly that in the end only a rebuilding of our economy can save us, he cannot free himself from the superstitious belief in the sanctity of interest, and therefore he depicts state bankruptcy entirely in accord with the interest of Mammonism, as a completely terrifying catastrophe.

It is interesting to observe that Röhr, in spite of better historical knowledge, cannot free himself from the Mammonistic view, and notes in his closing word: "If the ruinous economic catastrophe is not averted, no one will be spared by it," while on page 81 he admits that the consequences of public financial mismanagement have been partially reversed very quickly, and on page 68 he says that in any case there should be no doubt that Russia (in the last century) overcame these currency-crises without lasting problems. On page 76 he says, while examining the effects of state bankruptcies, that although, of course, profound economic problems etc. have occurred, by and large, neither the destruction of the state nor that of its economic strength resulted. On the contrary, a rapid revival of the national economy and a recovery of public finances have been observed often enough. When the author then continues for three more lines saying that state-bankruptcy absolutely means economic catastrophe and causes infinite misery; I regret being unable to follow this logic.

But back to our case! Which would be more honest? To speak pharisaical of the unassailability of war-bonds while oppressing the people with an egregious tax-burden? Or, if a finance-minister had the courage to approach the people openly and to declare, "I cannot make the interest-payments on the war-bonds, or I can only if I collect the same amount in taxes from you. "... But back then during the war I absolutely needed money; nothing smarter (see England) occurred to me, and so I did the swindle with the high-interest war bonds. You must forgive me, beloved folk; it was ultimately all for you, but if we wish to play hide-and-seek no more... I, the state, shall pay no more interest, and you, the taxpayer, need not pay taxes to cover these interest payments... That thoroughly simplifies our transactions; we avoid the enormous tax-bureaucracy and likewise the enormous interest-paying bureaucracy, thus conserving an immense quantity of money and work-potential."

I have lingered long on exposing this swindle, but I consider it fundamental here at no point in losing sight of the big picture.

According to Bavarian tax-returns, the circle of people that would suffer let us say, precisely those that according to their tax-returns received over 30,000 marks in interest-payments are 822 people, who is only 0.4% of those obliged to pay taxes (Bayr. St-Z. 1913) in all Germany, therefore, approximately 10,000. (The upper 10,000!).

Let us clarify for ourselves now as briefly as possible the most important aspects of this revolutionary demand, and indeed let us consider the questions first from our national perspective.

For this, there is first need to a clear look at our current situation. Secretary of State Eugen Schiffer, in his big speech in the Berlin Chamber of Commerce, has declared it "impossible to ignore." That is only partially correct. Possible to ignore is the enormous indebtedness of our national economy, and the unprecedented devaluation of our currency in short, the fact that we have become an impoverished people overnight.

The burdens that are being imposed on us through the peace-treaty, however, cannot be ignored. The currently existing certificates of indebtedness, as we have seen, amount to around 250 billion. Let us assume first that the Entente imposes on us an additional 50 billion in war-reparations in some form: that makes a total of around 300 billion in debt.

However heavily it may strain the narrow confines of this treatise, nonetheless some words must be said about the magnitude of German national wealth. The investigations of Helferrich and Steinmann-Bucher assess the German national wealth at around 350 billion. One can only attribute very limited value to such findings, however carefully they may have been derived. They are valid only four times of undisturbed economic activity. But they are also quite misleading since state and municipal properties are included, thus for example also road-repairs, waterway-modifications, and so on. Although the production of such works may have cost enormous money, nonetheless; they have strictly spoken no intrinsic value. A better yardstick for national wealth is so-called taxable wealth as it emerges from the tax-returns for the defense-contribution or the wartime wealth-tax. For this, a sum-total of 192 billion results, thus much less by far than Helffferich's figure. To this sum, nonetheless about 10% may be added, according to experience, for the legally tax-free small fortunes, and about an equal amount for "silent reserves."[5]

In any case, it seems to me overly optimistic to speak of a national wealth of more than 250 billion. But even this number has only a very limited importance. The most correct thing would be to break away entirely from the idea of a national wealth that is at all numerically graspable, and to penetrate to the recognition that national wealth finds its expression exclusively in the mental and physical work potential of the entire nation, and thus belongs to orders of magnitude that have no relation to the narrower concept of capital. Indeed, we must still see a further source of national wealth in the presence of mineral resources, the riches of the forest, and fertile soil, but these things also cannot be grasped numerically, since their value fluctuates between zero and infinity, depending on whether the mineral resources lie unexploited, or based on a geological report, can be reckoned for billions of tons of coal and so on.

Let us not forget that Germany really is a poor country. Of monopolies, it possesses almost none. In wealth of mineral resources, it stands far behind most of its neighbors, to say nothing of the unparalleled mineral resources of the Chinese, Indian, and American empires. In fertility of the soil, it falls far short compared to the blessed fields of Russia's black soil and compared to the effortlessly productive stretches of tropical and subtropical land. Therefore, in the end we have always only the potential and will of our people to work, as well as the availability of sufficient work, and we must clearly understand that in this situation there can be no talk of secured debts, of collateral for our debt instruments...

Whether interest-bearing war-bonds or non-interest-bearing Reich banknotes, behind them stands only and solely the tax-potential of the entire people and what is tax-potential other than a function of the work-power of the total working population?

We must now clarify for ourselves yet another relevant complex of questions, and of course the chief entries of our state revenue-sources and expenditures. There is a remarkable contrast between the broad space that the concern for making money occupies in our private lives, and the attention that we give to the great questions of our state financial management, and yet between individual economy and national economy no essential difference exists whatsoever.

The chief entries for state revenue are: first, the net profits of the post-offices and railroads; second, those of the mines, forestry-administrations, and other state enterprises; third, tolls and indirect taxes; fourth, direct taxes.

So as not to foster purely theoretical discussions in such eminently practical questions, I want to elucidate the individual entries from the Bavarian state budget of the year 1911 according to their order of magnitude. Post, telegraph, and railroads brought 120 million; forests, mines, etc., around 40 million; indirect taxes, 53 million; direct taxes, 60 million. An additional 67 million flowed from stamp-duties, fees, inheritance-taxes, land-taxes, revenue-transfers from the Reich, and so on.

What about expenditures? We find here in the first place the payments for interest on the state debt, including the railroad-debts with 85 million. For the royal house, 5 million administration of justice, 27 million internal administration, 40 million churches and schools, 51 million; financial administration, 13 million expenditures for Reich-related purposes, 50 million; pensions, 36 million. Miscellaneous expenditures 5 million. Back then, in this fortunate year of Bavarian finances, the annual budget left a revenue-surplus of 27 million.

In the scope of our thought, however, only those expenditures concern us that can be omitted through the abolition of interest-slavery. Here the interest-payment on the state debt naturally stands in first place at 85 million marks; add to that the greatest part of our payment for financial administration at about 10 million; furthermore, a large part of the payments for Reich-related purposes, of which let us add half, 25 million, and finally the 5 million in payments for the royal house are now gone: a total of 125 million.

The disappearance of these entries means the possibility of renouncing imposition of all direct and indirect taxes, which, as we saw, brought in 53 million and 60 million marks, a total of 113 million marks!

We are now not at all the opinion that one should entirely abolish direct and indirect taxes; unquestionably within reasonable limits, they serve on the one hand to educate, on the other hand, to regulate. It is certainly not more than right and fair that the profits from property owned free and clear remain subject to a moderate, graduated tax, since the state, of course, must also maintain secure ownership with its policing agencies. It seems just as advisable that trade and industry be required to make tax-contributions corresponding to their working profits, since the state also must care for the maintenance and development of public paths of commerce for them. A corresponding minimum poll-tax for every citizen entitled to vote is likewise a requirement of fairness since care for the security of the person and his property is also required from the state.

In the area of indirect taxes, a strong expansion of all pure luxury-taxes has a regulatory effect in the best sense, while all simple foodstuffs and necessities of the people should be kept free of taxes!

The result of such a tax-policy would be found less in high revenues about which there can be no talk, since for the great mass of the population taxation should be not a real burden but only a reminder that the person is not only an individual essence but also a citizen of the state, and that in addition to civil rights he also has civil duties.

Tax-revenues should be less necessary for paying off the debts of state-owned businesses, whose net-profits, as we have seen, suffice to cover the normal expenditures of the state for schools, universities, administration of justice, internal administration, etc. Tax-revenues should be used to advance special cultural tasks of the state for which adequate resources were never available in the scope of the normal state budget. Here I am thinking primarily about orphanages, institutes for the blind and the crippled, daycare centers, care for expectant mothers, the battles against tuberculosis, alcohol, and venereal diseases, and the construction of garden-cities and settlements, especially for the accommodation and humane care of our war-disabled.

Our view broadens. We see virgin land. Could the abolition of interest-slavery mean the cancellation of all taxes? It would mean that, if we had come out of this gigantic struggle as a victorious people. As things are, let us not celebrate too early; the burdens imposed on us by our enemies will make sure that we do not. But in any case, we see virgin land based on the indeed quite simple example of our Bavarian state budget that we just used...

In general, we find quite similar relationships in the other German federal states, and it is not too much to say that from the surpluses of the state-owned businesses, the railroads, post-offices, telegraphs, forests, mines, and so on, all state expenditures for the entire administration of justice, for all internal administration, including state construction-projects, all outlays for schools and universities, just as for cultural purposes, could be covered without difficulty. Thus, a perfectly ideal condition.

Why is that not the case? Interest has crept in. Because of the payment of interest, the population's foodstuffs become expensive; because of interest sugar and salt, beer and wine, matchsticks and tobacco and countless other necessities of daily need carry indirect taxes. Because of interest, direct taxes must be raised, which are divided into land-taxes that are passed on in the form of higher prices for grain, house-taxes that drive up rent, business-taxes that burden productive labor, income-taxes that unavoidably depress the living-standards of civil servants and people on fixed salaries, and finally at the very end, modest in giving but insatiable in taking, loan-capital pays taxes on capital dividends. According to the tax-returns of the year 1911, out of 253 million in capital dividends received in Bavaria, all of 8.1 million was paid in state taxes.

We have seen that all capital dividends, all interest in capital, ultimately must be raised through the labor of the entire people. We have seen that the interest payment on public debts constitutes the largest entry in our state budget, and we have seen that those obliged to pay taxes on interest-payments make only an extremely limited contribution to state revenues.

In terms of relative magnitude, the capitalist paid 8 million out of a total of 60 million in direct taxes, which is only an eighth to a sixth of the direct state taxes paid in Bavaria in 1911. Direct taxes, however, are only about a fifth of the total state revenue. Therefore, loan-capital contributes only about a thirtieth to a forty-eighth share of the state's total needs.

It should not be denied that tax-legislation during the war, especially in the last years, resorted to a stronger tax on capital dividends, but stronger indirect taxation has kept pace with it, so that the relative size has hardly changed.

The picture becomes dire when we consider the budget of the Reich. Here, the proportions in themselves are already much less favorable. The Reich does not have the same tax-sources as the individual federal states. Direct taxes are reserved for the federal states; the enterprises of the Reich are limited to the Reich's post-office and railroad (note that this does not include the Prussian state railroads), and consequently only tolls and indirect taxes remain.

The orders of magnitude of the Reich's revenue-sources (see Statistisches Jahrbuch für das Deutsche Reich for the years 1917 and 1918) were, in the year 1915, 1 billion in indirect taxes, 0.8 billion in special revenues (war-contribution, matricular fees), and so on. Here too, the same picture again. More than a third, 1.3 billion to be specific, was devoured already in the year 1915 by payment of interest on the Reich's debt. Here too, loan-capital pushed its way in again. Here too, it requires all direct taxes to satisfy it. Sugar pays 163 million, salt 61 million, beer 128 million, tobacco, schnapps, sparkling wine, lamp-fuel, matches, playing cards, and countless other items had to be taxed to scrape together a billion marks that then flows completely into the pockets of the capitalists.

Today, how to pay the interest on the Reich's debt is a riddle. Interest-payments alone devour 8 billion (annually), based on 100 billion in war-bonds plus other war credits. Revenues from the post-office and railroad can hardly be further increased. A further increase in tolls will hardly be tolerated; therefore, probably only a five-or tenfold increase in indirect taxes is left an impossibility! or the clear insight that only and solely the abolition of enslavement to interest on money can bring us salvation. An enormous self-deception is what the entire war bond economy was. The German nation borrowed a hundred billion from itself for its war. For that, it promised 5 billion in interest to itself; it must therefore pay 5 billion in taxes. All benefit goes to the big capitalist, who draws so much in capital dividends that he cannot possibly use it up, and yet only a quite modest percentage is taken away through the tax on capital dividends, as we have seen.

I hope now, through the main thrusts of my presentation already, to have dispelled the humanly comprehensible terror that many readers may have of eventually losing the interest-income from their pretty certificates. Let it just be demonstrated very briefly with one example that the whole interest-economy is a big self-deception, and along with that I want to look at an upper level of solid middle-class income.

Assume that the head of a household has an income from labor of 10,000 marks, and on top of that, another 5000 marks from capital dividends. In the first place, about 1500 marks of this will be paid in direct taxes; then at least 1000-1200 marks in the form of high rents will be stripped away for eternal interest. Another 1000 marks are likely to be drained off in the form of indirect taxes for a family of five or six, and already now one realizes that not much is left of the lovely capital dividends that the small and middle-sized capitalists enjoyed under the happy tax rates of earlier years. Indeed, already today there can be no more talk of "surplus"; on the contrary, if one examines for oneself today the current fantastic tax-proposals, considerably more income from labor will probably be taxed away.

Naturally, the situation seems to be quite different for the big capitalist, who, let us say, for example, collects only 1 million in capital dividends. (Such people are fairly numerous in Germany today.) Of the tax on capital dividends, this fortunate man pays at the most 50-60 thousand marks. Of indirect taxes, he also pays no more than the family-father of the previous example. On his budget, after all, he can still live quite comfortably indeed with 40-50 thousand marks, even in the current expensive era. If roughly a nice 900,000 marks cash remain to him, for that with 5% interest on loans, he will get another 45,000 marks in the next year and that, by law, at the expense of the working population.

The small pensioner who only lives in his interest undoubtedly would be harmed. If he can work, then he must, of course, resolve to earn an income from labor. With that, he then situates himself very much better than the millions of his folk-comrades who have nothing other than their physical or mental work-potential. If he does not want that, then he must eat into his wealth. Ultimately, he has 20 years to nibble at it again and again, if he continues to consume the annual sum that he has been receiving at 5% interest. For persons that are not able to work, or are weakened by illness or age, obviously an appropriate livelihood must be arranged through the development of social welfare for all segments of the population.

I visualize social welfare as follows:

Let us assume that an older lady, a widow, who hitherto had to live on the interest from a capital investment of 60,000 marks, is, through the legally proclaimed abolition of interest-slavery, deprived of her source of income. Here, through the broadest expansion of the pension-system, opportunity would be given the person to draw a pension corresponding to her capital, wherewith the annual pension could even be increased relative to the previous interest-yield, so as also to give a certain compensation for the diminished value of money even to this circle of people. Thus, for example, in exchange for the surrendered 60,000 marks in debt-instruments of the Reich, of the states, or in covered bonds, an annual lifelong pension of 4000 marks could be given. If the widow has children and she wants to will a portion of the wealth to them, then it can be allowed to her that only 40,000 marks be transformed into a pension, while the remaining 20,000 would be kept for the children. Out of the 40,000 marks, depending on the age of the pension-applicant, up to 1/12 of the received capital could be given annually. Furthermore, let it also be noted here that, with the discontinuation of oppressive taxes because of the abolition of interest-slavery, the widow's cost of living will be quite considerably decreased.

It would greatly exceed the scope of this essay to examine in detail the personal interests of each stratum of the population. Such a revolutionary demand cannot be about personal interests; nevertheless, as the idea takes effect, one will find that the healthful consequences personally benefit every individual in the end.

Precisely by the problem already isolated above, of how to achieve release from interest on war-bonds, I have tried to make it clear already that small capitalists by which I mean all the hundreds of thousands that have been induced through a hyper-American advertising campaign to devote their savings for subscription to war-bonds not only receive no benefit from interest, since of course they must pay for it themselves with taxes, but, with tax-legislation tailored for the protection of big capital, must support interest-payments for million-mark subscriptions.

It seems to me that, apart from these immediate considerations, an appeal to all for the sake of their children's wellbeing, must persuade the anxious bondholder to accept as Completely natural the renunciation of eternal interest from the Reich's debts. In this case, what does the patriot, who has given 10,000 marks to his fatherland in direst need, really lose, other than a usurious claim to draw 50,000 marks in interest within a hundred years, without even diminishing the principal? Eternally, his children and grandchildren must work, just to pay all the interest.

The question of repayment of the lent sums can be solved in various ways. In my briefly stated main ideas about the problem at hand, which I submitted to the government of the People's State of Bavaria (under Kurt Eisner) on 20

November of last year (1918), I proposed simply to have repayment take the place of interest-payment at the rate of 5% annually for 20 years. I believe that in what follows I can even make a much better suggestion, which because of its simplicity certainly deserves preference: "The war-bond certificates upon cancellation of interest will be declared to be currency." That is the Egg of Columbus. The advantage of this measure is in the first place that nobody really feels anything about it. The war-bond certificates continue to lie at rest in the depots; but no young people get them, any more than a book, or a cabinet, or some otherwise useful object that somebody would lend to his friend.

If one needs money, then one simply whips out a war-bond note and pays with that. War-bond notes have, after all, just as much beauty and paper-value as our other 10, 20, 100, and 1000-mark notes. There can certainly be no talk of the market's being flooded with currency in such a bump-free transition from the interest-economy into the interest-free national economy. All the war-bond certificates are indeed already well protected and stored in bank-vaults, or other places of concealment considered secure by the people, such as a woolen stocking or a manure-heap. Indeed, it cannot be denied that our issued paper currency, as much as about 40 billion, is also not in circulation but for the most part is hoarded in the manner described above. Our need for currency in the times of economic boom before the war was also only about 4-6 billion, and it is inconceivable that we would need more than twice that much today in the ever more customary cashless economy.[6]

The cancellation of interest is to be done in precisely the same manner for all fixed-interest assets. For these assets, just as for dividend-yielding assets, the originally proposed "repayment" in 20 or 25-year annual pensions is recommended, especially for mortgages.

The abolition of interest-slavery for mortgages means, without a doubt, the solution of the housing problem, the liberation from exorbitant rents. It is not at all evident why the holder of a mortgage should have the eternal benefit of interest from a sum lent once, why an effortless and endless influx of goods should be granted to him, why the great mass of a people, only for this unhealthy principle of interest, should pay high rents year in, year out. Let it be interjected very briefly that self-evidently there can be no talk of a complete cancellation of rent, since of course the management and upkeep of houses demands constant labor and money. A lowering of rents thus can only occur so far as it results of its own accord through the accomplished repayment of mortgages.

Only one thing should be sharply emphasized, that the abolition of enslavement to interest has not the slightest thing to do with our total value-producing labor, insofar as no hindrance is posed in any way to the entrepreneurial spirit, to productive labor, to the manufacture of goods, to the acquisition of wealth. On the contrary, as we have seen, the entire working folk are liberated from a stifling, unreasonable, heavy burden; our soul-life is purged of an intoxicating poison.

We can tell how correctly the fruitfulness of the interest-problem has been recognized in the course of history, by the fact that minds in all ages and all peoples have been occupied with it...

In various passages of the Old Testament, such as Leviticus 25 and Deuteronomy 15, we find regulations about the cessation of interest in the form that the seventh year should always be an acceptilation or jubilee, in which all debts of folk-comrades should be abated.

Solon in the year 594B.C. Abolished personal debt-slavery through legislation. This law was called the great Seisachtheia (shaking off burdens).

In ancient Rome, the Lex Gemicia of the year 332 B.C. abruptly forbade Roman citizens entirely from charging any interest.

Under Justinian, a prohibition on compound interest was enacted, with the regulation that no more interest whatsoever should be demanded when overdue interest has accumulated to the level of the sum originally lent.

Pope Leo I (the Great) decreed in the year 443 a general prohibition on taking interest; until then, only clerics had been prohibited from demanding interest on a loan. The ban on interest was now part of Canon Law and a binding regulation for the laity. Secular legislation also gradually fell in line with canonic views, and even threatened punishment for charging interest. We find this in the police ordinances of the Holy Roman Empire for the years 1500, 1530, and 1577.

Of course, such laws were now much opposed and frequently circumvented, and in this quite short historical retrospective it may only be mentioned as an astonishing historical fact that although under the canon law of the 11th to 17th centuries the charging of interest was forbidden to Christians, it was permitted to Jews.

It would be extraordinarily charming to investigate in each instance what economic tumors led to these powerful shedding of burdens. It would be especially valuable to see which powers and forces have violated the prohibitions of interest again and again.

In the Middle Ages, certainly short work was often made of usurers; the farmers or citizens having been bled dry got together and beat the profiteers to death. Today we have entered a completely different phase of the interest-problem. Such pogroms are most deeply disapproved.

Also, it is no longer a matter of individual locally confined symptoms of illness that could be combated by excising the pus-pocket; what is happening is a serious sickening of all humanity.

It should be most emphatically stressed that precisely our contemporary culture, precisely the internationality of economic relations, make the interest-principle so murderous. The foregoing historical retrospective should also not be regarded as providing an analogy for the circumstances of today. When the Babylonians overcame the Assyrians, the Romans, the Carthaginians, the Germans, the Romans, then there was no continuation of enslavement to interest; there were no international world-powers. The wars were also not financed through borrowing but with treasures accumulated during peace. David Hume gives a very nice overview of this in his Essay on Public Credit. Only the modern age, with its continuity of ownership and its international law, allows loan-capital to escalate into infinity. The penny that was invested in interest at the time of the birth of Christ exists no more, because since then all rights of ownership have had to give way to violence several times; by contrast, the penny that old Rothschild invested in interest still exists, and will exist, if there is international law, for all eternity.

In addition, it ought to be considered that broad stretches of the Earth have only in the modern age gone over from natural economy to money-economy. It is quite especially important in this connection that only in the middle of the 19th century were all restrictions on charging interest, and likewise all prohibitions on interest, abolished: thus, England in the year 1854, Denmark 1856, Belgium 1865, Austria 1868.

Thus, today's concept of interest as inseparable from the possession of money is not much older than half a century. But precisely, this interest-concept has, for the first time, completely caused money to turn into the demonic power of such universal coercion that we have come to know.

The incipient and then ever-increasing indebtedness of states to capitalists likewise dates only to the middle of the 19th century. Only since that time do we see the state degraded from being the trustee of the folk-community into being the trustee of capitalistic interests. This development has reached its highpoint in war-bonds, which we encounter in all lands, which exclusively, as we have recognized, serve only Mammonistic interests, which should be crowned with the gigantic credit-edifice of a world-loan.

These brief retrospectives should make it easier for us finally to break away from the supposition that unto loan-capital must be lent the supra-mundane power to grow eternally and interminably from itself. Gifted with a terrifying potential for sucking dry. We must break away from the notion that loan-capital, unaffected by worldly deeds and misdeeds, should be able to sit enthroned above the clouds, unaffected by transitoriness, unaffected by the forces of destruction, unaffected by the shots of our giant guns. For, should even houses and huts, railroads and bridges shattered by shells sink into dust and ash, the mortgages will still exist; the railroad bonds and public certificates of indebtedness are not erased. Should villages and cities, entire provinces, fall victim to the insane destruction of war? What is the result? New certificates of indebtedness are what it means. With eyes flashing with greed, the Gold International enthroned above the clouds watches the mad rush of humanity. And not long distant is the time when all humanity finally shall serve only as interest-slaves to Mammonism.

The idea is international; it must liberate the entire world. Hail to the nation that first dares the bold step. Soon others will follow.

The question often directed to me, whether the idea is nationally realizable at all, I answer with yes. We are internally indebted.

Against foreign interest-claims, we are naturally powerless for now; these must simply be paid. Excessive capital-outflow must be blocked to the extent possible, but, as little as the lawgiver refrains from working out laws against murder, manslaughter, fraud, etc., because there would still always be scoundrels, just as little should a people in its totality restrain itself from taking a step recognized as necessary for the healing of its public finances, just because of the fact that not exactly the best elements of the folk are trying to carry their loot into safety outside the country. If we assume that hundreds of millions, even billions, in war bond certificates would be spent abroad; even this could still not be a significant impetus for failing to abolish interest-slavery; for proportionally, of the more than 250 billion marks in fixed-interest domestic investment-assets, by far the majority must still be in the country.

Let us again summarize briefly. The abolition of enslavement to interest is the radical means for the final and permanent healing of our public finances. The abolition of the interest-community means the possibility of renouncing oppressive direct and indirect taxes because the state-owned businesses, especially after the socialization of further suitable sectors (inland navigation, electricity, air-traffic, etc.), will give sufficient surpluses to the public coffers to support all social and cultural tasks of the state.

Aside from this financial consideration, the abolition of the interest-community will grant to productive labor in all fields of endeavor the priority that it deserves. Money is returned once again to the role appropriate to it, to be a servant in the powerful drive of our national economy. It will become again what it is, a voucher for completed labor, and there with the path is cleared for a higher goal, for abstention from the raging money-lust of our age.

The idea points toward the establishment of a united front of the entire working population: from the unpropertied laborer who, as we have seen, is very heavily burdened with indirect taxes for the satisfaction of loan-capital, through the entire bourgeois class of civil servants and employees, of the farming and small-trades middle class, which get to feel the pitiless tyranny of money in the form of wretched housing, farmland-rental, bank-interest, and so on, all the way up to the leading heads, inventors, and directors of our big industry, who are one and all more or less stuck together in the claws of big loan-capital, for whom the first task of life is always to work for the sake of pensions, dividends, and interest for the money-powers playing behind the scenes. No less do all circles of the intelligentsia artists, writers, actors, scholars, as well as other independent professionals also belong to this group.

Although big loan-capital, as a group of natural persons or as the personification of the interest-principle, seeks consciously or instinctively to conceal the fact of its boundless lust for control, and although our entire legal tradition based upon Roman law, thus upon law serving for the protection of a plutocracy, has ever so strongly emphasized the protection of property and therewith permeated our people's sense of justice, the abolition of thralldom of interest on money must come, as the only way out of the threatening economic enslavement of the entire world by the Gold International, as one of the ways to drive out the poison of Mammonism with its corruption and contamination of the mentality of our age.

War-Bonds Into Bank-Credit

The demand in §1, for the conversion of war-bond certificates etc. into legal tender, has on many occasions been met with the objection that it would mean excessively flooding the market with currency. This objection is quite erroneous. Inflation occurs through the mere existence of war-bond.

It is however true that, despite its wrongheadedness, the concern about the physical presence of these papers declared to be currency is not going away, and therefore despite being unrealistic this concern might generate unfortunate side effects, as if in fact a new inflation had taken place. Therefore, amending § 1, we demand, after legislative cancellation of the obligation to pay interest, conversion of war-bond certificates, along with other public debenture-bonds, (not into currency but) into bank-credit.

This formulation has the great advantage that the physical existence of war-bonds as paper would cease; the war-bond certificates would be delivered to the Reichsbank by banks, bankers, thrift-institutions, etc., and would be destroyed after a credit-note for the face-value is issued. Therewith, nearly every person in Germany would receive a bank-credit, an open bank-account that he could use.

Such a procedure would also have the great advantage that the retention of larger investments in private possession would not be possible, since after the expiration of a specified deadline, the undelivered certificates would be declared void.

It would at least be possible to control how much war-bond is spent outside the country (thus affecting Germany's trade-balance). The last point, however, must not in any way block fulfillment of the abolition of enslavement to interest. Since we really feel too weak compared to foreign countries, we must satisfy (only) the interest-demands that confront us from abroad. Personally, I am entirely of the opinion that we should also uphold the cancellation of interest even for foreign bondholders. We need not fear that foreign interest-claims would be enforced by force of arms, since there has been so much progress in returning (from war-madness) to something resembling self-awareness, and never yet in history has a warlike action been undertaken against a great state because of financial measures affecting private persons. It also ought not to be imagined that even the French people would issue an ultimatum to Germany because of the interest-claims of Messrs. Mayer, Schulze, and Cohn from Germany, based on their German war-bonds carried across the border.

Beyond this it would be possible, to avoid even the appearance to the rest of the world of a state bankruptcy, to conduct a lottery of the war bond, which then of course could easily be rigged based on statistics obtained through the required delivery of certificates, so that at first just the numbers presumably belonging to people abroad would be drawn and paid off in Reich banknotes.

Yet a third thing would be the welcome ascertainment of the distribution of war bonds, and the accompanying opportunity that still exists for an extraordinarily simple collection of the wealth-tax, while the bursaries of course would need only to instruct the Reichsbank offices to charge the account of Mr. N.N. with so and so many marks in tax. In this manner, tax payments would be more painless by far, although, of course, the taxpayers' right of appeal would continue to exist to its full extent.

With such a transformation (conversion) of war-bonds into bank-credits a certain social leveling could also be accomplished, insofar as smaller investments in war bonds, thus all small subscriptions of all of those for whom the subscription of war-bonds really is to be accounted a patriotic deed; let us say up to 5 or 10 thousand marks would be made good at par, while all larger subscriptions could be credited at a rate to be established. The credits for all other government papers would be handled precisely the same.

Special Demands

On § 1

It is completely indispensable that all state and municipal debt-subscriptions be treated in the same way, since only such a unitary large-scale regulation of our entire monetary system, hand in hand with the abolition of interest-slavery, can be implemented.

On § 2

It is already clear that the abolition of interest-slavery must be applied simultaneously to all the other fixed-interest papers, so as not to cause an absurd boom in these papers, which obviously would occur if the public papers alone were declared interest-free. The reduction of the debt as such would be accomplished through annual repayment, whereby a constant and consistent undebting of all debt-laden objects would be accomplished.

On § 3

This paragraph is very closely related to the preceding ones, as well as with the demand for nationalization of mortgage-lending in § 5. The farmer or homeowner burdened with mortgages continues, after as before, to pay the amount that he had to pay to his creditors, but no longer as eternal interest, rather as repayment. Thus, after 20, 25, or 30 years, depending on the preexisting interest-rate, ownership of land and home will be freed from debt. (The mortgage-bank for its part can naturally likewise only during this time continue correspondingly to pay interest on covered bonds to covered-bondholders.) Hand in hand with this liberation from debt arises the community's right of ownership in the real-estate freed from mortgages.

A universal registry of dwellings, or rather a real-estate cadaster, would have to come first; because debt-free real-estate ownership naturally also has the right to repayment of invested capital, and a permanent claim on a portion of the rent, to pay all the charges, expenses, and so on that come with real-estate ownership, as well as appropriate compensation for work that the owner himself does.[7]

Let us consider this in broad outlines with the example of an urban apartment house. The house has a value of 100,000 marks. Against that is recorded a mortgage-bank's investment of 50,000 marks at 4% in position 1, a non-corporate investment of 20,000 marks at 5% in position 2, and 30,000 marks is the amount put up by the house-owner himself. The revenues from rent are 7000 marks. From this must be paid 2000 marks for the first mortgage, 1000 marks for the second mortgage, and 1000 marks for expenses, outlays, and so on: in all 4000 marks. Thus, 3000 marks remain to the house-proprietor as an interest-payment (so to speak) for his own invested capital of 30,000 marks.

Following implementation of the legal abolition of interest on money, the situation after ten years is as follows: 1st mortgage 30,000 marks, 2nd mortgage 10,000 marks. The house-owner has completely recovered his capital-investment, but on the other hand there is a new, public right of ownership in the amount of 50,000 marks. With that, the right of the state to have a say about further income from rent and to determine the amount of rent begins.[8]

It would be unjust now, regarding repayment, to put the house-proprietor on the same level as mortgages. For his capital is not pure loan-capital in the narrower sense that should be affected by the abolition of interest-slavery; here we are talking about "risk" capital, specifically about money converted into a valuable good, specifically a house. It is therefore up to the owner of the house whether to grant a longer duration of payments, or a corresponding percentage permanently included in the operating expenses of the house.

It cannot be the purpose here to make any binding proposals; here only suggestions are being made as to how a frictionless transition of the interest of economy into the interest-free economy could occur even around real estate.

To complete the example, let the status after 25 years be presumed as follows: by that time, all mortgages are paid off; only the permanent expenses are the same or, because of the greater age of the house, increased from 1000 marks to perhaps 1500 marks. Let the return afforded to the house-proprietor from this sum also be about 1000 to 1500 marks; thus accordingly, it appears that around 3000 marks of the rent-revenues go to cover non-negotiable charges, while the remaining 4000 of the original 7000 in rent-revenues would be freely disposable. The state thus has the possibility of lowering the rents by more than half; it will do this e.g., in workers' dwellings, or the state may cut rents by only 20, 30, or 40%, and thus gain from the difference an enormous source of revenue for other public necessities, above all naturally for publicly conducted home-construction. For mansions the rents are not lowered, or not lowered much, whence very great additional means become available also for the better construction of homes, or for special social purposes. This future situation however reveals, and I hold this for a very fruitful prospect the inner justification for the community (state) even now to take part in determining the amount of rent in the manner that I sketched above, with a lowering of rent for workers' dwellings.

In the growing right of the state to take part in real estate-ownership also lies the foundation for a sound bank of issue, and issue of credit to mortgage creditors.

On § 4 & 5

These paragraphs demand the socialization of the entire monetary system. Money is only and exclusively a voucher for completed labor issued by a community that has its own state. To issue money-tokens is one of the sovereign fundamental rights of the state. The counterfeiting of the state's money-tokens is subject to the most severe punishments; thus, it is a quite forceful social demand that the monetary system be placed under the control of the collectivity. The work-power of the collectivity is the sole substrate of money-tokens, and only the failure to appreciate this fundamental fact has led in general to the deterioration of our public finances and to complete anarchy of the monetary system in general.

With the surrender of personal and commercial credit by private bankers, proposed in § 5, a deeper incision is made into the total credit-system. For the state credit-system, as well as for municipal and even real-estate credit, one must cleave to the abolition of interest-slavery with utmost rigor and energy, because it is the indispensable prerequisite for the social state in general.

The situation is different from personal credit. We also demand, in and for itself, the interest less-ness of personal credit; yet this demand does not carry the same enormous and principal importance. We remember the 250 billion in fixed-interest loan-capital compared to the only 12 billion in dividend-paying stocks.

All such credits, stocks, participation-certificates, mining shares, equity-holdings, and so on, are risk capital. The yield of this capital depends on the industry and efficiency of those persons to whom the money was entrusted. Here, the element of risk and danger of loss thus comes into play, along with the question of personal trust. For that, a certain compensation of a special kind still appears indispensable. The owner of stocks and so on is in no way compensated or benefited if the enterprise to which he entrusted his money earns nothing. He loses his money entirely if the enterprise collapses.

It is otherwise with, for example, the owner of debenture-bonds of the Reicheisenbahn. The Reich's railroads (in Elsaß-Lothringen) are completely lost with the loss of Elsaß-Lothringen. Nonetheless, the holder of railroad-bonds continues to receive his interest-payments. From whom? From the taxes of the collectivity. The railroads may work with a deficit balance of any magnitude as in Prussia and Bavaria in the last year; yet the bondholders receive their interest payments just the same. From whom? From tribute paid out of the work-potential and consumption of the working population.

One would just like to make this fundamental distinction perfectly clear, in order finally to recognize where it is that the vampire sucks from the work-potential of the people.

Thus, personal credit should remain, or rather be allocated again, to personal dealing through the private bank. The personal efficiency of the credit-seeker, with which the banker is personally familiar, should again become the determining factor for personal credit. The fees set by the state will regulate themselves by themselves, in accord with the fluidity of money that will in any case commence with the abolition of interest-slavery.

On § 6

The main point of § 5 is also valid for dividend-assets. In the interest of the social state-community it must be demanded that a repayment of the capital once lent be attempted also for the great industrial enterprises to bring about here to a reduction of the indebtedness of the individual industrial works toward those that are only investors. For in fact, what we were able to observe in the relationship of loan-capital toward all peoples repeats itself here on a smaller scale. Here too, the capitalist exploits the worker, the foreman, the engineer, the entrepreneur, all equally, because the compulsion to have to earn dividends takes priority.[9]

If, however we attain the liberation of industries and businesses from the eternal interest-sucker, then the way is clear for the lowering of prices of products, and for the delivery and distribution of surplus value, partly to the community, partly to the laborers, middle management, and boards of directors of the enterprises, thus to those that alone create manufacturing and values.

On § 7

In this paragraph, naturally, the entire field of insurance also comes into play, which can be constructed on an analogous interest-free basis. The premiums paid cannot grow through addition of interest; rather the insurance-companies will become thrift-institutions; in other words, the risk and advantage of insurance are retained. For this the political community must be responsible.

On § 8

About the devaluation of our money, which has resulted only through the enormous mass of our innumerable certificates of indebtedness, we demand a strongly graduated wealth-tax. We lay the emphasis in this on "strongly graduated."

A (flat) wealth-tax (for the purpose of) reduction of the number of notes and so forth would be nothing but a self-deception whereby one throws sand into the eyes of the people. For if I also confiscate half of all the wealth everywhere and receive payment in bonds and pulp these, all that is really accomplished thereby is a diminution of the amount of paper, while in return a conversion-factor will increase the fictive value of the totality of circulating paper to the same level as before. Real value belongs always only to goods for consumption and goods for use, never to the paper vouchers for completed labor.

Another question is whether the foreign exchange-rate of our mark-currency can be improved. But even this improvement of the exchange-rate is again in the final analysis only dependent on work-potential and production, in other words the possibility for production of our total national economy.

Objection & Refutation

Never yet has an idea been able to establish itself without opposition, least of all an idea that makes such a radical departure from the long-established assumptions about the sanctity and inviolability of interest. With the objections already raised and those expected there is always a two-fold observation to be made: it must be asked, first, what part of the objections being made is based on a deliberate distortion of the idea of abolition of interest-slavery, and second, what ought to be said in response to all sincere and fact-based misgivings?

The most frequent objection is the assertion: without the charging of interest, nobody will lend money. We do not, in fact, want anyone to lend his money anymore. Credit was the trick, was the trap, into which our economy entered, and in which it is now helplessly ensnared.

If the folk urgently need greater capital, then it gets the needed moneys interest free at the central state treasury, with only repayment required. Eventually it will issue new banknotes. Why should it issue interest-bearing certificates?! Whether the paper bears interest or not makes no difference! Its only and sole backing is the work-potential and tax-potential of the folk. Why burden every public expenditure from the beginning with the leaden weight of eternal interest?

Yes, but how should the state fulfill its cultural labors for the community? It still needs money and can be fair in this task only by way of loans that charge interest.

This assertion is based on an entirely Mammonistic way of thinking. It would have to be deliberately calculated for misdirection after thorough reading of this Manifesto; for in the first place, we have proven that after the abolition of interest-slavery all cultural and social tasks of the state can be covered out of state-owned businesses, out of the revenues of the postal service, railroad, mines, forests, and so on, without anything further. In the second place the sovereign people's state (Volksstaat) has the power, at any time, to take care of special cultural tasks through the issue of interest-free value-tokens in lieu of the interest-bearing certificates declared to be the rule in the Mammonistic state. It is thoroughly impossible to see why the state should make special cultural tasks, e.g., railroad, canal, and hydroelectric construction, costlier for itself with an eternal promise of interest that is completely unnecessary. If it cannot pay the costs of construction from the revenues of its current state-owned businesses, then there is no reason to see why the state should not create the money; the sovereign people must indeed pay for it, while it precisely recognizes this money as a means of payment. Why however should the folk, with its entire work-and tax potential, stand behind another slip of paper (the interest-bearing loan), which imposes on the folk in its totality only an eternal interest-obligation for the benefit of the capitalist!? Therefore, away with this obsession of the Mammonistic state!

The capitalists then will just take up the issued paper notes and accumulate paper money.

This is refuted in two ways. First, the demand that mere possession of money should be rendered unprofitable would then of course be already fulfilled, and the abolition of interest-slavery voluntarily undertaken by the capitalists themselves, since the capitalist renounces interest of his own accord if he piles up his paper notes at home. Second, the capitalists' fear for his money makes it unlikely; one need only imagine the sleepless nights of the currency-hoarder who keeps great sums of money piled up at home and must constantly see his possession threatened by thieves, robbers, burglars, house-searches, fire, and flood. I am convinced that the upright citizen would become tired of these worries in a short time and would soon find his way to the state bank. The state bank issues a receipt and is now legally responsible for the account, but not for any interest payments. Otherwise of course a third possibility still remains open to everyone, specifically to work with his money, to create values and to manufacture goods, to participate in industrial undertakings, to render his life ever richer and finer, to support art and scholarship, in short to make beneficial use of his money while rejecting the Cult of Mammon.

It can, however, still happen that private need of capital for some goals urgently presents itself, e.g., for testing of inventions, founding of businesses by young, competent craftsmen or businessmen, etc.

To begin with, this has nothing whatsoever to do with the abolition of Interest-Slavery! For, in the first place, one must logically assume that the capitalist, who after the abolition of interest-slavery of course has no more opportunity to invest his moneys in a bombproof manner and to expect idle consumption of interest, will rather, as in an earlier age, be inclined to risk his money for such purposes, so that a lack or need in this direction will therefore occur much less than hitherto. Or has one not heard on the contrary again and again from the efficient businesspeople, from the cleverest inventors, precisely the complaint of how difficult it is to get money in the Mammonistic state for such purposes unless a "dividend" could be guaranteed? In the second place, it must be the task of the coming state to foster every competent force through generous support. There were indeed even before now already beginnings toward this in the old bureaucratic state, but so small-hearted that, instead of a stimulus, an inhibition and reluctance resulted, because of the harassing regulations that accompanied the granting of public support. In the third place, let it be noted that with the allocation of several million marks, enormously much could be achieved. The joy of labor, the industriousness and tenacity of the German inventor, engineer, craftsman, etc. is so great that, through the state's right of participation in the results of fortunate inventions, the expenditures most likely would be richly rewarded (England as an example).

The abolition of interest-slavery leads necessarily to the exhaustion of wealth.

Oho! Who claims that? But of course! Whoever has adapted his life to the consumption of his interest-payments on capital and cannot resolve to work, with him it is certainly true: consuming 5% annually he will have completely exhausted his wealth in 20 years. Of course, but that is indeed completely in order! What we want is precisely the abolition of interest-slavery; we want living on a pension to cease being the citizen's highest ideal. We want to end this Mammonistic decadence; indeed, we want no longer to tolerate that one, that many, can live in comfort permanently only from interest-payments on loans in other words at the expense of others!

I repeat it is also not true at all that the abolition of the lordship of interest would lead to the elimination and exhaustion of wealth. On the contrary, the abolition of interest-slavery would promote the creation of wealth based on labor that manufactures goods and produces value, unburdened, and liberated from eternal interest-outlays. The abolition of interest-slavery leads, as we have seen, to a comprehensive lowering of costs in all of life; it unburdens us from the excessive weight of taxation so that for every working man, the possibility of accumulating savings must be greater in the future than hitherto. One more thing! The goods and values-producing national-economic labor of industry, commerce, and trade is in no way hindered, but fostered to the utmost through the abolition of Interest-Slavery.

What does the worker get if capitalists receive no more interest-payments?

This question really ought not to be coming up anymore! In the first place, of course, it was the constant battle cry of labor that the capitalists would exploit the workers; in the second place we have indeed clearly and plainly seen that it is the laborer more than anyone else that is required to pay the interest on loans. (In other words, what the worker gets is lower taxes and a lower cost of living.)

The bonds of family are weakened and damaged if one can leave no wealth behind for the children.

Yes, what is the reality here? Quite generally, I think that money has little or nothing to do with the sense of family. Or has one heard that the children of wealthier parents cleave to their parents more than those of poor parents? Or do rich parents love their children more than the less propertied? What is likely to be more important for the children, that their parents arrange for them the best possible upbringing and have them learn some discipline, raising them into industrious and healthy and courageous people, or that they leave behind for them the biggest possible moneybag?

Cases, a justified striving to secure the children's financial future undoubtedly will have to be acknowledged. This striving, and thus the thriftiness of the parents for their children, will be in no way adversely affected by the abolition of interest-slavery; on the contrary. The possibility of saving will become greater when our national economy will be liberated from the all-encompassing pressure of interest-slavery.

We have seen from the example of the man with earnings of 10,000 marks and pension-income of 5000 marks that all medium-sized and smaller fortunes are in fact robbed of any beneficial effect by the circuitous route of the direct and indirect taxes of housing-rent and so on. I cannot repeat often enough: interest on bonds for possessors of small and medium amounts of wealth is a swindle, a self-deception, a running around in circles, but big capital through its devoted press has quite diabolically propagated and proclaimed in all the world the faith in the sanctity and inviolability of interest. It allows everyone seemingly to take part in the lovely, anaesthetizing consumption of interest, to lull to sleep the bad conscience that must invariably accompany idle, labor less consumption of interest and to recruit comrades for the struggle, for the defense of this highest good of Mammonism.

The civil servant, the statesman, will say: the state cannot renounce the obligation that it has undertaken toward its creditors.

What does "obligations" mean? Is it in any way moral to enter obligations about which the state must know from the beginning that it can only fulfill these obligations if it takes the interest away from the creditors through direct and indirect taxes in precisely the same amount? Where is the morality in that? Or is it not perhaps more honest to admit: "I can only pay the interest if I collect just as much in taxes but back during the war I absolutely had to have money, and for that I did the swindle with the war-bond; you have to forgive me, beloved folk; it was ultimately for you, and now we want to play no more hide-and-seek; I, the state, am paying no interest and you, the taxpayer, need not pay taxes for the interest; that will substantially simplify our transactions. Thus, we shall do without the enormous tax-bureaucracy and likewise the extraordinary interest-serving bureaucracy. Right? Do we have a deal?" And you, Herr Scheidemann, do not again post your name on every advertising pillar as the secretary of the state of the old, compromised government amid foolish declarations relating to the security and inviolability of the war-bond. You only embarrass yourself: the benefit of the entire swindle has indeed gone only and solely to big loan-capital.

Financial officials and banking professionals are declaring that the abolition of enslavement to interest on war-bonds and public debts is impossible because it is synonymous with public bankruptcy.

You will forgive me: according to your speeches, we are indeed publicly bankrupt anyway or must become so. An overt declaration of public bankruptcy, however, would be the greatest stupidity that we could commit to the actual incompetence of the current powerholders, it would add prematurely the historical confirmation of this incompetence.

Why declares bankruptcy? If I have put 3 marks from the right pants-pocket into the left, I must still not, on that account, declare the bankruptcy of the right pants pocket!

It was indeed no different with the war-loan! The Reich took out of the people's pockets the first present billions, then the moneys flowed back again; then came the new loan and again the money streamed back; once again came the pump and sucked the billions and again they ebbed back, until, after the game had been repeated nine times, the state had merrily generated 100 billion in debt. For that, the people had 100 billion in finely printed paper in their hands. At first, the folk imagined that it had become so much richer; then came the state and said: "It is horrible; I have 100 billion in debt and face bankruptcy." Yes, but why? That is in any case only a self-deception! I can indeed never become bankrupt if every so often I take my money from the one pocket and place it in the other. Therefore, we can rest at ease about state bankruptcy regarding our internal war-bond debts. Therefore, we really need not declare public bankruptcy and we can really spare ourselves the gigantic labor with the stupid interest-payments and the big, but even stupider, taxes.

Let us indeed finally free ourselves from doing the bidding of big loan-capital! Only big loan-capital benefits from this loan-interest tax-swindle, since a lovelier lump of gold is left over for it and the laboring folk pays this surplus in the form of indirect taxes; meanwhile, however, the small and middle-sized capitalist simply chases his own tail.

The global economic official says: The abolition of interest-slavery is not possible for us to accomplish in Germany alone; it must be done internationally; otherwise, we shall lose all credit, capital will flow away, and we will still have to fulfill our interest-obligations toward the rest of the world.

I confess that I was at a loss about this question for the longest time. It is the most difficult question because it involves our relationship with the rest of the world; meanwhile, the matter has two sides. On the one hand, the idea of the abolition of interest-slavery is the battle cry of all productive peoples, against international enslavement to interest on money; on the other hand, it is the radical cure for our internal financial woe. But it is really no reason to refrain from using a cure, just because the equally sick neighbor does not employ it at the same time. It would, however, be added stupidity if we in Germany continued to run in a crazy circle and pay taxes and interest when we have clearly recognized that this ridiculous activity benefits only the big capitalists and nobody else. Therefore, let us lead the way by our liberating example; let us liberate ourselves from the enslavement to interest on money, and we shall soon see that the force of this victorious liberating idea will stimulate the peoples of the world to follow us.

I am convinced that our initiative, if this initiative is not suppressed by the German Mammonists, will sweep the other peoples along with irresistible necessity. The Spartacist says: The whole idea only amounts to a protection of capital; it remains then as it was: the poor man has nothing, and the rich remain.

Yes, my friend; it is in general very hard to have a discussion with you if you really are in the depths of your soul a Communist, and will therefore actually maintain that "all things belongs to all men"[10], and if along with that you are indeed familiar with the actual ideas of the great Bolshevik leaders in Russia, especially Lenin, and regard them as correct, and accordingly regard the next tasks of the Soviet Republic designated by Lenin, "universal tendering of accounts and control of all production and distribution," as humanly possible.

If however you are completely clear about the fact that this task is really only feasible, if at all, under a horrible tyranny, and you still remain at the bottom of your heart a convinced Communist or Spartacist and so on, then let us not dispute further with each other; we just do not understand each other and are speaking different languages, and the future will decide, either for the strait-jacket state that can ultimately result from the chaos of Bolshevism, or the new state for which I hope, with a national economy liberated from interest-slavery.

But if, at the bottom of your Communist heart if you are honest you find that you still think about, long for wife and child, for a human soul that stands closer to you than an Eskimo or a Zulu kaffir, if during factory-labor commanded by the soviet-director you think that it would still be nice to possess your own little cottage, a little garden-plot, if indeed in the very depth of your soul it would really give no true satisfaction that you should be entitled like a dog on the street to use every bitch that crosses your path, if you want to call somebody your wife, if you merely think about saving something from your wage, which then should belong to you alone, then you are already no longer a Communist; then you have already in your heart broken from your so loudly proclaimed catchphrase, "All things belong to all men"; then precisely what you do not want is that all things should belong to all men; you want that precisely what you wish for yourself wife, child, house, farm, savings whether you already have it or only hope to get it, even then should belong to you alone.

And do you see, my friend, if you only suspect in your heart that it might make a difference to you, if some random individual came and simply took your savings away from you in the name of "all," and if he brought another child for you and took with him yours because all children belonged to "all," then my friend, let us not continue to speak completely past each other.

Perhaps I could ask you to contemplate whether in fact the Communist message that all things should belong to all men would not necessarily mean the end of every culture, because the lack of any concept of ownership must with compelling logic force man down to the level of the beast.

If all things belong to all men, if a tendering of accounts and control of all aboveground production and distribution in Lenin's sense could be coerced, then in the best-case scenario, an ant-colony would result. But in that case, we can also do without language, soul, and thought, mutely and instinctively, we can perform our forced labor. *The end of man is there.*[11]

But enough now, friend Spartacus. Let this fundamental consideration sink deeply into your head and heart. A more exact answer to your question will then result during conversation with the other parties.

And now, you comrades of the two socialist orientations, moderate and independent!

I cannot imagine that serious contradiction or objections against the abolition of interest-slavery would come from your side, and yet I must deal with you categorically, along with the entire socialist world of ideas, from Marx up to the current leaders Ebert, Scheidemann, Kautsky, and so forth.

1. The socialist will: elevation of the working class is an idea unconditionally bound to prevail; so far, we agree.
2. The paths trodden for the attainment of this great goal are almost entirely wrong, because they are based on false assumptions.
3. The (Marxist) socialist idea of the state leads necessarily to Communism, thus, to decline.
4. Because however Social-Democracy has a different goal, the elevation of the working class, of all working people in general, it faces a terrible inner conflict, because the logical consequences of Marxism lead to the direct opposite of the practical goal of the workers' movement.
5. From this inner division results the overt uncertainty in the direction of the government.
6. For the sake of the great practical goal (elevation of the working class) a sharper line must be drawn against Spartacus and Bolshevistic Communism, and their methods must be combated with all our might. But Social Democracy, organized through labor-unions, feels weak today before these radical groups, because it has taken up Marxist thinking as its fundamental principle of education, and because all Marxist ways of thinking logically lead to Communism.

Now the proof: point 2 says that the paths trodden by Social-Democracy are almost entirely wrong.

The whole agitation conducted throughout the country has led to a deep division within the population of our nation. The constantly repeated slanders against employers of every kind, indeed of every bourgeois calling whatsoever, as exploiters and bloodsuckers of the manual laborer working ostensibly unassisted, have led to an unjustified embitterment and to the haughtiness of labor, which today necessarily finds its expression in the demand for the "dictatorship of the proletariat" (Communist Manifesto). The essential demand of the Erfurt Program, the transfer of the means of production from private ownership into the ownership and operation of the community, has today been compressed into the cry for "socialization."

It is completely clear to every serious politician that full socialization of our economic ruin would mean complete state bankruptcy. But one dare does not confess this openly and freely to the people.

Not socialization, but desocialization would have to be the motto now. Thus, one attempts to compensate the blatant miscarriage of every socialization through delusional tax-projects and by this route to "expropriate the expropriators" for the second time. All that means nothing other than abandoning the entire national economy to utter ruin. Instead of growth (a doubling of production, as the entire socialist literature for the period after the revolution promised, is out of the question) the exact opposite has occurred.

The worst thing, however, would be if the current socialist government thought of accepting big foreign loans. With that, not only would our economic decline be sealed, but we would furthermore quite entirely deliver ourselves into interest-slavery to the Entente, from which there would be no return.

The fundamental failure, the basic error, upon which this whole wrong chain of treaties, demands, and promises to the people has been constructed, is an entirely wrong attitude toward industrial capital and loan-capital. The Communist Manifesto, the Erfurt Program, Marx, Engels, Lasalle, Kautsky, have not recognized the radical difference between industrial capital and loan-capital.

On this point, the entire Social-Democracy must relearn; this fundamental error must be clearly recognized and frankly admitted without reservation.

Then, however, one must also relentlessly draw the only possible conclusions. These, however, signify a radical renunciation of the pointless, because completely mistaken, rage against industry, against the employer. Worker and work-giver belong together; they have the same goal work, production; for without production, without work, there can be no life, no culture, no forward, and not upward. The self-evident and unavoidable oppositions that exist among humans, just because they are humans, are much less important than the great shared interest of employer and employee. These oppositions are and have been resolvable by means of wage-contracts and trade-organizations to the mutual satisfaction of both sides.

But let us not pursue further these questions that are trivial in the scope of our treatise on the largest political lines of force and let us only emphasize that the interest of labor collectively is perfectly aligned with our national industry, with the national economy of our people.

Whoever teaches otherwise and presents the oppositions between employer and employees as more important reveals himself as irresponsible precisely regarding the workers; for he thereby lays the axe to the roots of the tree that nourishes and supports the worker.

Social-Democracy, however, has done that, and with that it has incurred eternal guilt before German labor; with that it has brought unspeakable misery upon our folk, because it cannot keep all its promises, because it cannot bring to us the peace of mutual understanding, because it cannot create work for us, because it must even set up an armed force against us, because it cannot get by without the civil service, because it must demand the obligation to work, because universal equal and direct suffrage for men and women over the age of 20 helps nobody to earn a living, because without the state's guarantee of the security of person and property chaotic circumstances must occur, because without integration and subordination of the individual into society no vitality of the state is possible.

Thus, a deep, despair-filled wave of disappointment passes through the entire people. If individuals still do not understand it, ministers, members of parliament and people's delegates continue cheerfully lying to each other that the "gains of the revolution" must be defended against "reaction": what these two terms mean, if anything, no sincere statesman would be able to tell the people clearly.

The negative actions of the revolution, the deposing of a series of antiquated dynasties, deposing of officers, abolition of the nobility, dissolution of the army, in short, the "Great Demolition," is indeed no "gain."

And reaction?! The swept-away, rotten doctrine of divine right does not have anywhere in the entire folk enough moral support to result in any forceful action; the bourgeoisie, as regards the real bourgeois, is much too cowardly, much too morally corrupt, to rally against class-conscious labor: therefore, it is not necessary for the ruling class of the workers to be worried about a dynastic or bourgeois reaction.

But the deep disappointment of the people about the so-called gains of the revolution, in other words about the lack of any real improvement of the people's situation, that is the great danger. This disappointment leads to the streaming away of great masses ever farther to the left, where the promises already made are outbid by far.

Ultimately, one can no longer make promises such as "all things to all men." That is pure madness, but every idea, every phenomenon, every activity stretched and exaggerated to the extreme becomes madness in the end, and then changes into its opposite. So, goes it likewise with the Communist idea that all should belong to all, for this ultimately comes to an end and resolves into all ... having nothing. Hunger, despair, misery, sickness, and need have arrived in Russia; people have lost the last remnant of courage and joy in living.

I repeat: the enormous fundamental error in the socialist idea-world is ultimately to be traced back to the failure to recognize the deep essential difference between industrial capital and loan-capital. Interest-devouring loan-capital is the scourge of humanity. It is the eternal effortless and endless growth of big loan capital, not productive, goods-manufacturing, industrial working-capital, that leads to the exploitation of peoples.

I cannot forgo here the examination of the question of why this essential difference has not been recognized; whether it really has not been recognized, or whether it perhaps has been obscured for the benefit of big loan-capital; whether the leaders and chiefs in the struggle against capitalism, whether the authors of the Communist Manifesto, of the Erfurt Program, and the current leaders always have proceeded with the conscientiousness.

It is the most grave and terrible thing when one casts doubt on the absolute earnestness and firm conviction of another; it seems all the graver, the more carefully one seeks after the causes and relationships pertaining to life's occurrences. I want therefore also to give no answer at all to this question itself, rather only to allude to big, obscure connections by citing an utterance of Disraeli, the greatest English Prime Minister, Lord Beaconsfield. This he writes in his novel Endymion:

"No man will treat with indifference the principle of race. It is the key to history, and why history is often so confused is that it has been written by men who were ignorant of this principle and all the knowledge it involves." (Baron Sergius to Endymion)

The Bourgeois

The bourgeois, to whom rest appears as his bourgeois duty, is certainly disturbed by every new revolutionary demand, as always with every new idea. It means unrest for him; for perhaps he would even have to think something about it. All change is odious to him; he wants to have his rest, and woe unto him that covets his moneybag. Now indeed one does want from him his interest-payments, his income from rent on houses, the interest-payments from his covered bonds, the interest that he collects on mortgages; in short, what constitutes his rest, his contentment, and his good fortune.

Even so, we must inquire what the members of the classes owning loan-capital will have to say. They form, apart from the true bourgeois... Bourgeois is a human type, with which nothing further is to be initiated; the bourgeois is a branch on the tree of humanity that should be lopped off, the sooner the better. These are the smug, self-satisfied Babbitts with their deplorably narrow horizons, who are capable of no enthusiasm. They while away their days in eternal monotony with coffee, morning newspaper, morning drink, noon paper, lunch, afternoon nap, coupon-clipping, afternoon drink, friends at the pub, and occasionally the movie house. Lacking comprehension for all that moves the world, all for which youth longs, all that distresses the folk, the state, and society, untroubled about war and victory, they vegetate and decay, simultaneously arrogant and obsequious – but the bourgeoisie is such a broad class that it cannot be ignored.

Thus, through the abolition of interest-slavery, thrift is destroyed; people end up in the poorhouse.

That the abolition of interest-slavery quite generally may have its influence on thrift must be decisively denied. Thrift has just as little to do with the prevailing economic views as e.g., wastefulness. Thrift and wastefulness are human qualities that either are present or not, indifferent to whether an age approves or frowns upon the idea of interest.

In times of transition, perhaps an increase or diminution of thrift can be promoted. In the given case, however, I tend much more to the view that a rational, economically minded person will say to himself the following: "I can no longer in the future count on living on my interest alone. I want, however, to live in later years and still leave something behind for my children; therefore, I must now save more." The abolition of interest-slavery must, in my opinion, exert this effect on most people. As for the elderly, of course they will be referred to as public support.

Here too I must once again stress emphatically that, given the current burden of direct taxes on property and the burden of indirect taxes on every lifestyle, nothing of the lovely interest-payments remains, except in the case of that person for whom and it is indeed something iniquitous and to be combated all income flows only from eternal interest-payments. Therefore, a decline in thrift is probably not to be feared.

Is (loathsome) big capital so utterly unfruitful? Has it not also created the means to large-scale progress that bears fruits for humanity greater than what the interest on loan-capital destroys?

No! The posing of the question only proves that Mammonistic phraseology has clouded our clear vision.

Big capital has not created the means to large-scale progress; rather big capital has grown from labor! All capital is accumulated labor. Big capital is unproductive because plain money by itself is a thoroughly unfruitful thing. From mind, labor, and available or already developed raw materials or mineral resources, values are produced, and goods are manufactured through labor and only through labor. For if one pours so much money onto the most fertile farmland, into the richest coalmine, the farmland does not, on that account, bear grain, nor the coalmine spit out coals by itself! Let us conclusively affirm this. If people have invented money, it is accordingly quite useful and reasonable; for in every complex economy, one needs this (universally recognized) "voucher for completed labor." But that a potential should inhere in these "money-empires" to grow eternally from themselves into enormity and money does that. If it can bear interest, it is that against which the core of our being rebels; it is that which exalts money far above all other earthly manifestations; it is that which makes money into an idol. And all of that is indeed only the most enormous self-deception of humanity!

Nothing, nothing at all, can come from money alone. Table, cabinet, clothing, house, tool, and in short, everything around us has some value; in the end, one can still use a broken piece of furniture as firewood to warm oneself, but with a twenty-mark note, one cannot do anything; I cannot even wrap a piece of cheese in it. Only after people have sensibly agreed on the facilitation of the exchange of goods for consumption, to write vouchers for completed labor, only with that does the slip of paper receive meaning and purpose, and it is very reasonable that the farmer for his grain receives from the coal mining company does not coal but money, thus a voucher for other completed labor, e.g., pitchforks, crockery, plough, and scythe. But with that, the power of money should end.

Thus, the large-scale progress of humanity has been made not by money but by the men themselves, their bold spirit, their proud daring, their clever mind, the strength of their hands, their shared, therefore social, industrious labor. So proudly and so clearly must we see. The men were the thing, certainly not the pitiful pieces of paper that men invented for the simplification of commerce.

Further Program

Although the abolition of interest-slavery is not the final goal of the new statecraft; it is truly the most incisive deed, the only deed that is able to unite all peoples into a true league of nations, against the tyranny of Mammonism that encompasses all peoples. But it is not the end. On the contrary, the abolition of interest-slavery must lead to further steps, because, as we have seen, it lays hold of the global evil by the root, and indeed by the main root.

Only when the ground laying demand for abolition of interest-slavery is fulfilled, is the path cleared for the first time for the social state. This must be clearly recognized, and it must be accomplished despite all Mammonistic powers. The cry for socialization (while interest-slavery persists) is nothing more than the attempt to bring about the formation of a trust of all industries and to create giant conglomerates everywhere, over which big loan-capital, despite all wealth taxes, will naturally also have the deciding influence again in the future. A socialistic state on a Mammonistic foundation is an absurdity and leads by nature to a compromise between Social-Democracy, already strongly contaminated with Mammonism, and big capital.

We, by contrast, demand radical rejection of the Mammonistic state and a reconstruction of the state according to the true spirit of socialism, in which the ruling basic idea is the obligation to nourish in which an old basic demand of Communism can find its rational and useful satisfaction in the form that every member of the folk shall receive his assigned entitlement to the soil of the homeland through the state's allocation of the most important foodstuffs.

We further demand, as a skeleton for the new state, a representation of the people through the Chamber of People's Representatives, which is to be elected on the broadest basis, and next to that a permanent Chamber of Labor, the central council in which the nation's workers have a voice in proportion to their distribution by profession and economic class. Finally, we demand the highest accountability for the directors of the state. This new construction of the state on a socialist-aristocratic basis will be treated in an additional work that will appear soon from the same publisher.

The prerequisite for all this construction, however, remains the abolition of interest-slavery.

My unshakable belief, and my knowledge makes me recognize clearly that the abolition of interest-slavery is not only enforceable but will and must be taken up everywhere with indescribable jubilation. For bear in mind: in contrast to all other ideas and movements and endeavors, however well intentioned, that aim at the improvement of mankind, my proposal does not want to try to improve human nature; rather it applies itself against a toxic substance, against a phenomenon that was artfully no, diabolically invented, completely contrary to the deepest feeling of man, to make humanity ill, to ensnare humanity in materialism, to rob from it the best thing that it has, the soul. Hand in hand next to it goes the frightful, pitiless tyranny of the money-powers, for which people are only interest-slaves, exist only to work for the dividend, for interest.

Deeply troubled, we recognize the frightful clarity and truth of the old Biblical proverbs, according to which the god of the Jews Yahweh promises to his chosen people: "I want to grant to you to own all treasures of the world; at your feet shall lie all peoples of the Earth and you shall rule over them."

This global question is now laid out before all of you. Global questions are not solved with a wave of the hand, but the idea is clear as day. And the deed must be diligently propagated; we must understand clearly that we face the most formidable enemy, the world-encompassing money-powers. All force on the other side, on our side only justice, the eternal justice of productive labor.

Extend your hands to me, working people of all countries, unite!

CHAPTER 11

THE GERMAN STATE ON NATIONAL SOCIALIST FOUNDATIONS

Foreword by Adolf Hitler

Every great idea needs two things: the will to power and clear goals. The will to power, to liberation, lies glowing and strong in our hearts. Gottfried Feder has in his book The German State on a national and socialist foundation, presented our goals clearly and simply and in a way understandable to everybody. In it, the hope and longing of millions has found a form and powerful expression. The literature of our movement has in it got its catechism.

— Adolf Hitler, Munich, November 8th, 1923

Preface to the Fifth Edition

Here my work, The German State on a national and socialist foundation, appears within the series of the "National Socialist Library." The text has remained essentially and basically unchanged but the passages that referred to circumstances of the time when this work appeared (1923) and borrowed examples there from were deleted and the explanations of the Jewish question shortened since a special work will be dedicated to the latter.

The new edition should especially give evidence of the fact that nothing in the least was changed in the basic Program.

— Gottfried Feder, Murnau, October 1931

'Blessed are the people to whom a stark necessity

imposes a lofty political idea which,

being great and simple,

forces every other idea of the age into its service.'

— Heinrich von Treitschke

Introduction

We look into the future full of strong hope and longing. Germany will live, Germany cannot go down. The overpowering birth-pangs of a new age shake Germany. The horrid shackles of self-guilt, as well as the foreign tormentors, will fall away and will be shaken off with a powerful shrug, and Germany will march at the head of the nations.

If so much suffering and distress were not connected with the collapse and downfall, we could participate with a certain feeling of happiness in the days of creation of a new age. If we cast our glance upon the degradations of the day, in the confusion of the present, we see everywhere a powerful will, serious work, inspired intuition. The German soul moves its wings to a new topflight.

The tasks today are powerful, greater, and harder than ever in the so painful history of the Germans.

So, it is necessary to solve the twofold task -not just to "rebuild" the state and economy but to give them a new form. And a new form, also for the cultural and intellectual life of our people.

The old German longing for a united Germany must finally become a reality, a new economic law will arise and sweep away the nightmarish form of interest in capitalistic economics.

So comprehensive and overpowering are the tasks that await us. Grave and admonishing stands the spirit of the past behind us; filled with awe before that which has occurred historically, on the solid ground of the best German tradition, based on the earliest Aryan wisdom, the people and the state, economics and culture must be created anew.

Here the workers must be conscious of their enormous responsibility, indeed they are borne by the hope of the entire nation towards freedom!

But the National Socialist idea is much more than only a return or a detour into old ancestral customs, it breaks the chains of the Marxist state and economic form, it, as the first and most determined idea, consciously fights the hardest battle against the Mammonistic powers, against the world-encompassing power of the all-Jewish imperialism, against the spirit of rapacity, selfishness, and indifference.

This universal and great German freedom movement finds its most powerful, strong-willed, and goal-conscious campaigner in the National Socialist German Workers' Party. The party has outlined its goals in a short Program that summarizes in a pithy way the fundamental demands of the movement in 25 clauses. Alfred Rosenberg, the chief editor of the Nationalist Observer[13], the polemical organ of the National Socialist movement of Greater Germany, has, in a manner worthy of thanks, explained the Program points individually in a quick work.

Based on this work, it is at least possible to say to friends and enemies what the National Socialist German Workers' Party wants. There is lacking in the literature of National Socialism a comprehensive work that would recount the political and economic ideas from which National Socialism proceeds, what paths it intends to forge regarding national politics to arrive at its final goal, that of the National Socialist German state, the state of work and performance. The present work wishes to fulfil this task. We will therefore have to illumine the point of departure, the way, and the goal of National Socialism, we shall show wherein the German National Socialist state will essentially differ from the existing state, which fields will remain essentially untouched, on which fields there will be substantial reforms, and where essentially new paths will have to be entered upon.

We shall have to reveal new ways for public life, especially for the national financial policy, to treat the racial question and the questions connected with it. We shall further have to deal with hostile objections, distortions and lies that have already become loud.

The task that we have set to ourselves is extremely great and yet only a small part of the entire scope of Germany's renewal.

All effort would be in vain if a determinedness unto death and the unrestrained will of a leader did not work for the efficacy of the ideas.

The strongest "will" would be wasted uselessly if we did not bear in our hearts unshakably a clear image of what this German state -Germany, the land of our fathers and children—should look like under our will after our victory!

The Moral Foundations

The foundation of National Socialist statecraft is a complete responsibility regarding the people and regarding oneself.

"Public interest before self-interest" is the first law of National Socialism.

It may seem strange that such a principle must be established for a state, for we recognize from history periods in which the welfare of the whole was in the mind of the rulers as the foundation of their state leadership. If it is necessary today to set this principle before all other considerations, this is only the expression of the fact that the present-day public conditions are anything but the expression of this sole correct political sentiment. We see equally in this first principle how intimately morality and economics are involved with each other.

Public interest before self-interest is first a moral demand. But it expresses at the same time with excellent linguistic clarity the hierarchical ordering between the welfare of the whole and the justified striving of the individual for personal acquisition and property. This National Socialist principle therefore in no way excludes private property. On the contrary: National Socialism acknowledges fully and completely the significance of property. It knows that personal property and a right to dispose of an acquisition freely is the foundation of economics, and beyond that, of every higher culture; but National Socialism has recognized equally that for the acknowledgement of private property it is necessary to draw quite definite limits, where property becomes a mere instrument of power and is applied exploitative against the welfare of the whole.

There is perhaps hardly one seriously thinking person who would like to contradict this first principle in this general form. The difficulty will lie in the right assessment of public interests against those of the individual private person. Despite the doubtlessly existing agreement that the considerations of the public interest must go before the private interests, remarkably there has been, according to the legal ideas valid among us, precisely regarding the form of the use of property, no moral limitation determined beyond the criminal. It is, to be sure, forbidden to act with violence against one's fellow man (extortion -murder manslaughter -betrayal and illegitimate enrichment, etc.), but it has never and nowhere been forbidden to pile up immeasurable wealth and to make use of the often quite dubious banking and stock-exchange technical means. Further, the law gives every creditor the right to ruthlessly deprive a delinquent debtor of his home and possessions when adverse conditions illness, death, malformation, poor harvests, and famine -make the fulfillment of incurred obligations impossible. Every experienced judge can relate numberless cases in which our rigid law has destroyed economic existences where every healthy sense of justice has revolted against delivering a hardworking, diligent man who has, however, been dogged by bad luck temporarily to the brutal pressure and grasp of the creditor.

The limitless acknowledgement of personal right to properly and legal claims overall must logically lead to the damaging of the public interest through the selfish exploitation of this basically inverted anti-social, legal idea in opposition to our state principle "Public interest before self-interest."

In contrast to the false fundamental formulation ruling among us, the capitalistic, is the other extreme, the Marxist idea of the state and economics. The fundamental idea of this economic form is the denial of private property. The Marxist doctrine explains property directly as "theft" (Proudhon). It demands, in the foreign jargon that is so unclear, especially to German proletarians, the "expropriation of the expropriators"[16] the dispossession of property! This state, people, culture, and economy destroying doctrine has found its extreme but logical realization in Russian Bolshevism. In its economic aspect, this extreme can be summarized in the sentence:

"Everything belongs to everybody."

We have here to do with a depersonalization of property, with a transfer of all property to the anonymous property of the whole.

The extreme still ruling among us of an unlimited right to property has led us already to the last step before the temple of the god Mammon, on whose door stands in golden letters: "Everything belongs to One." Even this frightening economic form must equally lead to a depersonalization of property -only in another way in that, finally, all working mankind is here pressed into a frightful debt slavery to an anonymous financial power.

In starkest contrast to the just described economic extremes of Marxist socialism and high capitalist Mammonism of the western democrats, the economic ideal of National Socialism demands the realization of the principle, "To each his own."

Precisely in this principle are morality and economics, once again, most intimately interconnected. The removal of moral principles from the commercial life is indeed so characteristic of the present-day economy in which just the superior power of greater possession, greater cunning, the art of avoiding the state authority even in the most hazardous dealings, tips the balance. A glance at the thousands of mostly dark existences that conduct their mischief in all big cities, who dispose of fantastic sums, a glance at the several suits that come to a trial despite all the resistance of the participants, shows us how frightfully depraved the present-day commercial morality is. Let us consider, in contrast to that, the frightful misery in the circles of the middle-class and of the married working people who can no longer pay for milk and bread for their infants and growing children, let us be clear that in many, many cases with honorable work hardly the necessities for life can be earned, especially when there are children to be looked after and raised. The distress of the intellectual and free professions exceeds all measures; artists of the very first rank, especially when their orientation does not correspond to the Jewish orientation of taste that rules today, are flatly delivered to hunger; genuine German poems can achieve no public performance. But quite indescribable is the distress of those who have, through the mismanagement of the state regarding financial policy, been cheated of their savings, the small capital pensioners and retirees, the war disabled, those forced to charity help, as well as all those who have relied on the certainty of public bonds and on the stability of our national currency and the gold coverage of the mark. Such a condition is a decomposition of the economy -anarchy. Industriousness is repaid with insufficient remuneration, laziness is rewarded, honorable trade suffers distress, unhealthy trade, intermediary trade, profiteering prospers best of all. The more superior in cultural aspects of a production is so much, the worse is the remuneration that can be got. Trust is repaid with betrayal, and indeed by the state, which should be the protector of law and justice, the attorney of public morality.

We do not at all need any more to point to the corruption in public life, the Judaization and the impoverishment of the press and the miserably powerless and unworthy leadership of our foreign policy to show the extreme debasement of our public life and our economic morality.

Against this materialistic impoverishment and contamination of the public life, the National Socialist idea of the state sets the long-tested principle of state and economy: "To each his own" but above all "Public interest before self-interest." With the raising of this principle to the guiding principle of the National Socialist state, National Socialism binds itself to the best and most glorious periods of German history.

"Suum cuique" was already the economic principle of the healthy German early Middle Ages, but especially for a long period, it was ensured through the ordering of the guilds that to each was allotted his own. The commonalty of work of master and apprentice for half or a third of a penny at least ensured the worker his income, better work and performance found their acknowledgement and their reward and, in cases of outstanding performance, fame and rich earnings.

"Suum cuique" adorns also the highest Prussian order, the Order of the Black Eagle, though here in the special sense that to special merit is due its crown. Precisely this interpretation corresponds especially to National Socialism -not so much because it is here a matter of courtly decoration pieces or the one-sided honoring of military service but because the moral content of the rewarded fulfillment of duty regarding the state and people finds its expression a fulfillment of duty which is done selflessly without design and without a previous regard for clinking wages, with a relegation of personal interests to the background, born of an inner interesting feeling of responsibility towards the state and the people.

National Socialists extend this principle also in the other direction, we add to the "to each his own" of the German Middle Ages and to the idea of "To merit its crown" of Friedrich's state, with greatest emphasis: "To the criminal his punishment!." To each his own, to merit its crown, to every orderly and honorable work its adequate payment, to every special performance its higher remuneration, to every poor person and every person who has fallen innocently into distress sufficient help from public funds, but equally to all those who act against public morality and economic respectability -the deserved punishment.

However, we stress it does not lie within duties of the National Socialist state to supervise the state citizen individually in economic matters, that the economy prospers best free as far as possible from bureaucratic tutelage. We know also that a decrease of risk with every individual state citizen through the state -rather in the sense of Naumann's "risk-free man", of a man for whose basic existence the state should provide -would achieve precisely the opposite of that which Naumann expected of it.[18] The duty of the state must be limited to creating the preconditions for an economy which holds itself as free as possible from the frightful usurious phenomena which we know in the present-day interest capitalistic state.

The welfare of the state must therefore become once again the highest law, the efficiency of the state must set the principle "Public interest before self-interest" before all other considerations.

Now this principle, however, makes necessary among the state leaders, the state employees and those who stand in outstanding positions in the public life, a characteristic that has today almost completely disappeared from government and public life-responsibility.

Our entire public life stands today directly under the sign of irresponsibility. The delegates are not responsible for one says "immune to" what they do and speak in parliament. A desperate term when one remembers that this expression is taken from medicine in which it is said that a body is already so saturated with poisons that newly infused poisons harm the body much less or not at all, whereas a healthy body would die of them. The fractions are not responsible for the decisions of the majority, the ministers are not responsible for the discharge of their office, for they are only functionaries of the parties that take part precisely in the formation of a government. If something goes wrong, the people indeed suffer the worst damages, but the so-called responsible minister is only replaced by another equally irresponsible party functionary.

Of real responsibility, there is no mention.

Already the appeal to the Almighty in the divine's age right of kings was unfortunately often a quite special form of the irresponsibility of the ruling lords (rare exceptions for whom the responsibility to their god was synonymous with their feeling of responsibility towards their people are expressly acknowledged). However, this dear god was always, in the final analysis, only a comfortable protective shield behind which could hide, on the stepladder of the official responsible only to his superior, of the minister responsible only to his king and of the ruler responsible only to his god, the most incredible irresponsibility of the ruling class and its representatives regarding the actual life-necessities of the people.

National Socialism will have to radically clear away this state sanctioned irresponsibility.

'Highest responsibility' will stand in iron letters over the entrance gate to the National Socialist state. One who has the honor to stand in a leading position for the interests of a great person cannot be reminded strongly enough of his responsibility. Indeed, only he can be a leader who bears this deepest feeling of responsibility in his breast. For all state employees and for those who stand in public life, this responsibility is to be especially stipulated and carried out with ruthless strictness. Only in this way can a recovery be compelled, so to speak. Only in this way can the most precious thing be revived and grow that may allow the leader and the people once again to become a real national and historical community -trust. And from trust then can the faith grow once again which, with the responsibility of the leader, will bring forth a recovery and renewal of Germany, a reawakening of the German soul, in a nationalist state of work and performance in which each will find his own.

The Economic Foundations

In a healthy economic body, morality and national economy cannot be separated. Otherwise, the economy suffers in the most severe manner, especially regarding the most honorable task of every economy the fulfilment of demand. Without faith in commerce, without industriousness, without the loyalty of the officials and workers, no work can prosper.

Efficiency, justice, entrepreneurial spirit, energy, mutual trust between all taking part in an economic task are the indispensable preconditions for the prospering of every economy. All these things need to be said only to be acknowledged in their exceptional significance. Everybody who has had to be economically active in the present and the recent past knows to what extent these fine things are lacking today.

And who finally suffers the damages of the salvation doctrines of Marxism and its operational methods, the strikes, sabotage, and negligent and slovenly work? But in the end only the population itself which, through such state-and people-disintegrating doctrines, lost all feeling of community and sees its most important work in class-struggle. Therefore, to this quarter must also be directed the complaints which ring out especially from the nationalist camps that we are no longer a people, that we should first become a people once again if we wished to reacquire our lost position of power and international standing.

These complaints are justified, but with complaints, one does not go forward. Marxism did not hesitate to realize its economic and political ideal when it had the power to do so, it did not shy away from brutal suppression of dissidents: in Russia it silenced its enemies forever by slaughtering the entire bourgeois intelligentsia, among us through the laws for protecting the republic. The acquisition of political power is obviously the precondition of every economic or national political reform. That we know as well as the Communists and the Social Democrats, but we want political power not for its own sake, not to exploit the gained position of power against a certain class but to create the preconditions for an economic peace among the national comrades bound into a work community.

The fulfilment of demand is the national economy not profitability, which is today almost solely decisive in the production of goods. With this fundamental attitude of National Socialism, we enter definite opposition to the basic economic ideas of the capitalist state. Not what was necessary was produced in the first place, but what was profitable.

Anything that did not promise to yield sufficient interests and dividends was from the start not taken up. As an especially clear example of the profitability madness of the present interest, capitalistic economy may serve the fact that housing construction, despite the frightful need for housing thus despite the most urgent need is simply not carried out because it is not profitable! That housing construction considered in a national political way in a higher sense would indeed be profitable requires in this place no further explanation but is straightaway clear from what has been said, especially regarding the social tasks of the state.

Further, if the people hunger and freeze, then a capitalist economy directed to profit does not see its duty in fulfilling this need through the production of cheap and good shoes, clothes, and underwear, etc., for with the lowered purchasing capacity of the population this is not "profitable." The luxuries industry in all fields is fully busy, for never was effortlessly gained wealth so eager to surround itself with sheer luxury as today. But the capitalist idea of profitability becomes an economic nonsense in the branches of our economy that today rule everything, in the banking and stock-exchange system. The fact of the ruling position of the banks proves most strikingly the economic senselessness of the capitalist idea. With the "productions" of the banks and stock-exchanges, never yet has a child been fed, never yet has a freezing person been clothed never has even the smallest requirement that is necessary for life been supplied. This statement is not at all a demagogic catchphrase, it does not even include the dispensability of the institutions of monetary transactions, it only shows with all clarity what an enormous difference there exists between a national economic fulfilment of demand, such as National Socialist wishes, and a completely private-capitalistically oriented profit-based economy.

The National Socialist state will have its banks and other financial institutions, but they will no longer be the rulers of the national economy but their servants, money will no longer be the lord of the state and people but only the aid for the exchange of goods. We know precisely that this battle against the bank and stock exchange capital will mean the hardest battle for the National Socialist movement because today the most enormous plenitude of power that the globe has ever borne is concentrated in the bank and stock exchange capital. Here it is a question of a life and death battle for power, this the opponent knows better than most of our friends and followers. This battle will be so much more difficult in that entire sections of the population are still caught in the profitability madness.

A fundamental question which should be answered in this place once again with all clarity is the question of how National Socialism basically stands in relation to property. From the fundamental observations of the first chapter and especially from the fundamental opposition described there to Marxist Socialism, there results with natural consequence for National Socialism the fundamental acknowledgement of property. This acknowledgement of private property is too deeply anchored in Aryan life. The creative mind which recognizes the environment, which contemplates the environment to create and form therefrom its world, the creative man who wrests its fruits from the earth through hard work, who settles down, builds for himself homes and cities, who, having become settled and rooted in the circle of his kinsmen, his racial comrades, the man who then proceeds on such an infrastructure rooted in the soil to higher culture and creates for himself his the world in a higher intellectual sense, in the fields of philosophy, poetry, music, art and sculpture this man certainly cannot conceive of it differently than that the works of his hand, which have been born out of his own, are also his property. From this knowledge of the creative man arises directly the respect for the property of others, and law arises.

In fundamental and irreconcilable opposition to the creative mind stands the avaricious thieving mind of other men disposed differently, who have never known the breath of creation, who move restlessly from place to place, who could never put down roots anywhere, who did not rise expansively, and from the soil, in a long development to ever higher culture but, with their restlessly moving mind and with their money, moved from country to country, when they had "grazed" the individual cities or tracts of land. Even in the fields of the creative nations the Jew essentially stood quite far removed from the actual productions, we do not know the Jew as a farmer, not as tradesmen, not as engineers or master-builders, not as factory and wage workers, and true creative genius is foreign to him even in the fine arts and in the sciences. The moving mind begins its characteristic activity only where a work has been created by a creative hand, an object has been produced, there the avaricious mind knows to procure these goods for itself and to move them to its pecuniary advantage. Not to supply the national economic demand but to strike as high a profit as possible for itself from this traffic of production to consumption, it set itself up between producer and consumer the trader arose. Today the trader and moneychanger has become the board of directors and banking lord. The economy of the entire world has been turned upside down in the most senseless manner. The clever, inventive, daring, creative, and productive mind no longer rules; the crooked mind, incapable of creating anything of its own, exploitative, and avaricious rules. Money rules over work and blood.

The moving mind of the Jew has made everything mobile, even the land through mortgages, the largest long-established industries through anonymization and through the stock company, and, through the state bond economy, international capital has even separated the governments from their peoples. Today the governments are all dependent on large loan capital and in relation to their peoples they are only the interest collectors for their anonymous lords on Wall Street, the City of London and Paris.

These brief observations have shown us the deepest secret of the irreconcilable opposition between creative peoples and the avaricious Jew. "The Aryan creates, the Jew grabs the world for himself."

Here, it may be briefly added further that there is a very fine difference between property and possession. Possession need not at all be property, possession cannot be self-created. With a possession, the origin of the possession is not questioned. The Jew has seized possession of the property of the Aryan peoples and now rules the creators through his financial power. This abstracted form of property as legal claims, bonds, mortgages, etc.

has made the entire world today subject to interest to capital. The interest capitalistic economic form knows no limits of possession, it suffers entire nations with all their work to become subject to interest to a handful of bank and stock exchange magnates.

Against this not a little frightening interest-capitalistic robber economy National Socialism sets the limitation of the right to property. The principle for this limitation lies in the sentence:

"Public interest before self-interest."

That this limit for property moreover can be raised very high emerges from the fact that National Socialism will not reject even the largest industrial works, so long as they remain in the private possession of the creators (we think of Krupp, Mannesmann, Thyssen, etc.), as contradicting the interests of the whole, especially when the owners of these large works have a feel for and understanding of social questions and can find the right limits between self-gain from production, an adequate pricing for the sales and the fulfilment of demand of the national economy, and a corresponding and worthy form of participation of the workforce in the revenues of the works.

Here, we come to brief fundamental observations on the external forms of production. The powerfully rising German economy before the war was distinguished by a very fortunate mixture of big, medium and small businesses. Now in the tendency to big business there indeed lies a danger for the national economy where the next step above the big business, that no longer serves the fulfilment of demand but the high capitalistic interests of the domination of the market and of the dictatorship of prices. It is plainly conceded that certain industries can work only as big businesses. This applies to those industrial branches that we designate as heavy industries. Without wishing to go into details, it may be basically stated that the National Socialist state has no reason to strive for fundamental changes in these external forms of the economy. National Socialism rejects many "socialization or nationalization" in the Marxist sense. Our economic ideal demands as large several economically free existences precisely in the medium and small businesses. We know that only the free and independent men who can freely dispose of their work and their work income are filled with a serious feeling of responsibility regarding their work, that only on this soil do powerful personalities arise and that only on the soil of freedom and responsibility prospers the sense of the community which unites those bound through common work to a community of life and destiny and therewith makes them a free, self-conscious nation. Only on such a soil can the welfare of the individual be united with the welfare of the whole.

Boundaries of the State & Economy

Manchesterism and State Socialism are the opposites when it comes to establishing the limits which the state must observe in its intervention in the economy. The first doctrine demands as much freedom as possible from every state guardianship. It would like best to see the state relegated to the role of a night-watchman. State Socialism believes that most businesses are best conducted and administered by the state itself. The most extreme forms of socialization or nationalization, which is the Russian term for the running of the enterprises by all, have shown to everybody who has observed the Socialist experiments impartially, with conclusive clarity, that such Communistic forms of production are in the long run unfeasible. One who has followed our explanations of the foundations of the economy will recognize without difficulty the inner reasons for this phenomenon. On the one hand, the suppression of the entrepreneurial initiative, the lack of the profit motive, the removal of competition the compulsion to work which was exercised with ruthless force by the Soviets must reduce the advantage of production to a minimum.

The gradual, milder form of "state-control" of businesses as we know it from our German economic life is to be applied successfully to advantage only in different fields of the public economy. In the fields which are conducted in competition with the free economy, especially in large industrial production (coal), the commercial success is strongly limited compared to the free economy, which can take all important decisions more quickly and independently than is necessarily possible with state enterprises. To have a right judgement of what businesses are suited for state control, we must be clear of what position the state assumes the total operation of a national economy.

We have explained that National Socialism sees economics in the fulfilment of demand. Producer and consumer, manufacturer, and user, are the two chief participants in every economy. Now we know that the use is, in the final analysis, always and everywhere purely individual, or expressed clearly: every piece of bread can indeed be consumed only by one person, clothes are also destined only for personal use, a fiat provides a roof only to a small, connected circle, the work-place gives a position to only a perhaps greater but still limited number of work comrades, so we cannot at all speak of a common consumption or use of products. If, therefore, consumption is, in the final analysis, individual, the same is true also of production, of the production of goods. The more valuable the product of productive work is, the clearer it is that this arises only from a highly personal creative force. For the works of the mind in the fields of science and the fine arts, in technical inventions and discoveries this is immediately clear, but even with assembled work in factory-like enterprises, in which the mechanization through machines suppresses almost entirely human individual work, it is finally still valid that the pair of shoes that precisely this worker manufactures can be manufactured only by this one and not by another. The quality of the products, however, sinks with increasing mechanization. Already in the agricultural business the old rule is valid:

"The eye of the lord fattens the cattle", only the personal care of the breeder gets the highest results.

All attempts of the Communist economy have ended every time in a complete failure. We must, therefore, declare that both consumption and production go against socialization. Now, as soon as mankind abandoned the original economic forms of individual economy in the family and moved to more complicated economic forms through division of labor and had formed great state communities, there intervened between production and consumption something new trade and commerce and the financial system.

This very plain economic, philosophical observation gives us the clearest evidence of the fields in which the state must limit its economic activity. It is indeed immediately clear that it is here a question of matters in which every individual is equally interested. And it is only logical that here the state will find its scope of duties as the embodiment of the common interests.

If our economic philosophy is right, the state must have performed something exemplary in one of these fields in case it has tried its hand at one already, such as transportation. The performances of the German railway authorities before the war were just exemplary, and they are that even today, if the old fidelity to duty and conscientiousness still rule. One also often credits the non-state railway system in America with special perfection; this is also accurate in a certain context where the traffic occurs rather more freely, and many minor difficulties which are with us bound to the bureaucratic system could hardly have been avoided. Even the building of locomotives of great dimensions in America evoked astonishment amongst us earlier, but the chief reason for this was that the broader gauge of the American railway network made this indeed more easily possible technically. But this is not an aspect of transport but a technical fact which does not belong to our observations. Much more important to our question is the security of the transport in the railways. In this field, the German railways were constantly aware of this uppermost task of the state transport and can also claim the reputation for itself for having done, technically and organizationally, everything that was possible. With what irresponsible recklessness the life of the passengers was endangered in this field precisely in the American and French railways emerges from the history of railway accidents on American railways and on French railways before the nationalization if these served the reckless pursuit of profit of the Paris Rothschilds. Even here, therefore, we see once again the fundamental opposition between the capitalistic idea of profitability and the idea of a duty of the demand fulfilment economy.

Commerce is, in the first place, to serve the national economy through the secure, quick, and cheap transfer of goods and persons to the places of use or work. The question of profitability comes only in the second place in a state enterprise, or it is only a question of tariff policy. To commerce belongs naturally also the post and telegraph system. Even here, it requires only the honorable memory of the performances of the German post and telegraph administration to show how securely, quickly, and reliably, this important national economic task was fulfilled by the state.

Trade has always been considered as the exclusive task of private entrepreneurial initiative. Now, trade cannot be spoken of so unequivocally as the transport system. For a state regulation, there comes into consideration from the start only a certain type of goods, indeed mass-consumption goods. As little understanding as one could expect before the war of a state regulation of trade in the most important food products since the free trade doctrine ruled our national economical way of thought, so little can one expect today, in view of the shameless usury in the most important food products during the still unforgotten postwar period, that the idea that it is the state to provide for the preparation, transfer and distribution of the most important food products will fall on fertile soil. Exceptionally, we find, even among our antipodes in the economic field, the Bolshevists, attempts to solve this problem through the state control of production and its distribution. What is wrong there, as we have already shown, wants to conduct the production or to understand it always in a state-controlled way. The right distribution of the production is doubtless an especially important state task. Remarkably, in Russia the only bourgeois organizations that have remained preserved were the agricultural production and consumer cooperatives, thus those organizations that had precisely set themselves storing and collecting the most important food products in the common interest and of supplying the consumer in the common interest. A survey of our German economic life shows us know that, even among us, this idea is not completely new but that the cooperative idea has been increasingly taking hold everywhere and therewith creating the preconditions that National Socialism has in mind for regulating this extraordinarily important question. The cooperative utilization of agricultural products ensures, on the one hand, to the farmer the removal of his products at adequate prices, it ensures the cooperative purchase of fertilizers, agricultural implements, etc., and it especially attempts to ensure the fulfilment of demand through the establishment of agricultural warehouses. The consumer unions have taken completely practical steps to supply the products to the consumers as directly as possible and above all with the suppression of intermediary trade. A merging of the production cooperatives and the consumer cooperatives under state supervision will solve this question.

Even here, the core of the question is once again: not profitability, but the fulfilment of demand is the first task of the economy.

For trade, there remains more than enough to occupy it, especially in all the fields where the personal factor of risk comes into question. For a food product which is secure always, and in all the circumstances of the sales, the factors that characterize the businessman are from the start eliminated.

The financial system is the third and most important thing that is to be brought under state regulation. Money is explained by many financial theorists to exchange for the exchange of products; this explanation is indeed not false but also not comprehensive and not clear. This definition expresses the right feeling that money is an aid for the traffic in goods. That the state claims the privilege of coinage for itself already proves that the state considers money as an especially important field of public life. That the state has produced an entire series of sections in the penal code that deals with counterfeiting proves similarly that it is a matter of a public matter of the first importance.

In fact, the state has also for a long time determined through its own authority what is to be valid as money in public commerce. A special orientation of financial theoreticians the Chartalists[22] represents the state theory of money, which summarily declares:

"Money is what the state declares to be money."

Therewith, money is entirely separated from the substance of money, and the seal of the state sovereignty suffices to make "money" from iron, aluminum, porcelain and, above all, paper. The present teaches us that this theory has, in fact, become reality. The opponents of these financial theoreticians, the Metallists, cling to the old idea that money must have an inner value, thus must be from precious metal (gold and silver). The relations of the present do not bear this orientation out for, in fact, the state even makes money out of paper, and indeed money with which one can really buy something, even when the banknotes are made of quite worthless paper. But the question of the purchasing power of this money is another story. Here the sinking purchasing power of money that stands in inverse proportion to the swelling amount of paper money seems to prove the Metallists right, for the coins of gold and silver have not caused the loss of purchasing power of paper money. But this is due to another reason, namely to the commodity character of gold money. Not because the gold money is real gold does it maintain its purchasing power but because gold money is also a commodity. The twenty-mark coin today derives its purchasing power not at all from the stamped state currency sign '20 Marks' but from its content of the commodity of refined gold. But we cannot linger here longer on these financial theoretical controversial questions. We will have to speak at greater length on these questions in the representation of the state financial system according to the reasoning of the National Socialist reform. Here it is a matter of recognizing that the financial system, in the case of the question exercising us now of the boundaries of the state and economy, belongs in any case to the fields which, as an eminently important matter of the entire economic life, exactly like commerce and trade in the most important food products, must be subjected to the most careful fiduciary regulation on the part of the state.

The importance of the financial problem requires today no special explanation. The power of the large financial powers ruling everything lies manifest to anyone that wishes to see it. The perspicacious person has already for long recognized that precisely the incompetent, false way the state has positioned itself about the financial system is the basic reason for the present-day catastrophic conditions in the state finances. The fact that most of the so-called state central banks are not at all purely state institutes but stock companies in which the governments have retained for themselves only certain supervisory rights already give an idea of the muddled conditions in the field of the public financial system.

The National Political Foundations

No state without power and, without authority, no government. Nothing is more self-evident, and more immediately obvious to common sense. One must attribute it to the entire neglect of our public thought if, among us in the government circles, one still believes today that one can rule at all with a total lack of military and political power.

Power without an instrument of power is unthinkable; political power and military means of power condition each other mutually just as intimately as economy and morality may not be separated. To regain lost power, there is only the sole means of creating a military instrument of power.

How frightfully our poor fatherland has been punished because it has abjured the idea of power and given itself to the pacifistic fanfare, we experience now daily and hourly. "To prevent a worse situation" we have ourselves surrendered and destroyed our weapons, "to prevent a worse situation" we have signed the Versailles dictate, "to prevent a worse situation" the Berlin government has said yes and amen to everything that was demanded of us, "to prevent a worse situation" we have allowed every malice, every humiliation, every exploitation to be enacted against us. With this shameless catchword of cowardice and abjectness, the German people have been led into ever deeper misery. We fulfilled what was demanded of us, and a minister who wished to be a German, Dr. Rathenau, dared to declare publicly:

There is no absolute inability to fulfil, it is only a matter of how deep a people may be allowed to fall into distress!

This means although the words of Rathenau are already clear enough: the German nation is completely defenseless, it is politically completely powerless, intellectually it has been almost stultified, it can just continue to work. It has allowed itself to be burdened with such a gigantic burden of guilt that the members of the Chosen People can, on these reparations, forever lead a glamorous work-free life in all the countries of the world at the cost of German work. But now there is the danger that even the enormous workforce of the Germans may break under the fantastic burden. Therefore, the Germans must be kept alive constantly through stimulants and precisely in this way be maintained at the limit of their physical performance capacity that they may work summoning all strength always in the deceptive hope that they might one day free themselves from their burdens.

"It is only a matter of how deep a person may be allowed to fall into distress!"

This was the political sentiment of the Minister Rathenau, so celebrated by all republicans.

If we have recalled this paradigm of modern German statecraft, it was only to confirm this so frightful example lying so close to us of a defenseless and weapon-less nation having to simply put up with everything, even every derision. Against this is valid for us, the belief in an externally powerful state, which alone can guarantee peace and freedom. We dispense with historical reasons. This is not a manifesto, but a matter for the historian.

The counterpart of the idea of externally directed power politics is the internally directed rigid constitutional state. We came rather close to this ideal condition in the Bismarckian power state, but in the fields that concerned the financial system and the unlimited recognition of private property and the demands that were derived therefrom our legal ideas stood fully under the capitalistic idea.

It requires no special emphasis that, in terms of internal politics, National Socialism stands unconditionally on the standpoint of the law where everybody should be equal before the law and there should be no differences in social orders. But an essential transformation must be realized regarding the basic idea of the law which signifies to the German an inner need, a voluntary subordination to the higher interests of the whole, whereas the prescriptions of the law valid among us today appear simply as a commandment of power and indeed as commandments of a power that does not stand in the service of the whole but, precisely in relation to the questions of property, has placed the protection of property before protecting the person. The question of the new ordering of the public law will have to be discussed further in greater detail in another section.

Now we turn briefly to the questions of the external state form. A final decision on this question is not urgent. It can be solved only after a quite basic purging of our internal political conditions. The only possible way to this internal political purging seems to us to be only through a dictatorship which, with total determination, cuts off and burns the sources of decomposition and disease in our national body.

The demands that we place on such a leader are extraordinarily high; a passionate love for his people, an unbending will, a virtual somnambulistic certainty in all his decisions must distinguish him. That his intellectual capacities must rise above the average is self-evident, but knowledge and capacities in the different fields are not the decisive factor. Knowledge and learning can be realized by others how many men there are of high knowledge, great clarity of thought, of great intuition, the finest artistic talent -but if the last thing is lacking in them, the passionate will, the unswerving impulse, based on the deepest moral seriousness, then they will never stride forward at the head of nations, as trailblazers and leaders, to new heights.

We think of religious geniuses like Christ and Luther, Savonarola and Mohammed, state leaders like Bismarck and Cromwell, generals like Friedrich the Great and Yorck, etc. The dictator must be completely free of all unnecessary restrictions and hesitations, for him there cannot be any inevitabilities, for it must be he who makes history, and he seizes with a daring, determined hand when his hour strikes, he embodies the longing of the nation, and therefore he never errs and is borne by the fanatic love of those to whom his deed brings liberation. He must be able to hate, so strongly and ruthlessly, as he loves his people and his sacred task. In relation to his assistants and colleagues, he stands as the first among free and equal people.

This old German idea forms the foundation of this iron connection between the leader and his friends for the sake of the cause.

He is the leader because he has proved himself, and so long as he proves himself.

'Every power seems as it were redoubled by his presence

He draws forth every latent energy,

Showing to each his own peculiar talent,

Yet leaving all to be what nature made them,

And watching only that they be naught else

In the right place and time.'

— Wallenstein Schiller

He is strict and hard regarding himself; he orients himself according to his own laws. He has time for and listens to everybody, but he can quite differentiate between the important and the unimportant. For the accomplishment of his goal he may not be afraid of blood and war, he may not rest and relax until his goal is reached, then he secures his creation further than far as this is humanly possible, but he can himself withdraw, as the dictator Sulla did, and secures his work in a twofold manner in that he operates from a distance but still does not force everything through his strong personality to be measured by extraordinary standards; a freer and more independent following will develop if the Titan does not constantly determine the political daily life but remains the leader in the spiritual sense.

Such a brilliance of action and will distinguish the dictator who will again lead Germany to a height. If then the way out of the mire is found through the accomplishment of an extraordinary leader, the internal and external preconditions for an independent national life will have been regained, then the nation may once again decide regarding the external form of the state.

Our view of the future state will be essentially influenced by the way certain forms of the public life, especially the suffrage and the popular representation deriving therefrom, will be made up. We could certainly think of the possibility of a healthy republican state form, rather than in ancient Rome. Indeed, almost all historical memories in Germany point to the monarchical state form.

Now, with the monarchical state form is not inseparably bound the dynastic idea. Often dynastic interests have developed to the harm of nations. Another factor admonishes us to extreme caution in the question of a possible reintroduction of the monarchic state form -the consequence of heritability among dynasties. In the painful history of the German people, one may find repeatedly that the third generation after a significant ruler has squandered the heritage of its forefathers, damaged the honor and worthiness of the nation, lost the position of power of the empire, and destroyed the peace and welfare of the citizens. What the German imagines when he speaks of the advantages of the monarchy, especially under a hereditary ruling house, is always the thought of those to whom history has given the epithet "the Great." We think of Charles the Great, Otto the Great[28], Frederick the Great and the few who are ranked on a par with these actual rulers; but just a fleeting memory of the gallery of incapacity, indolence, selfishness, prodigality, fantasy, distance from the people, and other dangerous characteristics that are bound with the names of Louis the Pious[30], Otto III[31], Wenceslaus[32], Charles VI[33], Friedrich Wilhelm III[34], Wilhelm II[35] suffices to recognize clearly that the dynastic state form does not include a guarantee of the welfare of the nation.

That which expresses the inclination of the German to monarchy is the need of the German for a leader, and the readiness to subordinate himself to a leader. Precisely, this last characteristic is perhaps an especially typical characteristic of the German. We know only too well this trait of the German character in its good and bad aspects. The loyalty unto death allowed him fight for and win the most powerful victories, it allowed him to follow even foreign flags; but it includes also very much lack of independence among the weaker types, to the point of worthlessness and slavishness, love of things foreign and lack of judgement.

The question regarding the succession is, therefore, in Germany itself, easy to solve. The much harder question lies in the leader's problem.

The selection of the leader has up to now been always left to pure chance. The princely marital bed is indeed in no way a guarantee of the intellectual capacity and of the character traits that are to be demanded of a monarch. And if we remember the modern German economy, where mere membership in the party decides on the qualification for the highest official posts, we must give this question special attention.

The difficulty lies in the safeguarding of the moral and character qualities of the one in whose hands the destiny of the people should be laid. While however a dictator takes the leadership upon himself from himself, as the bearer of the national longing, a future leader must emerge from the conscious will of the nation as the best and most suited. It may remain completely open whether the highest worth should be united in one person or whether the state leadership should comprise two or more. One thing stands firm for us, that the one entrusted with the leadership of the highest state affairs, whether it be crowned heads or a "consular duumor triumvirate", the highest responsibility will, in the best possible case, be anchored in the constitution. Highest responsibility will therefore be the most essential national political foundation that will distinguish the National Socialist state from the previous forms of rule.

A special aspect of the national political foundations of the National Socialist state is the demand for a nationalist state in which the members of foreign countries and races are excluded from the leadership of the state affairs and from the assumption of public offices.

The great lesson of the whole of German history can be summarized because Germany was always poor, weak and miserable when its rulers pursued foreign interests and when the narrow small concerns of the individual provinces and cities were placed above the common affairs of the

Reich; and likewise, was Germany always strong and powerful when it was united, and its rulers thought and felt in a German way and the provinces and cities felt as members of the great common fatherland. Closing of the nation externally with all freedom and diversity internally. This is the correct idea of a German state. The Bismarck Reich already came very close to this ideal of the idea of the German state, only that our racial brothers in German Austria remained outside the Reich.

The unification of all German tribes in a closed national state is, therefore, our most distinguished national political goal. Internally politically, the federative and federal character of the larger provinces as it was produced historically is to be maintained or rebuilt. The national political base lines in this respect are: All functions of the Reich in which it is a question of the power political position of the German Reich regarding foreign countries are matters of the Reich. These are the Foreign Office, embassies and consulates, the passport system, the control of foreign trade, the customs system and, above all, the army and navy. Internally politically, the idea of the most far-reaching independence of the individual provinces or federal states is to be fostered. Financial independence is the precondition for the independent existence of the nation, so the tax legislation will have to be delegated mainly to the provinces.

The legislation for the civil-, trade-, and penal law will be regulated by the law of the Reich but subordinated in practice to the provincial justice and police authorities.

In a similar way, the transport institutions will certainly be regulated according to directives of the law of the Reich, but they will remain, in their finances and administratively and operationally, under the provincial sovereignty.

That the freedom of religion should remain fully upheld by the constitution requires no special mention; religions whose writings are not written fully in the German language and accessible to everybody and whose content contains doctrines dangerous to the state will not enjoy this protection.

The constitutional form of the basic socialist character of the Reich is stressed, especially in labor law and in the fields of illness-, accident-, old age-and disability insurance and will be better implemented than happens today.

Insights & Goal-Setting

If every thorough treatment of matters related to time demands an answer to the three questions: How is it now?

How did it come about? And what now?

For without this basic investigation a complete and conscientious work is never to be expected this is valid in a higher sense when it is a matter of building a new state. A description of the present-day situation within this work naturally has a place only where it is extracting the essential characteristics of the present-day critical conditions of the state and economy. In such a task, one must especially avoid taking any symptoms as causes. This is precisely the art of every diagnosis that is not deceived by externalities or excrescences but looks deeper into the reason for things.

This becomes most clear in the medical example or with a living man. If a swelling appears somewhere in the body, the cause is to be sought first in the ailment of the concerned part of the body; the fact that this part of the body is diseased has its cause in a poor condition of the blood; but even this knowledge is not to be considered as the last cause, but the poor condition of the blood will be the consequence of bad or insufficient nourishment. Now, the cure could not succeed if the doctor combated only the external phenomenon; a temporary alleviation would in the best case set in, a soothing of the pains, but the illness would continue. Even an attempt at a cure through a blood-purifying treatment could not bring a lasting cure if the basic cause, namely the deficient or bad nourishment or the other harmful circumstances, were not removed.

Only such a treatment from within outwards can bring a real cure. This is clear to everybody. Precisely so must the investigation be undertaken if we have to do with a sick national body?

Even here, it is very little useful if the external symptoms of the illness are combated. One feels only too well as a sad truth the well-known saying:

"The small rogues are hanged; the big ones are allowed to go free."

The frequency of violations against the common interest is only the external sign of the fact that behind the scenes, things are played out that harm the common welfare to a great degree. For, only if something is rotten in the state can such substantial damages persist and become a lasting danger in the existence of the state itself. If thus the state itself is sick, it is to be supposed with the greatest probability that the cause thereof is wrong intellectual attitudes regarding popular concerns and regarding the actual functions and authority of the state itself. A cure can therefore be expected, finally, from a new healthy idea of the state, through the creation of a healthy powerful state leadership which is fully independent and not burdened with the sins of the past. Every solution that takes its point of departure from a compromise with the existing powers or that seeks to bind itself again to the collapsed forms of the earlier state bears the seed of its own decay. In this connection one must also be warned against binding oneself to historical state forms that were indeed not bad in themselves but still very quickly succumbed to a collapse.

What now are the most striking characteristics of the present-day crisis?

Externally and superficially as with a fever high temperature or, translated into economic and political terms: agitation, tenseness on every occasion, unrest, and disorder. It is extremely significant that every stuffy and lazy person, but also the entire army of the actual debtors, has always praised with the loudest voice "rest and order" as the cure-all. Rest and order are naturally not a political goal in general, but only a condition that shows that healthy conditions rule within the national body. But if a nation is sick, it is quite natural and self-evident that this manifests itself in unrest and disorder.

A political attitude that preaches and seeks to establish only "rest and order" is therefore fully wrongly oriented; it only helps the illness to enter ever deeper until death enters with the most frightful cramps. Even ulcers and suppurations, thought of as personified, naturally wish likewise that the sick person would remain quiet, for the bacilli can then multiply so wonderfully quickly and spread over the entire body and fully putrefy it also internally. No, quite on the contrary: away with the suppurations! These must be cut out. One cannot adduce the pains of the operative attack as a counter-reason; the patient must be brought out of his dangerous environment, and above all he must receive a healthy diet.

The further symptoms are the filling of state positions with unsuitable elements, the disposal of state matters through majority decisions, the occurrence of such majority decisions in the parliament as do not bear any responsibility, the election of such parliaments according to a suffrage which externally is indeed the most free and universal but internally speculates on the lack of judgement of the masses and simply suppresses better insight and higher feeling of responsibility. A government that depends on parliamentary majorities–which come about purely by chance and for which only the party-political considerations are decisive can naturally for its part no longer be the aim guardian of the common welfare, but it is the stamping ground for ambitious party politicians and obstinate doctrinaires. All these symptoms may be summed up in the word "parliamentarianism."

This parliamentarianism is the great democratic lie of the capacity of the people for self-government. Of course, we may think that responsibility-conscious state citizens are completely capable of judging in an authoritative way on public matters and of leading the fate of their community or country, but a suffrage like the universal one, direct and secret for persons above 21 years of both sexes, bears necessarily the seed of the vile rule of the inferior and unscrupulous.

Along with the vile rule of the parliaments and the governments depending thereupon, there are rules today in reality, despite all the anticapitalistic slogans of the Marxists, large loan capital. High finance is the unrestricted ruler of the state and economy. No government dares to take any drastic measures against the profit interests of the banking and stock-exchange world. All the nations have become bound in interest and toll to this supra-national world power through quite gigantic national debts. The results are enormous. They shake the entire world to its foundations in economic and national political relations. Interest collection has indeed become the major work of the governments. This means for the nations a frightful tax exploitation and draining through the diverse methods of direct and, especially, indirect taxes, through an unstoppably progressive inflation which has led at its peak to a robbing of the entire middle-class of their savings. This unrestricted rule of the money-bag exercises, behind the mask of the legal claim to interest, the most brutal rule that has ever governed the world. It leads to an impoverishment and pauperization of the masses and especially of those circles to whom the acquisition of money is not a goal and therefore not the central point of their entire thought. Only from this arises the most frightful consequence of this absolute financial rule, the moral degradation of the peoples standing under this rule. All instincts are directed to acquisition and possession, all concepts of loyalty and faith sink in the ruthless pursuit of gain, the respectable man is forced to experience that, as a reward for his respectability, he must sink ever deeper down while unscrupulousness brings gigantic profits with all possible and impossible businesses. Desperately large circles struggle for their livelihood. A bearable income through work alone becomes increasingly more difficult.

In closed front lines the workers seek to extort ever higher wages, strikes shake the economic workplaces, lame their production and indirectly harm therewith most of all those who depend on the greatest possible production of goods for the national economy, precisely the workers themselves.

As a total phenomenon, we can summarize these conditions under the concept of "Mammonism."

The reverse side of this Mammonism is the Marxist worldview born of the intellectual mood of the victims of the Mammonistic violation. We know very well that the masterminds of the Marxists have cleverly been able to use this intellectual mood for themselves as handlers for international capital and, to divert from themselves the hatred of the exploited, but we must deal here with an intellectual disposition that stands not only in an obstructive but in a most highly hostile way against the re-establishment of a healthy national state.

The essence of Marxism we must glimpse because it denies private property and therewith cuts the ground from every economy and, beyond that, every higher culture; further, because it has fostered the idea of class-struggle and therewith torn the people apart into different classes mutually fighting one another. It is enough to point to the nameless misery of the Russian people, where, in the Soviet state, this erroneous nation-and economy-killing doctrine was translated into reality in the highest measure.

And if we now look for the actual pathogens of the disease, we strangely come up everywhere against Jews as leaders and chief beneficiaries.

The Jewish question is becoming a world-question on whose solution the welfare and woe of the nations will be dependent.

To this question, a special work will be devoted in this Library series.

A review of history shows us that the desperate nations have repeatedly sought to liberate themselves from this evil through bloody suppression and eradication of individual Jews but after some generations, the Jews have returned once again stronger and financially more powerful after such pogroms.

We must therefore avoid looking for the solution of the Jewish question in this primitive manner indeed one cannot kill the plague bacillus individually, one can only eradicate it by cutting off its life necessities from it.

The Anti-Semitism flaring up in the entire world is the torch-signal that the nations have recognized their greatest and most deadly enemy, but it is now our task to direct this correct emotive knowledge in a correct, reasonable way.

The battle against Marxism and therewith against the Jews succeeds through untiring education of the poisoned masses. It is the first stage of our battle.

The breaking of the interest-slavery is the last and hardest battle in the economic field for the liberation of the people and state from the golden network of the supra-national financial power.

Only after fighting through these stages, and when the victory has been fully wrested and secured, would it be time to carry out all the further reforms that will give the debilitated and sick national body a new will to live and new vital force that will first realize what is in all our minds, in which we all believe with glowing hearts and which we strive for with unbending will:

Germany's rebirth. A new, free, united Greater Germany in a healthy, firm, and powerful state of work and performance.

CHAPTER 12

THE PROGRAM

Origin

Every work requires a plan, every realization must be preceded by intellectual creation. The more clearly and better worked out the construction plans are, the more beautifully and quickly the building will be erected. Even new political structures require a clear construction plan. This is called here a political Program.

The demands that must be placed on a political Program are very high and very diverse. It is a question of a task of the highest responsibility, for the welfare and woe of one's own people depends on whether the plan was good. A Program must further deal, with the most concise brevity, with all the important fields of public life, must withstand every criticism, may not lose itself in detail, may not offer the opponents any unnecessary weak points, may not awaken any Utopian hopes that cannot later be satisfied. The Program must be a faithful image of the coming state and the new economy. It must show everybody in outlines the sketch of the state-and economic order that is desired, but it may not also constrain or anticipate the execution in its details.

Every Program also has a history and a development, but it is certainly a touchstone of the fundamental correctness of a movement if, after so many years, nothing essential must be changed in its basic features and only some obscurities must be removed. Only the most important and striking Program point of the old Program of 24th February 1923, no. 11, "Abolition of income without work and effort, breaking of the interest-slavery" urgently requires a thorough programmatic treatment in national, financial-and economic political terms. The detailed treatment of this point was at that time not such an absolute necessity because, at that time, the more detailed writings related to this, Manifesto for the breaking of the interest-slavery and the state bankruptcy, its solution, were almost the only existing writings and were fully known and familiar to the founders and first followers of the movement. In a way it was the intellectual content of these writings that added the socialist scope of activity with plans that had already at that time been determined in their fundamental features -to the will to renewal that had brought together a small circle around Anton Drexler[38] and Adolf Hitler, to the circle of nationalist and populist ideas.

It is precisely these Program points and demands through which the German freedom movement of National Socialism essentially and fundamentally differentiates itself from all other populist and nationalist groups, movements, and parties, and through which it differentiates itself especially from all so-called parliamentary parties which are, for their part, only a manifestation of the Mammonistic-plutocratic rule.

A further necessity in the new formulation of the Program was to obtain a clearer form and a clear structuring regarding the individual fields of public life. This has happened.

It is my duty here to think of yet another ground-breaking work which owes its origin to a parallel manifestation of National Socialism in Austria and Bohemia. I mean the book of the engineer Jung[39], representative of the Sudeten Germans in Czechoslovakia in the Prague Parliament.

Austrian National Socialism, in its beginnings, goes far back to the time before the war. Its scope of ideas rested more on the attempt to bring the socialist world of ideas into harmony with the nationalist idea, whereas the German National Socialism of the Reich that arose only after the collapse indeed without knowledge of the existence of this Austrian National Socialism adopted from the start a fundamental battle stance against Marxism.

Today, the two movements have come together in their common goals.

National & Economic Program

Our goal is Germany's rebirth in a German spirit to a German freedom. The way to this primary goal is:

1. **The National Political Principle:** The German Reich is the home of the Germans.

   A-1 | *In foreign policy:*

   i. The establishment of a closed national state that includes all Germans.
   ii. The powerful representation of German interests abroad.

2. **In Racial Policy:**

   - The removal of the Jews and all non-Germans from all responsible positions in public life.
   - Prohibition of immigration of eastern Jews and other parasitical foreigners. Troublesome foreigners and Jews may be deported.

3. **In Civic Policy:**

   - Only the German who pledges himself to the German culture and community can exercise state citizenship rights.
   - One who is not a German can live only as a guest in the German state and stands under foreign law.
   - The rights and interests of the Germans go before those of the members of foreign nations.

4. **The Economic-Political Principle:** the national economy is the fulfilment of demand and not as high a profitability as possible for loan capital.

   - National Socialism fundamentally recognizes private property and places it under state protection.
   - The welfare of the people, however, draws a limit to the immoderate hoarding of wealth in the hands of individuals.
   - All Germans form a work community for the promotion of the common welfare and culture.
   - Within this general work obligation of every German and with a fundamental acknowledgement of private property is allowed to every German a free possibility of acquisition and free disposal of his work income.
   - The healthy combination of small-, medium-and big businesses in all fields of the economic life, thus also in agriculture, remains upheld.
   - Gigantic enterprises (corporations, syndicates, and trusts) will be combated.
   - Usury and racketeering, as well as ruthless enrichment at the cost and harm of the people, will be punished with death.
   - The introduction of a year of compulsory work for every German.

5. **The Financial-Political Principle:** The financial system stands in the service of the state, the financial powers may not form a state within the state; thus, our goal: Breaking of the interest-slavery through:

   - Liberation of the state and therewith the people from its interest-bound debt to large loan capital.
   - Nationalization of the Reichsbank GmbH., and the central banks.
   - The financing of all large public tasks (development of hydro-energy, roadways, etc.) with avoidance of loans through the issuance of interest-free state treasury vouchers or through a cash-free method.
   - The introduction of a stable currency on a covered basis.
   - The creation of a non-profit Construction and Economic Bank (currency reform) for the granting of interest-free credit.
   - Thorough restructuring of the tax system according to socialist, national economic principles. Liberation of consumption from the burden of indirect taxes and production from constricting taxes (tax reform and tax exemption).

6. **The Social-Political Principle:** The common welfare is the highest law.

    - Generous development of old age insurance through nationalization of the life-annuity system. To every needy German national comrade, an adequate pension will be guaranteed from a certain age or in the case of a premature occurrence of permanent inability to earn a living.
    - The sharing of all people engaged in productive enterprises according to performance and age in the revenues of the work with an accompanying share in the responsibility for the fulfilment of the national economic tasks of the work.
    - The confiscation of all war-and revolution-profits is not based on honest work as well as of property acquired through hoarding and usury and their use for the development of social insurance.
    - Removal of the housing shortage through comprehensive new housing buildings throughout the Reich by means of the new nonprofit Construction and Economic Bank to be created according to Art. 21.

7. **In Cultural Policy:** A blossoming of all the sciences and fine arts on the foundation of a politically free, economically healthy state is our chief cultural goal.

    A-7 | This should be reached through:

    i. The education of the youth into physically healthy and intellectually free men according to the great traditions of German intellectual life.
    ii. Full freedom of religion and conscience.
    iii. Special protection of the Positive Christian faith.
    iv. Suppression and exclusion of religious doctrines that go against the German moral feeling and whose content bear a state and nation destroying character.
    v. Suppression of all harmful influences in literature and the press, stage, art, and cinema.
    vi. Freedom of instruction in the German universities, formation of a ruling class of men of character.

8. Militarily:

- Making the nation defensible through the introduction of military law for every free German.
- Abolition of mercenary troops.
- The creation of a militia army for the defense of the homeland under a professional officer corps to be built up through a strict hierarchical discipline.

9. Other Reforms:

- Reform of the press system. Suppression of all press instruments that contravene the concerns of the German people. The strictest responsibility for all news that is falsely or tendentiously distorted.
- Reform of the suffrage with the abolition of the current corrupting forms of election campaign and the lack of responsibility of the elected (immunity).
- Development of professional chambers.
- Reform of the judiciary in the field of Land law (fundamental recognition of the right to property in land, non-lease ability of land on the part of private capital, preemption right of the state, and reversion of land to the state in case of careless management).
- Civil law (far stricter protection of personal honor and of health, as against the one-sided legal protection of property ruling today).

10. Constitutional Reforms:

A-10 | *Constitution:*

i. The constitution corresponding to the German character is a sovereign state leadership focused on a highest position. Whether this highest position is occupied by a monarch to be elected by the people or by two or three responsible, highest Reich officials must be left for later determination by the people.
ii. Federal character of the Reich: The composition of the German people from different provinces internally bound through tribes and history conditions the comprehensive independence of the individual federal states with respect to their internal affairs.

The concern of the Reich is the representation of the German people externally, passports and tolls, and, further, the army and navy.

Three principal opponents stand in the way of the accomplishment of this national and economic Program of National Socialism. Marxism, parliamentarianism and, ranged above both large loan capital.

1. Our anti-Marxist battle is directed against the state-disintegrating doctrine of the Jew Karl Marx, against the people-disintegrating doctrine of class-struggle, against the economy-disintegrating doctrine of the denial of private property and against the purely economic, materialistic conception of history.

2. Our anti-parliamentarian battle is directed against the irresponsibility of the so-called popular representatives who -immune -never actually have to take responsibility for the consequences of their decisions, as well as against all damages produced therefrom (corruption, nepotism, bribability) and, as the worst consequence -a government dependent on such a parliament.

3. Our anti-Mammonistic battle, which is ranged above the other two battlefronts, is directed against the world-encompassing financial power, that is, against the permanent financial and economic bleeding and exploitation of our people through large loan capital.

This battle however is, on the other hand, also a powerful intellectual struggle against the soul-destroying materialistic spirit of egoism and avarice with all its concomitant corrupting manifestations in all fields of our public, economic, and cultural life.

In the last and deepest analysis, it is a matter of the battle of two worldviews that are expressed through two fundamentally different intellectual structures: the productive and creative spirit and the mobile avaricious spirit. The creative spirit rooted in the soil and yet again overcoming the world in metaphysical experience finds its principal representatives in Aryan man, the avaricious, rootless commercial and materialistic spirit directed purely to the-worldly finds its principal representative in the Jew.

National Socialism like Anti-Semitism glimpses in the Jewish materialistic spirit the primary root of the evil, but it also knows that this most powerful battle of world-history cannot remain standing in purely negative anti-Semitic demands, therefore the entire national and economic Program of

National Socialism rises far above the certainly ground-breaking but negative anti-Semitic battle by positively giving a creative, constructive image of how the National Socialist state of work and performance should look.

If this main goal is reached, then the National Socialist Party will be dissolved. National Socialism will then have become the life-content of the entire German people. The National Socialist German Workers' Party is indeed in general not a parliamentary party in the customary sense of the word, but only the determined, forward-looking and future-oriented section of the population that has gathered together around a leader strong in will and mind, to lead Germany out of shame and powerlessness externally, out of destruction and corruption internally, to a powerful and imposing position externally, and, internally, to an economically sound, culturally blooming, intellectually and morally high-standing national community.

We wish to build the Reich of German longing as Geibel[41] sings it:

"One externally, with a mighty sword,

Rallying round a high banner,

Internally rich and manifold,

Every tribe in its own way!"

CHAPTER

13

THE NATIONAL SOCIALIST STATE STRUCTURE

The National Socialist Idea

Already in the chapter on the power political foundations we have pointed to the fact that every deviation of the German rulers from their purely German tasks was accompanied by the most baneful consequences for the German people. If one surveys German history, one always finds the German longing for a closed national state realized only in short historical periods. Repeatedly, this German dream faded away, and repeatedly, Germany sank back in powerlessness and disintegration. Thereby there stands firm from the entire German history. One lesson that only the closing of the nation within a powerfully led state enables Germany to resist the enormous dangers which arise to it merely from its unfavorable geopolitical situation. Almost nowhere does Germany have natural boundaries. Almost everywhere it lies free and unprotected against hostile inroads. Neither the sea that girdles England nor the high mountains which separate Spain and Italy from its neighbors give Germany a natural defense. France has only one open side against us, Russia is the same. Only Germany lies in the middle between the other nations -as the heart -and as the battlefield of Europe. On German soil battled Spanish, French, English, Swedish, Russian, and Mongol armies, on German soil were the frightful religious wars of the Thirty Years' War fought, and conversely, Germans bled in foreign service for foreign interests in all the lands. Mother Germania bled from thousands of wounds that were struck by its foreign armies and -that were struck in her by the strife of her own sons. Endlessly tragic is German history, so tragic that the German longing for a unified, closed German Reich was included in fairy tales, in the sagas of old Barbarossa in the Kyffhäuser[42]. Through centuries the realization of the German state idea remained a longing and hope of the best people of the nation until, in 1871, a mighty smith forged the Germany unity. Much remained to be desired in the realization of the Great German state that was to include all Germans who live in territorial connection with the motherland. But already this partial realization of the German longing granted us a high flowering of German history as seldom before.

But we do not have to reckon with 'ifs' and 'buts', rather, we must learn from history. Politics is history that is becoming, and if from the "making of history" salvation should bloom for our people then our statecraft, our national politics must, with respect for that which has come about in history, avoid the mistakes of earlier times, and bind themselves to the best tradition. The man, the politician without a history who dogmatically makes history from his armchair, will be able to bring only calamity on a people as we have experienced it in the last years from the new German Marxist government-showmen. As disastrous and pernicious is the complete breakdown of the old social form, especially when this destruction is identical to the force of the Marxist movement, so little may the old be preserved merely because it is old. Herein lies once again the tragedy of the conservative spirit, that, creatively unfruitful and without imagination, it rejects everything new just because it is new, and because it holds fast tenaciously to outdated forms which have lost their substance a long time ago. People and state are not mummies and constructions but living entities; the clothes cut once do not suit forever. Only some quite large basic traits are drawn through the destiny of nations, and a neglect of such basic knowledge has always avenged itself bitterly on the nations. For us Germans, the fundamental historical national political doctrine is: "Be unified!"

The word "united"[43] however, does not mean "unity"[44] but "being in agreement."[45] Only from the agreement of the German tribes on the principles of external and internal politics can there grow as its finest flower an internally free state that is externally powerful with international weight.

For the German state, therefore, there may not be any European or international economic, church, or humanitarian motives, but only exclusively the welfare of the entire German nation. I mean "motives" for political action. Alongside there run naturally the influences of a church-, economic-and generally human character which must be adequately valued and considered. But the principle must be and remain that the German national state must represent only Germans and this in internal politics as well as in external.

Our national political goal, therefore, is:

1. The establishment of a closed national state which includes all Germans.
2. The powerful representation of all German interests abroad.

The Nationalist Idea

The precondition for the awakening or, better, for the reawakening of a strong national consciousness is the removal of all Jews and non-Germans from all responsible positions in public life.

The determined defensive battle against the invasion of the Jews in almost all fields of our public life is carried out with total energy only by National Socialism. The battle against Jewry is the conscious struggle for the German spirit and for German freedom.

The influence and effect of the Jews on their host peoples cannot at all be compared with the power relations and the battles of other peoples but only with the struggle for life and death between a healthy body and the deadly poisonous germs that have attacked it. When a living organism is attacked by poisonous bacilli, the question is only: either the healthy force of the body will become master of the foreign intruders then it cuts them out or it will no longer be master of them, then it will die on account of them. So also, for the host peoples of the Jews everywhere in the world, there is only this: either cut the Jews out of the national body -or die on account of the Jew.

Precisely the comparison with the human body and the germs shows us very graphically how lopsided the favorite misleading opinion is, that the Jews worked their way up everywhere only on account of their greater efficiency and it is highly wrong and unjust to attack and persecute them for that reason. One cannot simply say that the cholera bacillus is likewise so much stronger and efficient than the man and that is why it has overcome the healthy man no, it is a poison for the man. And, precisely as in this battle of the living organism against invading poisons, special symptoms of poisoning appear accompanied by fever conditions, cramps, symptoms of paralysis, etc., so the battle of the nations attacked by the Jew is expressed in quite similar symptoms of disease unrest and agitation in the civic and political life, powerful convulsions in the national body, turmoil, terror, civil war alternating with quite typical paralysis symptoms especially in the intellectual parts of the nations in the governments. Then there is only one question, whether the nationally conscious circles recognizing the enemy succeed in warning and enlightening the governments or in forming the government and neutralizing the Jews themselves, then the cure enters with certainty; if it fails in doing this, then national death enters equally certainly. There is no third way. A temporary isolation to remain with the medical imagery brings about only apparent remedies: sooner or later the bacilli break out anew into the blood vessels of the body. The end of this second struggle is then deadly for the patient.

Decisive for the final success, as in life in general, is the will to power. Without this will power without this will to the maintenance of the nation, the nation is helplessly delivered to a downfall. What does not literally go down becomes a slave, fellaheen, bondman, and servant of the all-Jewish world-power.

It is a life and death battle. Many efficient soldiers have set out, but most of our national comrades are still asleep. Education repeatedly, tireless, is the solution. What makes this education so especially difficult is the artlessness and softness of the Aryan precisely in these vital racial questions.

The strong racial mixture within our German people itself has doubtless almost completely buried the clear and high racial consciousness in too many, so that only an indefinite feeling of aversion against the racially foreign Jews has remained instead of a precise knowledge of racial laws. The Jew for his part has most strictly followed his racial laws for more than two thousand years in the clear knowledge of the outstanding importance of the maintenance of the purity of the blood for character and nation.[46]

On the other hand, he has been able to represent the racial agitation as outdated rubbish, which, about the racial mixture in Germany, was unfortunately possible for him with a certain appearance of justification. Instead of the Jewish contempt for racial science on the part of the Germans being opposed with complete determination, by the demand: "German, keep your blood pure!", the German was inferior even in this field to the psychagogic arts[47] of the Jew. The century of the Enlightenment with its humanitarian ideals indeed brought to the Jews emancipation from the chains which had been forged by our forefathers in their higher wisdom against the infestation of the Jewish spirit of robbery and usury, but to ourselves only confusion and uncertainty on this fundamental question. With the sentence: "the Jews are also men" a sentence which was and is indeed never disputed by anybody the entry of the Jews to civic equal rights was granted. The national-racial resistance against the Jewish foreign folk of an entirely different intellectual structure was therewith lulled and the battle against the civic emancipation was therewith crippled from the start.

From this platform now there took place the conquest of our entire economic and, recently, public life up to the present situation of the unrestricted rule of the Jews. An entire series of testimonies of the Jews themselves reveals that they feel as a state within a state, that they feel more closely bound to their racial comrades in other countries than to their host peoples. From this Jewish feeling of belonging closely together among peoples are directly produced dangers for the indigenous peoples in the field of the foreign political relations of nations in war and peace.

At first, however, the attention of the Jews was directed to the demand for economic advantages. Here once again, their unrestricted pursuit of profit, impaired by no social feelings for their host peoples, stood them in good stead.

As the inventors and bearers of the modern credit system, it was soon an easy matter for them to bring the entire financial economy of the states and, through bank and stock-exchange, also of the private sector for the most part under their influence.

From here, thus after the creation of their financial position, Jewry stretched its fingers also to the intellectual-cultural products of the nation;

here their moving spirit, their quick wit, their critical understanding characteristics that may often appear as definite advantages to the serious, heavy, down-to-earth Aryan spirit came to their help.

But it was only the thieving instinct, their lack of conscience and unscrupulousness which is already announced in their religious doctrines. For the Jew, according to the doctrines of the Schulchan Aruch[48], the property of the non-Jew is like property without a master there so that the Jew may appropriate it! The Jew set all the means of the banking and stock-exchange technique at his service. Anonymization the depersonalization of our economy through the stock-marketable form of the public limited company has to a certain degree separated capital from work, the shareholder knows in the rarest instances something of his factory, he has only the one-sided interest in the profitability of his money when he has invested it in the form of shares. This phenomenon must be mentioned in this place because with this depersonalization of our economy there goes hand in hand also its degradation. The entrepreneur and manufacturer who has built up his enterprise from scratch, who knows the requirements of his customers, who still has the old business honorableness and considers it as his duty to produce a solid, good, lasting product corresponding to the actual needs of the economy, this really solid entrepreneur is something so fundamentally different from the modern large share-holder who, with the purely capitalistic possession of a large share package knows only one interest, to aim at as high a return as possible. Whether in the enterprises good and cheap objects are manufactured, whether in general productive values are created by a stock company or, as in the case of the credit companies (banks) in general, no values are created is a matter of utmost indifference to the capitalist the shareholder. This has as its further consequence that the production is oriented less to the needs, that, much rather, only an apparent need needs to be stirred up through enormous advertising. Earlier it was entirely forbidden in the code of honor of the entrepreneurs to extol one's products; one who did this was a market-crier, and such a market-crier-like extolling of one's wares was considered by the solid businessman to be dishonest competition. The Jewish trader, however, conducted precisely this sort of market-crying trade businesses with total insistence, wherein his arts of persuasion came in handy. Today in place of the importunate Jewish crier has appeared Jewish advertising.

In the field of science there occurred a similar development, especially in the field of economic science the so-called national economics. Gradually the task of national economics was seen no longer to lie in the investigation of the national economic legitimacies and necessities and in the derivation of guidelines for the economic leadership from the results of the investigations but increasingly only a description of the situation was carried out without investigating whether the economic phenomena and forms encountered were also good and suitable and applicable to the actual needs of the national economy. In this way people succeeded, and succeed today more than ever, in effecting the frightful damages to the economy and, therewith, to the national community considered scientifically and, for this reason, in an unchangeable manner. In this field, there enters especially the doctrine of the state and private credit services industry, and especially the doctrine of interest. We have dealt with this question in detail in another place, here it may suffice to point to the fact that basically that which we call national economy today is only a private capitalistic instruction to personal enrichment and a well-arranged attempt at the justification of the usurious capitalistic robbery of the workforce of productive nations.

It is worth noting that among the lecturers of national economics, there is a very large percentage of Jews.

To the layman, more striking is the incursion of the Jews into the literary and artistic field.

One who considers our present-day theatre will be shocked at the baseness and cynicism that spreads there. Especially valid is this of the modern phenomenon of the cinema. The drama of lechers and rakes rules our stages; with subversive and clever dialectic, the good German is lectured that morality and ethics, honor and conscientiousness are basically sheer stupidity, without which one can go farther. These attacks on the public are accompanied by the Jewish theatre-agency nuisance, in which the knowledge of the artistically inclined tends to decide less than the gratitude to the theatre-and concert-agents of those seeking a position.

But then there followed on a wide scope the manipulation of public opinion through the daily press. Almost all the large newspapers gradually passed over to Jewish ownership. Therewith, the circle around the German people was closed. To the economic rule was added the intellectual rule. Everything that was detrimental to the Jewish interests was withheld and silenced, if possible, from the public; if ideas or performances asserted themselves, then began the real witch-hunt, at first through the attempt to make such efforts ridiculous, and, if even that did not help, lies and misrepresentation and personal denigration had to operate. Briberies, threats were attempted and finally one did not shy away even from economically mining the inconvenient opponent or admonisher, or from even killing him.

This last most frightful weapon was generally not used, or only seldom, against private persons, for hardly ever did the reaction of a real friend of the people without a political or state position of power to achieve a degree of effectiveness before he was already broken by the barrage of lies and calumny in the public organs of the Jews.

In the parties, the dissatisfaction of the masses was stoked through extreme exaggeration, and the class hatred against the propertied and their supposed protectors, the state authority, and the army, were kindled. Even here as everywhere in the case of these assaults on the national state it was Jews who mostly agitated and fomented. It need only be recalled that Karl Marx, the founder of the Marxist doctrine of class-struggle, was indeed a Jew (Mardochai was his real name). His herald in Germany, Ferdinand Lassalle[49], originally Feist Lasal, was likewise a Jew.

In the war and revolution, then the Jewish work of destruction against the German state was completed. The princes were driven away; the epaulettes torn from the officers; the officials made complaint through hunger so that they may make their manpower -indispensable even to the socialist-high-capitalist state of modern Germany available. In this way was the German nation disarmed, emasculated, robbed of its leaders, dispossessed, and violated, demoralized, and debilitated, while everywhere throughout public life, in economics and politics, in art and theatre, the Jews arrogated to themselves an unquestionable hegemony.

The foundation of their rule is their enormous wealth.

Despite their small number in relation to their host peoples, they have been able to bring all important posts of public life into the hands of their Jewish racial comrades or of Germans closely related to Jews. But a removal of the Jews from the German national body is completely possible, so much more so in that the real vitally important productive activity in industry and agriculture, in the professions and administration, is almost entirely free of Jews.

A removal of the Jews from our national body would neither disturb the agricultural production I have not yet seen any Jew behind the plough going round the furrow–nor would the factories have to come to a standstill through lack of workers the workforce will indeed know that no Jew hoists coal in hard work or stands at the forge our work places of the smith and metalworker, carpenter and cobbler, would not be orphaned the houses would not in any way have to remain as ruins after the expulsion of the Jews, the statistics do not mention anything of Jewish masons and carpenters, roofers or glazers. But even not in trade and commerce would a stagnation appear if the Jews were no longer there. In the field of the transport system, the state has already made up to now taken care of personal and goods traffic in an exemplary way and, anyway, who has seen Jews as railway conductors or locomotive drivers or as tram conductors, or as waggoneers or transport workers?

But even in the field of the typical predisposition of the Jew to trade and finance, the military administrative posts before the war have shown that they could conduct a careful storage and provision service, in trade itself hundreds of thousands of commercial clerks and German businessmen are active who understand the real aspects and necessities of trade, and in the state bank and the postal bank we possess institutions that could form the basis of a healthy national economy freed of the Jewish robber economy.

If we have seen in this rather brief survey that the Jews represent in no way an irreplaceable function in our state and national life, that they misuse their supremacy in the most ruthless way to the harm of their host peoples, then as an obvious and logical consequence is produced the demand for the expulsion of the Jews from our nation. Only one who pledges himself to the German national community can be a state citizen[50].

From this review of the racial question naturally and follow the other consequences of the prohibition of the immigration of eastern Jews. It is a complete lack of understanding of the Jewish question if one believes that it is sufficient to repel the eastern Jews through a prohibition of immigration. It is necessary to simultaneously place the Jews hostile to our people settled amongst us under an alien's act. The eastern Jews are, of course, the great reservoir from which the Jews constantly replenish themselves. The great danger that this immigration includes has been revealed with all clarity through the experiences of the last years. In a few years, these eastern Jews have been able, through all possible business tricks and flourishes, to come into possession of enormous wealth. Our courtrooms are full of frauds exercised by such foreign elements. The state does not have the least interest in the immigration of such people, who in no way make themselves useful productively.

This position of the National Socialist state to the eastern Jews does not exclude that even the members of other nations who are parasites on the national body can be expelled.

The discussion of these questions leads us now to the third section of the state policy of National Socialism: to the citizenship right.

The Citizenship Right

The citizenship right must be acquired. In this principle, National Socialism differs considerably from the right valid at present according to which every adult German above 20 years of male and female sex, can exercise state citizenship rights. Likewise, today, according to the Weimar constitution, this possibility is open to the members of the Jewish race. Similarly, this state membership can be acquired by any foreigner with the fulfilment of a few superficial formalities.

The Weimar constitution does not in general understand the concept of state citizen but speaks in Art. 110 of membership in a state, and in Art. 109 of equal rights before the law for all state members of male and female sex. The vagueness of this concept naturally excludes the demand for moral and racial preconditions for the acquisition of the citizenship right. In contrast to this, Art. 113 of the Reich constitution takes the foreign-speaking "sections of the nation" (!) under its special protection; they "may not be disadvantaged in their free traditional development, especially in the use of their mother-tongue in education, as well as in the internal administration and administration of justice."

If one compares with this most comprehensive consideration of foreign nationals the practice of our Law for the Protection of the Republic against one's own national comrades, the obligation to deliver the so-called war-criminals to the enemy, with the certainty guaranteed in Art. 1 12 that "no German of a foreign government may be delivered to persecution or punishment", and, if once compares precisely this last-mentioned article with the infamous judgements of the French against Krupp[51] and his directors, perhaps a reference to the fact that the author of this constitution was the Jew Preuss[52] suffices to set a definite light on all these events.

Not "the more fortunate future of the Poles", as Betthmann-Hollweg[53] said in one of his unfortunate parliamentary speeches, and not also the betterment of the Jews in Romania (according to Kuhlmann)[54] can be the leading idea of a German state but only the welfare of the German people.

This guiding theme is expressed in the national and economic Program of the NSDAP (The Program, p.35) under No. 7: "The rights and interests of the German precede those of the members of foreign nations" and under No.6: "One who is not a German can only live as a guest in Germany and stands under the aliens act."

According to this, the state citizenship right must be acquired. It can also be lost through unworthiness. It is a right from which the Jews are fundamentally excluded, from which also members of other nations can be excluded.

The internal condition for the applicant for German state citizenship is the pledge to the German culture and community. One who does not pledge himself to the German nation in this way, one who declares himself to be an enemy of the German state, one who feels more closely bound to members of other nations than with his people, cannot receive any German state citizenship rights, for he indeed does not wish to have anything to do with the German community.

It seems to be indeed a madness when people who declare quite publicly that they know no fatherland called Germany, as Crispien[55] and others did, still wish to advise on the fate of this country, when they claim as representatives of the people, as delegates to still enjoy special privileges and when they still enjoy the protection of especially strict laws (the protection of the republic) in case they are promoted from this parliament to government positions.

The National Socialist German state will demand precisely from such men the hardest reckoning and the members of the revolutionary governments and parliaments will retrospectively have to take responsibility for their actions or omissions. The laws that are to be developed on the responsibility of all persons who stand in public life will therefore have to be endowed with retrospective powers.

Here it is not, as in the case of the mistake of the German revolution, a matter of the battle for wages of the hungry "proletarians" against the sated and insatiable capitalists, thus not about the misleading of the healthy and correct feelings of the working people through the idea of class-struggle, but here it is a matter of the moral demand that the irresponsibility of the present beneficiaries of the present parliamentary and government system must come to an end, and that those who have enriched themselves in an immoderate way on the need of the people or those who have abetted the machinations of other circles will be brought to the deserved punishment.

The slogan: "The little rogues are hanged; the big ones are allowed to go free" should not be proved right. The National Socialist state will, on the contrary, in the case of the determination of the punishment, take into consideration the fact of the small rogues' being seduced as a very mitigating one and, on the other hand, bring the big criminals against the German people to justice with the total strictness of the law.

The purgative work of this state court cannot now in any way stop with those who first came to power with the revolution. It will also have to target those under the Imperial government who, through their negligence, made this German downfall possible. The chief responsible Bethmann-Hollweg has indeed been taken from his earthly judges, the same is true of the next most guilty Erzberger[56], who, as the father of the wretched parliamentary revolution of July 1917, raised once again the sinking will-to-win of the enemies. Even Eisner[57] and Rathenau have been removed from the scene of their nation-destroying activity, to be sure in an illegal way, but according to the iron laws of history. But many of those still live who, through the organization of the munitions strike in January 1918, thrust a dagger into the back of the fighting army, and those still live who through speech and writing broke the will to win, those still live who preached 'peace without winners and losers', those still live and accept it as right who misused the distress of the people in war and revolution for their own immoderate enrichment.

Certainly, such a national political demand will spread fear and horror, and tens of thousands will fear for their lives because they are not of pure heart. But for National Socialism with this demand for social justice stands and falls the question of destiny for the German people, whether the German people can find its way to a noble nation, or whether it will eke out a miserable life in degradation and corruption as a fellaheen nation. For the National Socialist movement, its raison d'être is also decided by this question.

The state citizenship right is accordingly not a thing that will be placed in the cradle of everybody born in Germany; much rather, this state citizenship right includes also the highest moral obligations towards the state and nation. The observance of this responsibility to the state and nation must, however, also be protected by the possibility that this right may again be lost in case of unworthiness.

On the other hand, the acquisition of the state citizenship right will not be an act of mercy, but a claim that every industrious German can raise who proves himself worthy of the German community and who pledges himself to the German racial and historical community. One who has fulfilled his army and work obligation, one who is active as an honorable worker in his profession, has a claim to the acquisition of the state citizenship right.

But with this state citizenship right is also bound the obligation not to forget in all one's work the view of the larger whole and to be always conscious in one's economic activity of the fact that one must fit one's work into the whole, that is, even with full freedom in particular areas, the activity of the German state citizen should not be directed against the welfare of the whole.

National Economy

The task of the national economy is the fulfilment of demand and not the attainment of as high an interest-yield for loan capital as possible.

One would think that this principle is taken for granted for every economy, and yet the National Socialist economy is different from the current interest capitalistic economy precisely in this guiding principle. It is not so easy for the guileless sense of the productive man to imagine a national economy that does not serve the fulfilment of demand; and yet it must be made clear now that for the current masters of the economy -the bank-and stock-exchange capital the fulfilment of demand is basically of very little importance. International capital has an interest in it only insofar as this fulfilment of demand can be exploited in a usurious capitalistic way.

We have, in fact, to do here with two fundamentally different attitudes to the economy. The only urgent demand on the entire economy from the side of the entire population is, naturally, the satisfaction of the need for food, then the fulfilment of the demand for housing and clothing, and only then are ranged in an assortment all the other daily requisites up to the higher arts and cultural pleasures. In between come the support services, the entire transport system and whatever relates to it, trade, and the financial system. The production of goods for its part has in a healthy economy the worthiest goal of covering the need in the best possible way through a payment which covers the production costs and includes a corresponding work income for the entrepreneur and a suitable profit-share from which both unavoidable losses and improvements and renovations in the enterprise can be defrayed.

The attention of the just entrepreneur is not directed to the attainment of immoderate profit in individual cases, even when fortunate accidents might make this possible. The just entrepreneur is completely conscious of his national economic tasks, to establish production in such a way that the need can be covered with the least costs for the user, that at the same time the enterprise grows and flourishes, that the production costs become ever smaller without the wages being reduced.

Perhaps the most illuminating example of such a true way of entrepreneurial thought is Ernst Abbe[58], the co-founder and director of the Zeiss works in Jena. This man has understood to a high degree of perfection this national economic task of the entrepreneur and sought to realize this to the best of his ability.

But in this respect, we have also, in general, no reason to make special complaints about our entrepreneurs before the war. Men like Alfred Krupp[59], Mannesmann[60], Werner Siemens[61], Thyssen[62], Borsig[63], Krauss, Maffei[64], etc. have secured for themselves even socially a place of honor in the history of German industry. They were all not ruled by one-sided pursuit of profit. They all remained simple and modest for themselves, only the prosperity of their works was their lodestar.

Indeed, the tireless productive and inventive power of the German industry has resulted in the fact that not only the gigantic increase in population found work and bread but that, despite rising wages, despite a comprehensives improvement of the standard of living of all sections of the population, the most important products could be made cheaper thanks to ever new improvements and inventions. The German manual worker should never forget that he owes this to the brainworkers.

And another thing must be stressed here again with all emphasis: that the foundation and precondition for this high blossoming of the German economy was the powerfully led Bismarck Reich. These two factors, the united and therefore powerful political situation of the German Reich and the unprecedented industriousness of the German entrepreneurs and workers made it possible that a comprehensive raising of the standard of living of the entire population was registered, that the gigantic increase in population of Germany could be fed, clothed, and housed and that the emigration from Germany sank to insignificant numbers.

The numbers of the German migration in the decades after 1870 included only the healthy surplus of the German entrepreneurial and merchant spirit that streamed out into the world as the pioneers of German industriousness and German performance.

For the most part, the entire national economy of the German Reich did justice to the fundamental demands that we also place on a healthy national economy. The demand was amply covered. Nevertheless, there appeared even at that time deep damages in our economy which were expressed in diverse ways.

1. Our state finances fell into ever greater debts at the same time in which the German people became ever richer and more powerful, in which the products of German industrial and trade efficiency conquered the sales markets of the world, at a time in which our internal economy strode from success to success and the medical and living conditions became better from year to year.

2. Now, it is naturally not a good sign if the debts become increasingly bigger. Such a phenomenon always points to the fact that something is not in order. For it must indeed be considered as fully absurd and nonsensical if a state whose citizens enjoy increasing wealth does not at the same time find itself in a condition of healthy and flourishing state finances. This must be so much more surprising when to the German Reich and the federal states extraordinarily large revenues flowed from their railways, post, and mining works, as well as from the state forests, etc., quite apart from the fact that the Reich and the federal states could, by virtue of their financial sovereignty, claim the considerable tax capacity of their citizens.

3. A further deep-seated economic damage was the progressive debt of our agricultural and urban real estate. The movement of land reform that was applied against that correctly recognized a very important part of the entire problem without unfortunately achieving complete efficacy.

4. The fact of the inflation of our industry through credit of all sorts should also have filled sharp-sighted observers with anxiety. Certainly, in times of increasing prosperity, the commercial and industrial enterprises take the acceptance of foreign monies and the interest obligation bound with that light, because indeed the strongly increased work and income possibility permits the bearing of these burdens.

5. But woe if economic crises set in! Then the use of interest-bound credit shows itself in its entire economic banefulness.

6. The form of a stock company that emerged in these years with the actual detachment of capital from work bound to it, that is, the separation of pure capitalistic interests in the profitability of money, on the part of the creditors, from the healthy cooperation of the individual entrepreneur and from the entire identification of his existence with his enterprise similarly sowed the seed of profound economic damages.

7. The growing position of power of the money-brokering institutes, the banks, should have filled the honorable friend of the nation with anxiety. From servants of the economy, the banks became the unrestricted masters of the entire national economy. In a noteworthy and significant way, this growing position of power of the banks was in no way accompanied by a concurrent prosperity of our national economy, but, on the contrary, the more lamentable our economy became, the more the banks aggrandized themselves.

We do not wish here to go further into this development, there will be much to say on it in the discussion of the purely financial-and monetary-economy. The mention of the fourfold root of the great national economic damage through the financial and credit system was of great importance because precisely this aspect of the entire economy has become the opposite of a true national economy, namely a one-sided robber economy of the financial powers.

One on whom the image of a body stricken with parasites does not spontaneously impose itself must be very interested in the retention of the present situation or dependent on the beneficiaries of this exploitative economy. Unfortunately, the last is the case among a very great number of men. That is why the internal resistance to this modern economic robber baron system does not emerge in a corresponding manner.

It is especially bad that even the science, and indeed especially the science, that must deal with these things dutifully is still, with a few exceptions (Othmar Spann[65]), within the spell of the current interest capitalistic economy and finds itself in dependence on it. The present-day national economy is not a leader towards the truth and to correct knowledge but has become the spokesman for national economic criminality.

Every simple man can understand and contemplate all great truths and wisdom in their essential aspects. Not to be confused with this is the fact that it is naturally not so simple to arrive at such fundamental knowledge. To be sure, the knowledge itself, the intuition, is like a bright light that shines in the soul, eternally thirsting for knowledge. Difficult, however is the subsequent work of the understanding which must strenuously pile up brick upon brick to build up, with the most careful selection of materials, the entire thought-structure so that the finished work appears to everybody as self-evident.

In such cases, there is then no finer praise than when one occasionally comes to such thoughts by oneself. Thus, did I receive, while I was working on this work (Summer 1923), an excellent work of a now old man, the Austrian engineer W. Schober[66], in which the entire disastrous development of the Austrian financial and credit situation was predicted with unprecedented clarity already 30 years ago.

Schober pointed to the fact that only a complete departure from the fundamentally false national economic doctrines could stop the disastrous development of the national economy unfortunately without the least success.

The chief reason lay at that time in the fact that Schober's friends, of the Christian-Socialist Party, after an initial enthusiastic agreement, turned away from him with lazy excuses: "The time is not yet ripe", but, because it did not suit the Christian high finance.

The bank stopped a long time ago, being the trusted intermediary between savings capital and the claims of the economy and the working capital. Today, the big banks have their directors and delegates sitting in all stock companies. Nothing can take place without the bank's knowing of it. And what interest does the bank now have in the economy? It has a sole interest in the capital yielding as high a profit as possible; in what way is quite indifferent to it? It does not see its task in the fertilization of the economy through the loan of money at the cheapest rates precisely when the national economy is threatened by crises of the worst sort this, however, would be its highest task; the big banks much rather tend to come forth precisely at that time with credit packages and credit notices when the manufacturing industry most urgently needs an anticipatory credit for its work.

One may further consider the following: What need do the banks cover? One will say the need for money. Of course. But how and under what conditions? The baker, the shoemaker, the factory owner, the businessman, indeed cover the real need of food, clothing, etc., and they receive for that the equivalent value, the price, in money or through a transfer of money. Therewith the need is covered, and the factory owner, etc. has again working capital for purchases, payment of wages, and further manufacture. Here we see an economic circle completed. The producer covers the need for the user; the money fulfils its proper task as the intermediary of an exchange business and fertilizes anew the economy in the hands of the producer.

It is quite different in the case of the money-lending business. First, there does not exist for any bank any obligation to give away its ware money the way such an obligation exists, for example, for every trader. It can therefore ensure that it gives money to only those who are favorable to it. Further, the bank demands, in the largest number of cases, securities that far exceed the value of the loan, it demands further a debt certificate according to which the debtor must pledge himself to the repayment of the debt with everything that he has and will earn. In other words, against the dispensing of money, the bank draws into its power-domain assets that are far greater than the loaned sum; it also lets a debt certificate be handed out, which exposes the work incomes of the debtor to its grasp. But that is not enough: for this double, and many times, secured loan of money, the bank lets itself be paid still more in the form of interests that become enormous overtime. We thus must do here with a procedure which, considered economically, is not a productive performance at all, the return payment pledge, debt certificate is given immediately, and, besides that, the debtor must agree to another continuing payment which in a few years exceeds the value of the received money, without the pledger becoming free or the debt being resolved. Such a financial business is naturally national economically an absurdity, it is unadulterated usury.

The true sense of credit, of the belief in the greater economic efficacy of another, is indeed that the owner of saved money does not see that he is able to use his money himself profitably, he therefore turns to someone whom he can trust that he can entrust this money to and who offers him the guarantee that he will again return to his savings to him at request fully and undiminished. If the loan strengthens the debtor in his economic work capacity that he could make considerably greater profits one can consider this as an act of fairness or gratitude if the debtor gives the creditor, apart from the return of the money, also a certain share of his profits. This conception of private monetary and credit economy rules the entire Middle Ages, it formed the core of the Church's doctrine of interest. The demand of interest was considered as usury. Today, the interest that was judged to be usury by the Church has become indeed axiomatic of our entire economy the national economic sense of credit has become a national economic nonsense. To be sure, for the moneyed man, such a doctrine is the source of lasting effortless enrichment. Not really because gold is as it would like to appear really a power that produces money from itself, a superhuman phenomenon that, freed from the earthly laws of perishability, forces everything under its spell imperishably and forever, but because it is felt in modern financial and international economics simply as a law that every sort of financial possession bears in itself a claim to interest, to a certain degree innate in money, is this most monstrous reversal of the relation between work and money accepted as a law, as something that cannot be touched, as something for which the science dealing with it has to produce a great number of justifying reasons.

Only in this way was it possible to divert the entire national economy from its sole and natural task of covering the need and therewith creating work and food for everybody and to misuse it primarily as an instrument for the personal enrichment of the owners of bank-and stock-exchange capital.

It is now a favorite trick of the political battle against our movement that this opposition of ours against the high capitalistic exploitation of our national economy and our battle for a national economy satisfying the demands of social justice is portrayed as an opposition between property and other forms of possession, that our demand "Public interest before self-interest" is decried as Communistic. Against this, we should constantly point to Art. 8 of the national and economic Program (The Program, p. 35):

"National Socialism fundamentally recognizes private property and places it under government protection."

It will, however, be the task of the legislation to draw the limits about the hoarding of immoderate wealth in the hands of individuals at the expense of the whole.

Positively and for the economy itself there arises, as a demand for the entire economy and its tasks in the spirit of National Socialism, demand No. 10 of the "National and Economic Program": All Germans form a work community for the promotion of the common welfare and culture of the German people.

From here is derived, in turn, the moral demand that every German must work intellectually and physically according to his strength, but that this work of his must be incorporated into the whole.

I stress that this is a moral demand. It is a matter, therefore, not of the establishment of a compulsion to work as has been introduced in Soviet

Russia. Something quite different is the introduction demanded by us of a year of compulsory work for every German before the acquisition of full state citizenship rights.

It is again quite different that our main goal aims precisely at securing a worry-free old age for all national comrades who have worked industriously in their youthful and adult years. Precisely in the case of a national economy which does not stand continuously under the blood-letting of an interest and toll obligation to loan capital it will, and must and can, be easily achieved that it gives away large surpluses in such a way that to all national comrades a suitable and adequate old age pension–similar to the retirement pay of officials; is ensured on reaching a certain age or in the case of a work disability that has occurred prematurely.

I bring in this social-political demand here because the fulfilment of this task belongs to the performances of the entire national economy, because it is the point that is not only able to say constantly to the worker in the widest sense of the word: You must work!, but because, behind the work compulsion, it establishes something comforting and reconciling -the prospect of a secured old age for everybody who has done his duty all his life long.

Within the scope of the fundamental recognition of private property as the foundation of our economy belongs naturally also the fact that every German is protected in his free possibility of earning a living and in the free disposal of his work-income and his acquired wealth (No. 11 of the "National and Economic Program"). Limiting this basic right is only permissible through the law, whereby the guideline should be followed that only such work is considered as work that is not directed against the interests of the community. Chain-trade and profiteering also doubtlessly cause much work; similarly, a burglar will often shed more drops of sweat in his "work" than the mason in the building of a house, but such "work" is directed indeed only to one-sided personal enrichment at the cost and harm of others. Such "work" is therefore generally harmful and must therefore be punished with all severity.

Such an express determination is in no way superfluous, for, from the practice of the law, is apparent all too often, and to a frightful extent, how many things are designated there as honest work. There are also an entire series of activities which are very close to the borderline, where it is difficult to say that this work still harmonizes "with the whole."

In any case, legal tools must be created so that all these activities or enterprises that are directed against the national health in a physical or intellectual way may be suppressed. The same is true of the exploitation of the distress of the population through profiteering and usury.For such vermin that are hostile to the nation, we demand the death penalty. Financial penalty or even imprisonment are ineffective against such unscrupulous people.

In short, therefore, the economic policy of National Socialism will work towards removing a basically false concentration of economics on profitability and, for that reason, to restore to honor the only right and reasonable task of national economics: the fulfilment of demand.

This does not in any way exclude income and profit for the trader, factory owner and the honest businessmen; on the contrary, in no way should difficulties be created for the justified striving for earnings so long as this striving is contained within the scope of the public interests.

It is a matter therefore of a purgative action, and then of the maintenance of the German economy, which is unobjectionable both in relation to its forms and with respect to its performances. By this is to be understood what No. 12 of the "National and Economic Program" demands: The healthy combination of big, medium, and small businesses in all fields of the economic life, thus also in agriculture, remains upheld.

Therewith is also given the fundamental position of National Socialism to the different social orders.

National Socialism will support and promote agriculturists through all means as the foundation of a powerful nation and of the nourishment of the population.

If point 17 of the Program contains a clause which envisages a free dispossession in special circumstances, by this was only meant, as Adolf Hitler proclaimed on April 13, 1928, the "creation of legal possibilities of confiscating, if necessary, land that was acquired in an illegal way or not administered according to the viewpoint of the welfare of the people. This is directed thus mainly against the Jewish land speculation companies." This clause was therefore designed only for the protection of the native population.

Especially dear to National Socialism also lies the prosperity and the independence of a healthy commercial and mercantile middle class.

And even in the forms of production of the so-called heavy industry there is, from the point of view of National Socialism, nothing essential to be objected to. Precisely, this large industry has rationalized everything in an exemplary way, that is, it has avoided no costs to bring about better and simpler production methods. The present overburdening of enterprises aiming at communization–with an excessive number of people who are dispensable (we are thinking here mainly of the necessity of maintaining one's own tax and insurance officers, etc.) naturally works directly against the nationalization effort of industry.

At the conclusion of these economic and political tasks of National Socialism stands another enormous organizational performance:

"The introduction of a year of work-service for every German."

Even here, it is a deeply moral principle that compels this demand duty.

One who wishes to exercise state-citizenship rights must have also served the state, he must also have proved himself duty-conscious and loyal to his state through deed and indeed without remuneration, that is, possibility of enrichment, exactly as the soldier serves his fatherland.

We glimpse into the idea of the compulsory work service a fully supplementary idea to the idea of universal military service.

As much as we would like to consider it possible to substantially reduce the training to become efficient soldiers compared to the earlier two and three-year long service period, so much do we consider it necessary and advisable that every young German be acquainted with one or more commercial activities in which he can serve the state.

The duty-consciousness about the quality of work has suffered so much under the rule of the machine and under the still more devastating doctrine of the class hostility of the workers against the entrepreneurs that a tutoring in this field under tight state direction according to uniform principles seems completely indispensable. Precisely, the entrepreneurs, in the good sense, will welcome such an institution and not consider it in any way as a competition. Such a work army cannot be a competition already because, according to experience, every productive economic activity of the state must be excessively burdened with its official apparatus, because the employment and training of a young inexperienced workforce consumes too much of its efficiency.

On the other hand, it will be the task of this year of work-service to better acquaint the young people in model state enterprises with all the progresses of technology. They should, if possible, cover the actual needs of the workforce and of the national comrades serving militarily.

Thus, a state competition with the rest of the national economy does not come into question, it could at most operate in certain fields as a price regulator with market prices that still leave to the free tradesmen and the free entrepreneurs a wide scope for a reasonable profit.

It cannot be the task of this manifesto to go further into details. Nevertheless, they must be sketched and illuminated briefly, for we know that a correct solution of this question will be of enormous advantage for the recovery of our economic morale, quite apart from the benefit that the entire economy will derive from the fact that the idea of duty about work will be awakened as a moral duty about the nation.

With respect to the position of the state-citizen about the national economy, Bismarck once declared:

"We do not live to be happy but live to do our duty."

This moral principle lies also at the basis of our position regarding the state and the economy.

National Financial Reform

"The rule of interest."

The demand for the breaking of the interest-slavery is groundbreaking new in a political Program. This fact alone would be enough for the widest circles to bring forward a most vehement opposition to National Socialism.

By far the largest part of the opponents is constituted of those who have indeed lost everything through the present interest capitalistic economy and who, brought up in these ideas, still fear the loss of already lost privileges. This opposition indeed possesses no impetus, for precisely the lack of any internal impetus is characteristic of the circle trapped in the capital pension ideal.

A further group is those who are dependent on loans or at least believe that they are. This group naturally fears not really the abolition of the obligation to pay interest, but it fears that it would not receive any more working capital unless everything remains as before.

Another group is the wonderful national economists for whom opposition to the problem of the liberation from interest is the alpha and omega of their national economic wisdom.

A further group is the malicious who are indeed not of a better viewpoint but who, for personal or party tactical reasons, combat this basic demand of National Socialism with false assertions and misrepresentations.

That the circles of international finance exercising the rule of interest are, precisely on account of this demand, our most irreconcilable and bitter enemies are self-evident.

Except for the malicious and the professionally interested opposition, the chief reasons for a hostile and mistrustful attitude are -ignorance and intellectual laziness, stupidity.

We must do here with quite powerful opponents, with opponents among whom any system that one may try to enforce fails, who draw back like jellyfish from the pressure of convincing explanations but immediately after the relaxation of the pressure flow back once again into the old ways of thought.

So, what is understood by "Interest-Slavery"? By Interest-Slavery is to be understood the interest-bound debt of the state and people to the supranational financial powers. Here therefore it is a matter of a new form of slavery, of the slavery to the rule of finance. This slavery is more frightful and cruel than any form of rule ever was under the rule of absolute princes because it is exercised in an impersonal way, without any human feeling, obsessed only with an insatiable instinct to expand and enlarge, with a greed for power without comparison.

The customary expression for the existence of this rule is: "Money moves the world." But here, money is only used as a symbol of mastery for financial power. Money itself, the metal and paper currencies, are in themselves naturally neither good nor bad, and exercise no sort of rule. Money as a currency is indispensable for the exchange of goods and services. That is why all attempts to deal with the rule of the financial powers from the side of money alone are from the start erroneous and doomed to ineffectiveness, because in the case of this rule we are not indeed dealing with a question of the narrow monetary system but with questions of power. Money as an instrument of power is. As mentioned, neither good nor bad, it depends only on its use. The fact that it can also be used murderously, that is, misused does not in any way neutralize its endlessly various and indispensable, useful usage possibilities. Even money, applied in a useful way, has a beneficial effect on the national economy. Money has not wrongly been called the blood in the national economic body. So long as money remains true to its task as a means of exchange, so long as money received or earned is again directed back to the economy, it cannot exercise any harmful influence on the national economy.

Now there comes in a factor: that is the desire to use money as a savings method. This desire is itself completely justified. On the contrary, it is only to be fully wished that the savings sense may be restored to honor again if yes, if savings were indeed possible at all in the present-day circumstances. The lasting, threatening devaluation of our German money through an irresponsible State financial policy indeed makes saving a stupidity, for, after a few weeks or days, the value of the money can have sunk to a fraction of its earlier value. Therefore, if money should fulfil its task as savings money, it must be of stable value.

Since the German money, for reasons that we shall still have to investigate, is not of stable value now and cannot be of stable value, the German saver looks around in every unstable period for such money of stable value. Such money of stable value is the so-called noble currencies, the dollars, the Swiss francs and Dutch gulden, the monies of the Scandinavian peoples, etc., as well as the metallic money from precious metals.

But now the national economic task of money as the working capital of the economy stands opposed to this desire for accumulation of stable money. To understand this question in its entire depth, we must adhere to the fact that money, according to its essence, is and should be nothing but a "token of performed work." The customary explanation: 'Money is a means of exchange' is in no way false, but it does not exhaust the question. It is a task of money, and indeed its most important one, to mediate the exchange of goods. But this task is fulfilled also by other things like the tea-packets of the Chinese, the cowry shells of the negroes, etc. The innermost essence of the money dispensed by the state today, as well as of the money surrogates, is that they are tokens one could also say vouchers of some work performed by other persons. By "performed work" we must understand quite comprehensively every economic product, thus also raw materials, for even these have commercial or sales value only if they are quarried and if they are brought to the market. To facilitate this exchange of goods among themselves, indeed, to make this possible at all in a complicated economy, a means of exchange had to be invented which would directly make it possible that the producer of only one ware would be able to satisfy his own manifold needs through this means of exchange, which had a general validity. A cobbler makes shoes and boots year in, year out -but he needs his daily bread, meat, milk, eggs, he needs clothing and so on. The baker, from whom the cobbler buys his bread, may indeed need one or two pairs of boots in a year, but he cannot really be paid the whole year through for all the bread that everybody eats with only boots, he must indeed also pay his miller and firewood supplier for flour and fuel, but these can also not use any more boots because they themselves already get boots and shoes from another cobbler. But the baker cannot naturally pay the miller for his flour with his own products, the baker must bake bread for the community. A pure exchange economy is quite impossible in a developed national economy with an extensive division of labor. An exchange intermediary is therefore indispensable. In the most general form, this exchange intermediary must be a recognized record, protected by the state, of the productions of the national economy; one must also be able to buy something with these records and everybody must be obliged to provide his commercial products for this exchange money.

It is, for example, also erroneous to say that money is a record of a performed work. Certainly, one accepts this money as a performed work, but not because an economic cycle is already completed therewith but because this money is indeed a record of every one of many performed work-activities records with which everybody can satisfy his requirement for life-necessities and his other needs. Only when this need is covered, and the money is fed back into the economy, is the basic cycle of money completed. But if the money remains lying as hoarded or saved money in one hand, then only half an exchange, only half a cycle is executed. The money has not yet fulfilled its goal. On the contrary, it has been withdrawn from the goal for which it was invented and for which it exists. We must fundamentally declare that this interruption of the national economic task of money is, for national economic and national political reasons, impermissible. It obviously cannot be that every financial amount received must be immediately given out, that the financial market must be provided so abundantly with money that every private person can make his economic arrangements in such a way that he preserves for himself sums for the covering of his monthly requirements or the amounts for larger onetime yearly services, but it must be declared as completely inadmissible national economically that the currency dispensed by the state for the welfare of the community is withdrawn from the public circulation as hoarded money.

To the financial system therefore corresponds also the duty to spend, that is, the duty to bring acquired money back into circulation.

One may also specify here again quite sharply that savings is therewith in no way made impossible. Savings, understood rightly, is in no way the avaricious and miserly hoarding of money but if one wishes to employ the favorite combination of the idea of savings with children's relief, it is the creation and acquisition of goods, the purchase or building of a small house, the purchase of valuable objects, of collections, books, pictures, household goods, the expansion and improvement of the business establishment, the extension of the stocks, etc., and that is a far better "savings" than the hoarding of gold.

Precisely, we Germans have had to undergo an education in worldview of the grandest style on this question. This correct "savings" just described has rewarded itself best; the false one focused on money has been bitterly avenged.

This unerringly correct feeling of the people, even for these matters, has been reflected quite correctly in sagas and fairy tales. The hoarded money is transformed into worthless clod, or it disappears, or it brings endless misfortune. On the other hand, always and everywhere, the one who, out of his industriousness, has "achieved something" and by that healthy reasoning always understands a blooming private economy, be it mercantile, commercial, or industrial has acquired respect and esteem. Such a development of wealth is unobjectionable, it is not directed against the spirit of money, it is, as a thriving member of the entire economy, social in the best sense.

After these brief but necessary, because essential, observations on the financial system let us return to the point of departure of our question: "What do we mean by interest-slavery?"

If, through the withholding of money in the hands of people who are not conscious of the national economic task of money, or still more in the hands of those who wish to use the collected money as an instrument of power, a deadlock arises, the money that remains in circulation becomes scarcer, there appears a money squeeze. But those who possess money still do not, in a national economically healthy manner, put their money back into circulation because they for their part satisfied continuing needs and had houses built or purchased other commercial or industrial products. They therefore do not take away from the businessman or the factory owner, who needs the working capital for the maintenance of his enterprise, his products but they give him the money withheld by them illegitimately, in a national economic sense, against a special toll against interest. The national economic squeeze begins.

The relation of the production of goods–the producer–of the national economic worker to money is, at one stroke, turned upside down. The money that was, according to its essence and its invention, to serve the economy has suddenly emancipated itself and exercises a squeeze on the production of goods. The financial rule begins. Certainly, the private economy is glad that it can maintain its enterprises at least in this way, for it feels itself bound to serve production national economically. The money hoarder derives from this feeling of national economic duty of the national economic worker a double benefit: first he has a debt certificate drawn up thus a legal title–according to which the debtor with his entire wealth is liable for the undiminished repayment of the loaned sums, in most cases other definite objects of wealth are quite especially pledged, and secondly, the debtor must pledge himself further to a continuous extra payment which one calls interest.

The guaranteed credit is thus not given for reasons which would correspond to the literal sense of the word credit, that is, to the trust in the greater economic efficacy and performance capacity, but purely with the intention of exploiting the need of the economic entrepreneur to procure for oneself without any effort a part of his work-income. The credit is also not given to therewith promote production, but solely to make the possession of money "profitable." To what businesses the credit is used is basically a matter of complete indifference to the creditor; if he is interested in it, this happens only to assure himself that his money is safe and, above all, that it is also effectively interest-bearing.

Observed generally, the credit system that is mediated by the banks is today built up in such a way that generally the capitalist, the possessor of money and credit, is fully detached from work. He has no relationship at all a personal nature to the different branches of production in which he "lets his money work", as the favorite misleading expression goes. What does the shareholder know of "Girmes", "Pöge", "Weser", "Riebeck Montan", "Otavi", "Salitrera", "Steaua Romana"[67], what does he know what is manufactured in these works? He does not have any interest in it, he has only the one-sided interest whether the shares rise or fall, and how high the dividends are that his capital yields. It is also a matter of complete indifference whether the stock companies or the other forms of capitalistic activity (joint-stock company, society with limited liability, union, etc.) serve production in general. The main thing, the only decisive thing, is the "profitability." A proof of the fact is the enormous popularity that the bank shares enjoy. The big banks, as well as every credit institution, perform in general no productive work in the sense of the production of goods. Here, in the big bank system, the idea of interest that is, the possibility of transferring a gigantic share of the incomes of productive work into the possession of the mere money-owner, and indeed, for the latter, completely effortlessly celebrates real orgies. Today there is almost no more enterprise that is not dependent in some form on the bank, that is not run in a purely interest-capitalistic form. The entire national economic work is dependent on the bank and stock-exchange capital and interest-bound to it.

The lords of the banks the high finance are therewith also the lords of production. It is dependent on them whether the work comes to a stop or whether the market is deluged with an enormous amount of rubbish. For the organized private sector, the fulfilment of demand is totally an incidental matter.

In the case of this interest capitalistic economic form of the modern credit system we thus have to do with the most complete national economic immorality, with a total perversion of the meaning of the financial and credit system as of a servant of the economy into the position of an absolute lord of the economy.

Creative and productive work has become the slave and the cunningly rapacious, eternally mobile Jewish spirit of usury rules the world. A piece of extortion is only possible through the conjuring up of an artificial state of emergency through a national economically illegitimate withholding of money. And that is considered today as just, as a right nobody dares touch because it brings him into conflict with the world-ruling power of large loan capital.

The thralldom of interest has been perfected!

It was perfected through the fact that the seductive arts of the mobile spirit succeeded in tying even the state, the given protector of the financial system, to the interest-slavery so that it too, with bound hands, acknowledges international capital as its lord and has allowed itself to be diverted from its actual task as the protector of the national economy into the position of the bailiff, the interest-collector for large loan capital.

The National Financial Economy

It is now our special task to trace this development of the national financial economy.

Even here, it will be the right way to start from a determination of the facts as they are found today.

The outstanding phenomenon in the national life of the nations of the western cultural circle is the enormous debt of all the states. Whether victor or vanquished, all bear gigantic debt burdens in their national economies affected severely by the war.

The most significant statistical work of the British Empire is The Statesman Yearbook; this official national yearbook gives for the individual states a precise overview of the condition of their public debts, etc.

According to it, the debt of England that is, of the English working class to international capital on March 31, 1930, was 7,596,000,000 pounds sterling with a yearly interest payment of around 350 million pounds sterling. It is quite useful to convert this sum into German marks, since one sees best in this way that in this interest question it is a matter of an international question of the widest scope.

France owes to its internal and foreign interest creditors around 279 billion gold francs.

The United States of North America, the blessed land of the dollar, bears a public debt burden of around 16 billion dollars.

In Canada, Australia, India, Italy, Czechoslovakia, Poland, everywhere we find the same miserable picture of a hopeless debt of the states and, therewith, of the peoples to international capital. Everywhere the national life revolves around one question: How do we pay the interest for our loans, that is, for our debts to international finance, to the large loan capital?

The finance ministries in all states are relentlessly occupied with tapping new tax sources. The parliaments advise for months on the new tax bills, but all resistance is useless. Before the majesty of the international usurious capital and its chartered "legal" claims to the interest payments, parliaments and governments collapse repeatedly and oppress their peoples with unprecedented tax burdens, instead of their daring to put an end to this enormous international fraud with a flat 'No'.

Injustice became the law, the lord a slave.

How things stand in our poor fatherland we experience daily and hourly.

Violently and powerfully did the young German work-giant rise after he had achieved a national unity through blood and iron. His tireless work, his creative spirit, brought ever new inventions. The German entrepreneurial spirit and daring conquered the markets of the world.

With amazed anxiety the French and English loan capital of the Rothschilds and the other bank magnates, as well as the trust capital of the American financial people, the Kahns, Loebs, Speyers, etc, saw itself threatened most seriously in its profitability. The value of the German mark, that is the quality and cheapness of German products, continued to rise, one could figure out when the mark would reach the value of the dollar until the English world trade would be surpassed by Germany, one saw how all over the world the German transport installations, the German educational institutions, the German sanitation organizations, the German urban administrations, the German military methods were taken as a model, one saw how everywhere in the world German engineers as pioneers of German work capacity built railways, bridges and streets. But all this meant that the profitability of the capital loaned out all over the world by international finance was threatened.

Then did international finance decide, with the help of international Freemasonry, to encircle Germany and, using all the means of lies and slander, to represent Germany as the enemy of the world. Edward VII was only a piece pushed forward in this chess game. The nationalist passions were stoked against Germany, in England as well as in France. Indicating the political prehistory of the world war does not belong here, but it is in any case certain that Germany's side, despite its military strength, was lost, because there cannot in general be any talk of a political counter-game against the game of intrigue of the Entente powers (cf. Rosenberg, International Freemasonry).

Even the only group that still had a foreign political instinct in Germany, the All German, did not have any idea that this powerful struggle between the armed nations was not about political success but was directed to the goal of the financial subjection of the German workers to the interest-slavery of international capital. The militaristic overpowering of Germany was naturally France's special goal, the destruction of the German navy the special goal of England, but above both these imperialistic goals of France and England always stood the striving for world-rule of international capital.

While thus the nations tore one another apart in wild struggle and the blood of the best flowed in streams on the battlefields, Jewry of the entire world was in movement. For All-Judah, the harvest time had come.

High finance financed the world war; in all the nations of the world, the Jewish scribes sat in the editorial offices of the international press and lied to and instigated the nations to ever new efforts against one another. 26 states were in this way led into the war against the Central Powers. From the east there flowed in a stream of eastern Jews over the German lands; these thrust themselves forward, haggled and hogged and enriched themselves, took possession of the flats in the cities and acquired everything that they could get.

In the military industrial companies, this business of the plundering and misrule of the German workforce was taken care of by the members of the Jewish race, and the Jews forced themselves forward and up into all positions of the state and economy. The internal demoralization was likewise consciously led by Jews, the Haases, Dittmanns, Cohns, Luxemburgs, Barths, then the Parvus-Helphands, Eisners, Leviens, Gradnauers agitated and incited, supported by ambitious people, fools, and power-hungry criminals against the German people.

In this way, did the German nation finally collapse from inside? Judah's star rose blood-red. The last nation that had firmly resisted the international finance and its witchcraft collapsed, it threw down its arms and bowed before the frightful yoke of the Versailles dictate. Bleeding from a thousand wounds, leaderless, not really on account of the expulsion of the princes, for precisely these had fully failed as real leaders, the German nation was led by its parliaments and parliamentary governments with the fateful sentence that can always be applied at such times, with the phrase, "To avoid the worst", into the interest-slavery to loan capital.

Versailles, Dawes Pact, & the Young Plan

The goal of the world war had been reached: Germany, the most industrious and efficient nation of the world removed as a competitor on the world market, militarily overpowered, made leaderless and seduced and poisoned by the false Marxist doctrines, morally dissipated, and buried under a mountain of debts that it can never again remove from itself, but had to serve forever as an interest slave to international capital.

According to the London payment plan, Germany has had to acknowledge an interest-bearing debt of 132 billion gold marks, and to this debt was added also the interests.

It would be ridiculous if it were not so frightfully serious and if the enemies did not take it so mercilessly precisely contrary to all the platitudes of the pacifists, "but it will not be so bad", and "reasonableness will triumph." No! It will not triumph! And the international finance will do everything to keep Germany continuously in this Interest-Slavery. Only we can free ourselves.

It is the deep tragedy of the German nation that, as efficient as it in general is in its narrow work circle, it immediately becomes uncertain when it raises its glance beyond the limits of the daily work and stands before the great world occurrences. Here, the conscientious and precise German loses all measure, he becomes a visionary and enthusiast. The "German professor", who performs outstanding things in his specialization, becomes, faced with the things of the world, an object of the comic papers, from the forgetting of his umbrella to the gushing prolixity of the ideologues the German officer, trusting in the excellent efficiency of his troops, is inclined to underestimate the spiritual imponderables of a political nature and the power of ideas, and thereby to place the final success in doubt; the German official tends to think of himself as a boss of the population instead of as the servant of the whole.

So, we see in great and small this disastrous trait in the German character: the Germans are specialists and dreamers. Individually more efficient and industrious in all special fields than any people, even completely capable of becoming enthusiastic about any great idea and with heroic bravery giving their life for an idea, but less skilled in seeing and hitting on the right solution within the intervening circle of international economic and political matters.

The reflection of such a fundamental character-trait in the German in the political field is his so oft lamented lack of national feeling and his political incompetence. The average German lacks, to a certain degree, the sense of large orderings; thus, he also does not mostly understand that those debt figures are really his destiny, that those figures, that the acknowledgement of this debt and the willingness and the attempt to pay this debt in money and material goods is the basic reason for the entire desperate situation of the German nation. Much fewer does he see, however, that the beneficiaries of this German payment obligation are not really the other nations but solely international finance.

To international finance, however, the repayment of the loan is in no way important, only the lasting obligation to interest. That and that alone is why international finance, which composed the Versailles dictate in its financial parts, set the basic sum so fantastically high from the start that a repayment can never be thought of but, even in an eventual reduction of the basic sum (in any case only with a simultaneous raising of the interest rate), Germany will permanently be held in interest-slavery.

The imposition of this interest rule over our poor industrious people was the final goal of the world war, it was the goal of high finance, and this goal has been fully reached.

The relevant clauses of the Versailles dictate are so frightful, they show so clearly the entire seriousness and the destructive hardness of this interest rule which delivers everything that we have and that we work for to the grasp of international finance that I cite them in excerpts in the following:

Art.231. The Allied and associated governments declare, and Germany acknowledges (!), that Germany and its allies are, as the originators (!), responsible for all the losses and damages that the Allies and associated governments and their members have suffered because of the war forced upon them by the attack of Germany and its allies.

Although it is quite cynically acknowledged in Art. 232 "that Germany's resources are not sufficient to ensure the complete restitution of all these losses and damages", the obligation is nevertheless demanded "that all these losses and damages be compensated."

Art.233 says: "*The extent of the damages will be determined by the Reparations Commission.*"

Art.234 says: "*The Reparations Commission will periodically test the payment capacity of Germany... But it cannot waive any amount without the approval of the different governments represented in the Commission.*"

Art.234 determines: "*Germany will pay before the determination of the final amount of the compensation claim... 20 billion marks in gold (in gold, goods, ships, securities or in other ways)*"

Germany will besides issue the bonds indicated in Art. 12c of Annex II.

And now comes, prettily stowed away and near the end in this Annex II Art. 12c in Section VIII of the so-called Versailles Peace Treaty, the financial, political strangulation of Germany. This Art. 12 says in its most important points as follows:

The Commission has all powers and exercises all authority that is guaranteed to it in this treaty.

The Commission has, in general, the most comprehensive power of supervision and enforcement with respect to the questions of the reparation. It must observe the following conditions and determinations:

a) Every part of the entire amount of the determined demands that is not paid in gold, ships, securities, or goods or in another way must be secured by Germany under the conditions determined by the Commission through the transfer of a corresponding amount to bonds or obligations of any sort to affect an acknowledgement of the owed amount.

b) The Commission will periodically evaluate Germany's payment capacity and examine the German tax system (!), so that, first, all revenues of Germany, including the revenues determined for the interest-and debt servicing of its domestic loans are preferably (!) used for the payment of the sums that it owes under the title or reparations, and secondly, to obtain the certainty that the German tax system is exactly (!) as oppressive as that of any other power represented in the Commission.

This paragraph is diabolically focused on the lasting suppression of Germany. It practically contains the possibility, with the reference to some small robber states in which unrestricted taxes are decreed, of simply stipulating the imposition of the same taxes even in Germany. But it also acknowledges at the same time with brutal frankness that even the other nations should be held in the same debt-slavery. And now comes the infamous paragraph c.

c) To facilitate and carry out the restoration of the economic life in the Allied and associated countries, the Commission will, as arranged in Art.232, receive a first payment from Germany as a guarantee and acknowledgement of its guilt, consisting of bonds to the holders, payable in gold, that are free of every tax or charge of any sort (!) that are introduced or can be introduced by the governments of the Reich or of the German states. These bonds are given as instalments (!) and that in three instalments as determined below: **1.** 20 billion gold marks are to be paid immediately **2.** 40 billion gold marks will be given in bonds that are to bear interest at an additional charge of 5% + 1% for amortization from 1926. **3.** A written obligation to pay 40 billion gold marks more in bonds, with 5% interest as coverage, will be given immediately.

This clause is the core of the entire Versailles dictate. We know that the London Ultimatum not only set fewer payments but, on the contrary, set the entire amount at 132 billion gold marks. Art. 16 then declares expressly: "From 1 May 1921 the German government has to pay for the interests on their debt." The interest rate is set at 5 percent.

Then follows Art. 17, which gives a handle to every violation:

Art. 17. *If Germany should be late in the fulfilment of any debt that the previous section of the treaty lays upon it, the Commission will immediately inform every participant power of this default and simultaneously propose the measures to be taken against it.*

And now follows one of the most outrageous clauses of the entire treaty:

Art. 18. Germany pledges not to interpret the measures that the Allied and associated powers are justified (and what would not be justified in the eyes of the enemies?) In adopting against an intentional (!) non-compliance of Germany as hostile treatment (!). These measures could consist of import prohibitions and economic and financial sanctions and in general (!) in all measures (!) that could appear to the concerned governments as demanded by circumstances.

With this clause naturally, the door and gate are opened to every, even the most brutal, terror, and the German government has further expressly signed that it may not consider even the greatest oppression, murder of Germans, the most brutal expulsions, plundering, destruction, etc.

"As hostile treatment"!

This written delivery of the German people to a cruel, vengeful, implacable enemy is, further, envisaged forever, for ***Art.23*** says:

The Commission will be dissolved when Germany and its allies have paid all the amounts that it owes for the implementation of the present treaty or according to the decisions of the Commission and when all these amounts or their equivalents are distributed to the participant's powers.

This is the eternal interest-slavery of Germany.

Perhaps our political friends and enemies will understand now what must be understood by interest-slavery. Perhaps one will understand why the breaking of this frightful interest-slavery stands at the center of our demands. Perhaps one will understand also why, in the case of this demand, it is a matter of an international question is of the very first order. It is for Germany simply a question of destiny and even for the other nations; it is the most decisive question for the recovery.

Compared to this international question, all the other questions sink into nothingness, for without the breaking of Interest-Slavery a rise of productive nations is in general not possible. If the interest-slavery now initiated is maintained, the god Mammon would have ascended the throne. God is dead, the souls of the nation's die, a human mess fills the world as interest slaves of international finance. Money rules the world.

The regulations of the Versailles dictate were essential points substituted in 1 924 by the Dawes Pact. Now, after the fears of inflation, the further plundering of Germany was to continue "on a more solid foundation." High finance allowed assurances of all sorts to be issued, among which the most significant and far-reaching are to be mentioned, the denationalization of the Reichsbank and Reich railways. Despite all the "silver cloud" prophecies, the German economy continued to collapse, the impossibility of the payments according to the Dawes Pact was finally perceived even by the blindly raging sadists of the implementation. The Young Plan entered in place of the Dawes Pact. It was supposed to bring "alleviations." Now the end has come.

On the horrors of the Dawes Pact Vol.7 of the National Socialist Library (Price 1.80 marks) gives the most precise information, which contains a reprint of the original text along with a comprehensive critical commentary. Vol.13 of the present series deals with the main points of the Young Plan.

The Loan Economy

"If the state needs money, it must borrow this money from those of its citizens who have more of it than they themselves can use. It must naturally pay interest for the return of this money, or else it will not receive the money. It has indeed already had enough difficulty in accommodating its loans."

This formulation was used by the former Socialist minister Dr. David[72] with me in a discussion in Berlin. I have placed this formulation here intentionally because it reflects in an exemplary way the interest capitalistic way of thought of our age; that he was, of all things, a Marxist gives the whole a special attraction.

Now I know from hundreds of discussions and lectures that the above formulation is derived so fully from the present interest capitalistic world of ideas that hardly anybody would feel the falseness of this explanation of the interest and debt economy of the state, let alone find a correct answer to it.

This has a very simple psychological reason, namely that the above explanation given above applies to the coverage of the monetary need of a private man within the scope of the interest-capitalistic form of the economy.

For the individual private man, as for the private economy in general, the sentence is true: "If anybody needs money, he must borrow this money against interest from those who possess more money than they themselves can use."

But we must indeed avoid answering questions about national financial economy from a private capitalistic viewpoint but from a state's viewpoint mainly. I mean, it would be indeed a major misfortune if one simply transferred this private economical way of thought unquestioningly to the national economy.

The state, with its instruments of power, its sovereign power is indeed not to be equated with any random private man. The state possesses three powerful possibilities through which, by virtue of its sovereignty, it can cover its need for the execution of its tasks. These are its service sovereignty, its coinage sovereignty, and its financial sovereignty.

By service, sovereignty is to be understood the sovereign right of the state to call on its citizens for free services. This sovereignty of the state over the individual is revealed in its most powerful scope in the compulsory military service and still more in the war service. Faced with the demands that the state can demand of its citizens in wartime, all private considerations must step back.

Family, profession, business and earnings, everything must be silent when the state calls its sons to the flag. But the state can call its citizens not only to war service, the state can call them even to great economic undertakings, we remember the auxiliary service law that however, unfortunately, quite in contrast to the military service, provided a high and ever-increasing payment for the performed services so that soon a deep cleft arose between the front soldiers, who had to offer their lives daily for the fatherland without payment, and those who were employed, in the homeland, protected behind the front, at a high wage. Just in passing, the strong performances of other nations that were based on service obligations may also be recalled: we recall the building of the Chinese Wall, the circumvallation of our mediaeval cities. Practically, therefore, it would stand completely within the power of sovereignty of the state to revive and expand the old hand and team service and to solve large economic tasks with them in this way for the disposal of existing forces.

The coinage sovereignty of the state is a second source of power from which the state can directly cover its money requirement. Nobody contests the state's right to mint coins or to issue treasury notes. Indeed, beyond that, the state has, by virtue of its sovereignty, produced money from every possible source.

From copper, nickel, iron, porcelain, aluminum and, above all, from paper. I need only to recall the time when our Reich government considered it justified to issue daily 100,000,000,000,000 marks and ever more new paper money. We shall not go in greater detail here into whether this was right and acceptable, we must state here only that the state can cover its need by virtue of its coinage sovereignty, and that it is not forced "to borrow money on interest from those of its citizens who have more of it than they themselves can use."

The financial sovereignty or the tax sovereignty of the state will likewise not be able to be contested by anybody, and one who contested this and sought to conduct it practically as an individual would be able to feel the authority of the state in the form of the bailiff. The financial or tax sovereignty of the state, that is, the right of the state to call on its citizens to financial services, is as obvious and as old as state structures. This form is also the most natural and healthy, even though in this field it has been reserved to our times to transform the reasonable sense of taxation into a complete nonsense and to make of the tax system a means for the total plundering of the people in favor of the supranational financial powers. Even here the question of the permissibility of taxes should not occupy us further but only the fact that the state is very well able to cover its money requirement by way of taxes, thus, again, by a way that is not open to the private economy, but which absolutely removes from the state the necessity of coming up with its money requirement through the adoption of an interest payment obligation to the capitalists.

Certainly, the state, like every private man, has naturally the further possibility of covering its need by incurring debts. But this is already for the private man a two-edged sword; for the state, however, it is, to express it in plain and good German, the stupidest thing that it can in general do. But it is not only the stupidest thing, but it is downright criminal with respect to the mission of the state as the protector of the common interests.

The loan economy of the states has virtually ruined the states and delivered them into the hands of international finance, it has delivered the wealth of the nations to the financial powers, and today the state loans are the frightful leech from which the nations are not able to free themselves and through which they will collapse helplessly if we do not determinedly put an end to this specter through the breaking of Interest-Slavery.

With this, we are in the middle of the field of national financial policy, thus in a field in which the normal German does not feel at home at all. What should one do now with all the many and large numbers? The normal state citizen does not in general read budget debates, and he has such a religious respect for the secret paths and misleading ways of the financial art that he would best like to be fully spared of these things. In the unconscious, this certainly is also related to the fact that every individual bears within himself such a slight feeling for the tax sovereignty of the state and nobody wishes to be reminded of numbers. Only when the tax papers fly into his house does the modern man remark that these things concern him considerably and that he is always the victim of every sort of false national financial policy.

Now it is extremely remarkable that basically the matters of national financial policy are not at all so opaque and mysterious as they appear at first glance, indeed that they are basically so clear and simple that they can be grasped by every average understanding at least in their broad outlines.

It therefore requires no great constitutional explanations that the state very well possesses the described possibilities to cover its money requirement, for everybody knows and has experienced in his own life what the nature of the service sovereignty of the state is, and everybody receives in his hand daily the paper notes issued by the state, and nobody is spared the tax. It would, therefore, be the most natural thing in the world if the state covered its money requirement exclusively in these three ways.

For the private man, however, these three ways are not open, for neither could he call on his neighbor successfully to work or tax service, nor would he be secure if he attempted to print money on his own and bring it into circulation. For him, there is indeed only the way of incurring debt on interest, if he already absolutely thinks that he can become happy only with other's monies and cannot avoid incurring debts.

But that the state in general sees as right the sole means of accepting interest-bearing loans thus debts, when it needs money and applies its other sovereign rights today only in an underhand manner to collect the incurred debts from the people, these are conditions for which one seeks in vain for a reasonable explanation. There is indeed no reasonable explanation for it, but only the fact that our entire thought, even in national financial political matters, is directed or corrupted in a private capitalistic manner. With such general pollution of public opinion, such apparently logical explanations for the loan policy of the state as I have reported play a great, indeed an all-important role.

The Jew has proved himself to be a master of psychagogy even in these matters. It is, in such cases, always very hard not to speak at once generally of direct corruption of the responsible statesmen, the presumption is obvious, and yet in most cases there has been no corruption but only uncertainty in matters of the financial and credit system, short-sightedness and complacency that have led to the fact that the state financial administrations have fallen slowly but surely into a loan delirium from which they up to now see no exit.

To this development of the circumstances has contributed in a very essential manner the fact that one at first considered the financing of large public works like railway building, etc., which promised to yield a revenue, through loans as harmless. One decided in the following manner: From the revenues of the railways or waterways, the interest can be immediately covered, then we indeed have the pricing under control. With its own resources, the state cannot draw such large works at one stroke from its treasury, so it thankfully accepts the offered credit help of the banks. This removes the trouble from the government of approving new taxes in the state parliament, the liquid resources of the state are not claimed, and the railways can easily pay the interests from the surpluses. The seductive arts of loan capital, which can do nothing with money if it does not find anybody who takes it away from it and pays it interest in addition, succeeded in turning black into white and in making the state itself an interest collector for private capital.

Even the simplest economic reflection on the part of a government or a parliament conscious of its responsibility however should have led to the following: If one builds the railways with foreign money and one must pay for it, year in year out, only 5% interest, with everything connected with it, one pays back in 20 years already the entire amount once, in 40 years already twice and yet the same debt remains outstanding. These extraordinary amounts which exceed many times the initial investment costs must indeed be raised once again indirectly from the people, the entire population, who must pay the railway transport tariffs raised precisely according to these interest amounts. A onetime announcement to the people of a large railway levy is, or would have been, better. Then these levies would, of course, have been rather oppressive for some years but also for not much longer, as the transport costs and the railways would have very soon become a debt-free asset of the state which would have later assured it large yearly revenues. But it is the old story that one would rather cut off the dog's tail bit by bit because one thinks it would be so much less painful for it. Naturally, the opposite is true. The investment costs of such a national undertaking must indeed be paid by the population, but if they are developed on loans, then there inevitably enter, in addition, the interests that amount in the course of the years too many times the debt itself. It is therefore a sheer financial stupidity to finance such public works through loans. Already here we may point to that which will rescue the state from its loan madness: nobody can forbid the state, for example, for such productive undertakings, to issue credit notes, state treasury credit notes, and pay for the works thereby. Such a creation of money of the state in cases where there can be no question of an inflation at all because there is a new value also for the new tokens, would resolve at one stroke all the difficulties and free the state and the people forever from the interest-bearing debt to private capital.

We shall have to go into greater detail about this problem in another place. A skilled financial administration should be able to arrange things in such a way that such large works are carried out from special taxes along with the use of other revenue sources of the state and only with a partial issue of new notes. This possibility would, of course occur to a considerable extent only if all other state expenditures, especially the so-called unproductive ones for administration, administration of justice, education, etc., could be covered from the surpluses of the state's commercial enterprises.

This may, in view of the present frantic deficit economy of the railways, post, etc., sound like an irony and yet we were not so far from such possibilities, as I already showed in 1919 in my first publication in the Süddeutsche Monatshefte (February), "What now?" under the heading "The radical means." Only the interest obligation of the state to private capital separated us from this ideal condition of a national financial economy. The delusion, already effective at that time, that the state, when it needs money, must simply pump money into itself at interest, has prevented this.

It is clear, and everybody should have been able to follow my explanations, that the state is in no way directed to foreign money, thus to the incurring of debt, when it wishes to undertake something, that it, for example, could demand work-and team-service and that it finally would be doubtless justified in issuing state treasury credit notes for such goals, to institute these works with them without a burdening of the people. Such a procedure would have the enormous advantage of freeing such works from the start from every interest-and toll-obligation; the works would become immediately free and debt-free state property. From the revenues of the works, the issued state treasury vouchers could indeed be redeemed and destroyed in a short time; the products of such works, or the freight and passenger transport prices, could be reduced quite considerably.

Thereby the greatest services could in general be rendered to the entire national economy, the state could have obtained quite significant revenue sources which would have been of the greatest use to the entire national community and would also have made the state itself quite independent of high finance. But it also should have been so. For the state is the master of the financial system and not high finance, that is, it will be so in the National Socialist state of the future.

It has been really a psychological fraudulent trick that the banks have succeeded in not allowing such obvious and self-evident thought processes which once expressed are no longer to be contradicted, and in befuddling the state and economy with the sentence cited above and roping them into the interest-slavery to capital.

I know that, even though these things are now clear as daylight, still many of my readers mistrust their healthy human understanding and simply do not wish to believe how such an absurdity could have been possible and would rather suppose: "*That cannot be right, our statesmen cannot have been so stupid, but I just cannot judge this.*" This confession to a lack of judgement about such a plain state incompetence in financial and political matters stands doubly in contradiction to the otherwise ready fault-finding and ranting on state measures and to the fact that it is a question here of matters that hit every individual most keenly in his wallet.

To these people, I would like to leave another viewpoint for consideration which is related to the method of credit approval through the provincial or Reich parliament.

Such large state tasks are indeed deliberated thoroughly in the parliaments. After long debates, the credits are finally "approved." The average state-citizen believes now that now everything is in order and that the state, which is indeed such a rich and powerful guy, already possesses the approved millions. Quite clever persons might still scratch behind their ear and say to themselves, 'That means new taxes again'. But I think I may boldly maintain that, apart from the initiated to whom neither the representatives nor the ministers need to belong, indeed perhaps only one at most becomes clear of the fact that this large credit approval in the provincial or Reich parliament signifies nothing but the permission to have this "credit" loaned to itself at interest in another way. This "credit approval of parliament" thus empowers only the concerned minister to get this credit at interest at the large banks. In this way the "credit approval of parliament" naturally becomes a farce, a comedy, for the entire population which must in the final analysis pay for capital and interest was not in a position also to really supply the "credit", no, it must first be created by large loan capital.

The only logical and natural thing would indeed be that, in the case of a credit approval through the parliament, simultaneously and automatically there would also be an approval that now the state bank would also pay out or authorize the approved sums based on payment orders from the implementing authorities to the concerned entrepreneurs.

The credits are approved, for the necessary currency something must be done; it is therefore senseless if as is now common first a loan must be written out and then the just "approved" credits are in a way given a second time by the capitalists.

Now one may be able to maintain that surplus money from the state is drawn just in this way and that this must have a beneficial influence on the general financial situation of the country, that thus such a credit management will operate in an inflation-reducing manner. But this is naturally in no way the case and indeed for reasons that cannot be contested by any banking expert. It may be admitted that a quite smaller part of such drafts and payments of such loans is paid in cash, it is a question here of the circle of small savers who find their way to the bank with such drafts, who have saved a pair of hundred or thousand marks that they would now like to invest in an interest certificate, in such a magic paper from which one needs to cut out only a piece every year to be paid out a certain amount without the certificate becoming less valuable thereby.

But the monies entering the bank in this way are quite negligible. In addition, the banks at which such monies are deposited for their part do not at all convey these cash amounts to the state treasury, but the transfer of such draft amounts is conducted exclusively by way of transfer or clearance.

But all larger drafts on such loans are conducted by the capitalists already from the start, in their banks, by way of transfer without cash or through the process of banking transactions, etc.

Therefore, no cash comes into the hands of the state and, if it receives such, it must immediately give it away for the execution of its works. This supposed advantage, therefore, does not exist. On the contrary, this follows: The state, as we know, issues for loaned amounts of so-called security certificates or bonds. These bonds of the state are finely, or not so finely, printed papers which contain a debt instrument endowed with all state safeguards on the received amounts, and in addition, the necessary determinations of the interest payment dates and, on their own coupon-sheets, the coupons on the basis of which the state pledges to pay quarter-yearly, half-yearly or annually the interests for the amounts noted in the coupon-sheet. Besides, to this coupon-sheet is added another so-called renewal certificate (talon) which entitles the owner to the receipt of a new coupon-sheet if the first has expired after a certain number of years.

Now such a security certificate that is issued by the state for which the state is liable for its entire wealth for capital and interest means certainly purchasing capacity in the hand of the owner. The owner of such state certificates can indeed buy something for himself with these certificates at any time, whether he gives these certificates directly as payment or sells these certificates at the stock-exchange or his banker and then pays cash with the proceeds.

Now there is no doubt at all that the issue of new security certificates by the state means the creation of additional purchasing capacity whether this is right or justified does not interest us here now, quite the same would occur if, for example, the state printed new paper money. The difference would consist in the fact that in one case security certificates are produced which burden the state, apart from the debt, with a lasting interest obligation, whereas in the case of the new issue of paper money an interest-obligation does not at all come into consideration. We see therefore already now that the last form in any case would be the more favorable for the state and the people.

But now, if we follow the method of such financings further, it emerges that a direct financing of a large state works with an avoidance of the loan route reveals further huge advantages.

We have seen that the currently adopted form of the financing of state works leads to the creation of additional purchasing capacity, which is represented by the issue of new security certificates. Here, naturally, the entire new loan amounts will and must be given out all at once, even if the railways, waterways, etc. to be built newly are only in a construction stage and still do not represent any real value worth mentioning.

If one moves to financing, such large state works in the way proposed by me, then the enormous advertising costs for the loan first disappear. One may remember what enormous amounts are devoured by the tenders in the newspapers alone. Further, the percentages that are granted to the banks and other credit institutions from the start disappear.

Even these are, again, millions. Further, one tends to issue the loans under the par value for a 1000-mark bond. Only 970 marks are to be paid by the purchaser of these certificates, and yet he receives the full amount with interest. Even these are losses that from the start become burdens to the state or the enterprise and in favor of the capitalist. Indeed, one tends "to decorate" such loans with other attractions, as the stock-exchange expression goes, by holding out in prospect special extra benefits which may even include a tax exemption. I recall here the mining premium loan that displayed the most fantastic of such attractions that a state ever stooped to.

The lottery and gambling devil was set in the service of the loan advertisement in that one promised to pay out winnings of millions on a very large number of 1000 mark bonds; besides, so-called bonus payments were held out, and further, an announced interest-rate at 5% that was however hedged in with clauses, and, in addition, in the case of a series of taxes the savings premium loan was exempt from every tax! From where one wished to obtain the enormous amounts to pay these premiums and benefits, these fabulous lottery winnings, nobody considered even though it had to be clear to every serious and perceptive man that all these amounts would have to be drawn out once again from the pockets of the people. For, the amounts received then were immediately used for the most urgent expenditures.

These are all financial political crimes against the people in which one must only wonder at the consummate insolence with which they are staged.

If one therefore does not at all, take the loan route, but directly the way of direct money creation, then all these hard and unjust burdens of the state budget would be removed one would not even have to raise the necessary amounts all at once in new paper money, but this could take place quite slowly, according as even the new works proceed. This would have the further enormous advantage that there could be no question of the issue of uncovered money, for new money will be given only when another considerable section of the works has been completed. We would have to do here with a money fully covered through real values, thus with money that is stable, with money that is matched by so many hours of performed work.

But even this form of a successive issue of new money for construction, which already appears much more favorable, is not in any way the final step. For it will not at all be proved necessary to bring an amount of money equivalent to the newly created works into circulation, for the newly issued notes indeed flow back again into the public state treasuries; they can thus be issued once again without new series having to be brought into circulation. And now let us go a step further, that is, let us declare the issue of one's own new money for such special state tasks as being in itself fundamentally not at all necessary, even if we could very well explain the permissibility, and also especially the clarity, of the financing process in the issue of one's own money for construction and wished to adhere to it for certain purposes.

This last step is the complete cashless financing of such state tasks. It is, as have already shown above, erroneous to assume that the state would, through the loan, come into cash with which it could pay the entrepreneur and workers of railway or electricity plant constructions. Nevertheless, the entrepreneurs will have to draw out weekly from their banks the necessary amounts for the payment of their work in cash. The banks, for their part, must cover these extraordinarily large demands on their treasury stocks once again from the central banks or the Reichsbank, etc.

Now, in normal times, the entire existing liquidity already suffices fully for the weekly wage payments of the entire workforce, and it is fundamentally a matter of indifference if temporarily, for example, larger workforces are concentrated in one place in the construction of the Bavarian Walchensee power plant, for, if they were not employed there, they would even when distributed in other enterprises have to expect and receive their weekly wage payments, or receive money by means of unemployment insurance. That means that it is a quite general state task to take care of the total need of means of payment for the entire national economy, no matter whether greater workforces are temporarily employed in one place for the execution of large state works or not.

The provision of means of payment for the wage payments and the implementation of the other cashless transfers to the entrepreneurs are tasks of payment transactions and have nothing at all to do causally with the credit situation.

It would therefore be the most obvious and natural thing if with the credit approval for some large state work through the lawful representation of the entire population were bound, at the same time, the authorization that the state bank may, based on these approved credits, carry out the necessary payments. Obviously in the normal way -that these payments are made only when the different contracted state authorities (agricultural departments, street and river engineering departments, railway construction sections, special departments for special purposes, etc.) have examined the payment amounts demanded by the entrepreneurs and, in accordance with the regulations and the contract, authorized payment.

The entire loan swindle that is thrown in for it is nothing, but the modern form of cheating a nation is completely useless and only harmful.

The Reichsbank Corporation

The Reichsbank is not, as every credulous state-citizen may, after all, believe, really a state bank but a stock company. The Reichsbank is thus in no way a state institution even if the state had, up to June 1922, when it was fully "autonomous" on the demands of the Entente, certain regulatory rights. Even the officials of the bank were named and paid by the Reich, but the advisory council was composed exclusively of representatives of the world of big banks and of international Jewry. The two are the same circle of people.

Already in its foundation in 1 873 the first advisory council recorded among around 15 members the following names: Baron Rothschild, Privy Councilor of Commerce Bleichröder, Privy Councilor of Commerce Mendelssohn, Theodor Plaut, Privy Councilor of Commerce Oppenheimer, Privy Councilor of Commerce Warschauer and Privy Councilor of Commerce

Zwicker, Councilor of Commerce Stern, Councilor of Commerce Gelpke; so eleven pure-bred big Jews and, as decoration, four more gentlemen with German names.

It was again a clever chess-move with which the banker advising Bismarck, Bleichröder, recommended to the old Reichschancellor that the Reichsbank be developed not as a pure state institution because thereby it would not be able to be appropriated by the enemy in case of war on the basis of the international! recognized security of private property, whereas as a pure state bank, it would stand immediately open to the attack of the enemy.

The clever Jew, along with the other big financiers, naturally wished only to get the principal financial institute of the Reich into his sphere of power. The gentlemen succeeded in this too and the Reich therewith totally renounced one of the most important fields of its coinage sovereignty: its right of issuing banknotes.

The Reichsbank occupies today a quite special position in the financial system of the German Reich, a position about which the least important people are clear even today regarding its frightful consequences for the state and the people.

It must be the task of an individual investigation to precisely examine in what way the big banks have misused their decisive influence on the Reichsbank, since its foundation, to their egoistic ends.

So long as Bismarck was in office, his state-manly view, and the respect for him kept the stock-exchange hyenas under control; only once in the entire history of the Reichsbank did Bismarck make use of the chancellor's veto provided for in the Reichsbank law, namely when he forbade the acceptance of Russian stocks. Today, the Reichsbank has, under the friendly pressure of the international bankers, as already mentioned at the start, been made fully independent. The Reichsgovernment thus has no further possibility of acting in a decisive way on the conduct of the business.

The interest-slavery of the nation's means the rule of the bank and stock-exchange. The breaking of interest-slavery is by far the greatest task of National Socialism.

Everything that happens today in the state and economy everything becomes a demand for interest of large capital against productive work. If a railway is built, there results a loan therefrom, if a war is conducted, war loans result therefrom, if natural resources or hydro energy are developed, their result hydro-energy loans therefrom, if a factory is expanded, new shares are issued, if a new enterprise is founded, some interest capitalistic company form is chosen that allows the work and the risk to flow to the entrepreneurs and the lion's share of the profits to the financiers. If it does not proceed any more by way of loans, the far simpler and more extensive way of money-printing is chosen, as in the time of the inflation of 1923, which likewise gathers in the greatest interests of large capital. As in the case of King Midas in the saga, for whom everything that he touched turned into gold, so today everything that happens turns into interest-bearing securities.

Unfortunately, the world-bankers have a damned good appetite and securities are indeed their favorite food, which obviously suits them excellently. We cannot count on their going hungry, like King Midas, for whom, as is well known, even the food in his mouth turned to gold. On the contrary, the workers will first go hungry before the interest lords will.

They also do not at all think of giving up or softening their rule, so this interest rule must be broken.

Now we must illuminate a third aspect that will complete and round off the picture of the interest capitalistic exploitation even for the layman, that is, inflation.

Inflation

Inflation is the clearly visible expression of our financial-political misery. Inflation affects everybody who must earn his livelihood with frightful severity.

But whence does inflation come?

To this question, one can hear numerous explanations which are partly taken from the narrow viewpoint of the person answering, partly from the dictionary of demagogic slogans, and partly indicate actual partial causes without, however, correctly hitting the ultimate motivating cause. When one hears these causes of inflation identified by the different parties, there is soon no social order and no profession any more that would not be designated by some side as the cause of inflation.

For those who have followed the explanations of the book on Interest-Slavery, the answer is not hard to find. The original guilt for inflation is borne by the interest obligation of work to capital.

Interest on debt leads to inflation, creating a logical chain of events that begins with the government's misguided and disastrous promise to pay interest. To fulfill these interest obligations, the government must extract money from the people through taxes. These taxes, which include all types of direct and indirect taxes as well as tariffs, and even the most problematic indirect taxes like those resulting from the issuance of uncovered banknotes, inevitably bring about inflation. This process creates an endless cycle.

Inflation demands ever-increasing government expenditures, and the government, caught in a cycle of debt, believes it can only cover these costs by taking on new loans. These new loans, in turn, carry new interest obligations, which necessitate additional taxes. Eventually, tax legislation collapses entirely because, during such currency crises, all tax revenues fall far behind the pace of currency devaluation. Now the state surrenders without resistance to the financial Bolshevism of the money printing press, as we have horribly experienced in the inflation of 1923.

My first polemical works were primarily dedicated to the uncovering of these connections. In the Manifesto for the breaking of Interest-Slavery[74] I developed in broad outlines generally the all-overarching significance of the interest problem, in the State bankruptcy: The solution I quite specifically revealed the stupidity of the state loan system and pointed to the innumerable tax laws which made more expensive the livelihood of the broad masses, whose productions had to be used completely for the interest service. In the work the coming tax strike, with the new flood of tax laws from 1920 to 1921, as well the Reichsbudget for 1918, the conclusive proof was offered that the entire financial administration of the Reich and the states is completely yoked to the interest service for large loan capital. In the last book, however, the way is already shown by a reversal of these completely squalid circumstances with a quite palpable example.

It is obvious that, through the flooding of a national economy with paper money, the purchasing power of this paper money must steadily go down.

Since money in its innermost character, as we have recognized, is a token of performed work, the so-called quantity theory of money, at least in its essential features, must be effective purchasing power is the total amount of all demand claims on the national economy which in the form of cash or in the form of securities are applied to the goods market and seek to transform themselves into material goods.

Potential purchasing power can be transformed at any time into effective, in the case of this phenomenon, one speaks of the "flight from the mark."

Acknowledged by us. This theory teaches that the amount of money found in circulation in a national economy must remain in a certain stable relationship if changes in purchasing power are not to emerge. The money stands to a certain extent against stocks of goods and calculated from the amount of goods a certain number of units of value of the customary currency is produced, that is, the average price of the goods.

Here I stress very strongly the adjective 'average'. Indeed, one must go farther and say: the average price level thus in no way the amount of the individual prices stands in a certain dependency on the amount of the purchasing power present in total in the country. But purchasing power is already a much more comprehensive concept than only the amount of cash assets.

But we do not wish to get lost here very much in economic details, for otherwise the question of effective and potential purchasing power in its effect on the prices must be broached here. Anyway, it is certain that, for example, a multiplication thousand times of the circulating currency must naturally bring with it a multiplication roughly thousand times of the prices. It is not the prices that have really risen, the purchasing power of the mark has just diminished in inverse relation to the multiplication of the amount of the currency.

The basic cause of inflation is the interest obligation of the state. This interest obligation makes taxes necessary, for the state can only give what it must again extract in some form from its citizens.

This form of robbery of its citizens by the state is, as we have seen, a threefold one either through direct taxes or in more effective form through indirect taxes or in the special indirect form of inflation. The last form is the most objectionable. It is also that with which bankrupt states seek to hold their head above water it is the most perfect counterfeiting. But this last form is especially so harmful because thereby the savings wealth of the most efficient and industrious part of the population is simply destroyed.

This is one of the most shocking chapters of the tragedy of the German people. Hundreds of thousands of industrious manual laborers, employees, officials, members of free professions, doctors, engineers, etc. Have all their life long, through tenacious tireless work, saved for themselves and for their families so that they could enjoy an old age free of care and independent.

They have collected their savings penny by penny and mark by mark, and every mark means the guarantee of the subsistence minimum for every day in old age. But the state, to which these unfortunate people have entrusted their savings, did not, in the inflation of 1923, pay in any way for a mark which had been entrusted to it in some way as savings even not when these saved pennies had been deposited at that time in shiny gold pieces–about 30 million papiermarks, but it availed itself of the decline of the currency caused by itself and said: a mark = a mark. Therewith it robbed all these men of the fruits of their lifelong work and pushed them into the most bitter distress.

They were then fobbed off by the state with pathetic and miserable handouts, private charity had to step in with help but precisely this form was especially shameful for those affected, for from the private hands these gifts remained actual handouts, charitable gifts for which these unfortunate people had to be thankful, even though it was a matter of organized robbery of well-earned rights. Of rights which, if they were restored, would not even make a "thanks" from the robbed necessary.

We have already pointed in other passages to the fact that a false principle avenged itself frightfully on these poor people -indeed the ideal of capital pension. Not as if these circles had deserved this fate. On the contrary, it will be an honorable duty of the National State to compensate these robbed people as well as possible. Yet, it remains to be hoped that this frightful lesson will nevertheless continue to vibrate in the unconscious of the people and that the capital pension ideal will sink and will help the right savings ideal–the purely German idea of old age care, care of women and children through the creation of a home of their own, field and garden, etc. to a breakthrough and victory.

The second form of robbery of the citizens by the state mentioned above is the indirect tax. Indirect tax is, in its consequences, indeed a social crime. Ruthlessly and relentlessly, in a form that nobody can avoid, it hits the great mass of the population with total severity, whereas the rich are, in general, hardly touched by the indirect taxes.

The direct tax is, if it is graded according to the economic performance capacity of the taxpayer, in itself a just and right to tax. A direct tax is also, as a contributory payment to the state for communal tasks, in no way a tax which must essentially make the production more expensive, for it should be taken only where actual surpluses beyond the coverage of the adequate life-necessities are present. But as direct tax is treated today, it, like inflation, amounts to a sheer robbery and places itself in direct contradiction to the guarantee of property expressed in Art. 153 of the Weimar constitution.

In summary, let it be once again pointed out that we must do here with an inflation which operates generally because of the interest obligation of the state to international finance. It is a matter here of a lasting blood-sucking from the economic body of our nation in favor of the supranational financial power for which our own state acts as a tax-collector.

It is a matter here of a quite special form of inflation the interest, capitalistic inflation. Natural inflation arises when insufficient harvest or an epidemic hit the country, when the natural demands are greater than the existing supply. Such an inflation is, however, always only of a temporary nature. The next fertile year removes the distress, and the prices return to their natural level.

The interest in capitalistic inflation, however, is like a devouring fire which is not extinguished until it has consumed all the treasures of the world and made the whole of mankind interest-slaves of international finance or until the interest-slavery is broken.

National Financial Reform

After such a thorough diagnosis of the illness of our state finances, as of our financial system in general, we may hope to be able to give the right prescriptions for the remedy.

Those regulations and measures that regulate the transition from the present situation to the future form do not belong within the scope of this work. For these measures is valid the general guideline that through these where possible every disturbance of the economic life must be avoided. Naturally, it will not happen without a certain severity here and there and without temporary interventions, but, even in the case of a most carefully prepared operation, it does not happen without a certain small loss of blood.

Our great shining final goal is the breaking of thralldom of interest.

The first and fundamental measure, which results from the surrender of the national financial system to a private institution, the Reichsbank, plc. Is the nationalization of the Reichsbank.

It must already be obvious from the scope of this bank that a "Reichsbank" has indeed to be an institution of the Reich, just as the Reichspost or the Reichscourt. It must be absolutely declared as a misleading of public opinion that the Reichsbank, pic, is allowed to bear this name.

The task of a real Reichsbank must correspondingly be a twofold one. First, the provision of financial businesses of the Reich must lie with it, insofar as these cannot be provided for by individual administrative positions themselves and directly, as this is indeed the case with the post and the railways, and, secondly, it must form the strong backing for the entire national economy in the fiduciary mediation of payment transactions. Its task must, further, be seen to it that constantly sufficient cash assets are present for monetary transactions.

For this range of tasks, it must be the executive organ of the national financial administration, which must be placed fully under it. The officials of the Reichsbank must be state officials, like the other officials, as well. An advisory council, which is constituted by representatives of big Jewry, as that of today, is naturally completely superfluous. It is indeed sufficient if a special state commissioner for the supervision of the financial conduct of the bank, who is responsible for the financial conduct of the bank, is appointed by the state. The tasks of the bank will be precisely circumscribed by its own Reichsbank law so that already the financial conduct of the bank would provide a guarantee that the institution of the Reichsbank serves only the national interests.

But we have now already a banking institution which corresponds completely to these demands that we must place upon the Reichsbank. This is the Bavarian State Bank. The Bavarian State Bank is a purely national bank, and nobody will be able to maintain that it has not fulfilled its tasks as a banking institution in an unobjectionable way. This naturally with the caveat that it has likewise worked according to the general customs of the interest capitalistic economy. But in any case, this bank has served the monetary transactions without considering profitability for the bank capital as the first task. It has thereby manifested the following very remarkable phenomenon that the bank, with its own extremely small capital of only 8,000,000 marks, was very well able to serve all the demands of monetary transactions and to manage revenues of billions.

It is not uninteresting to state that, in the Stock-exchange Yearbook (Saling's Stock-exchange Yearbook, A Handbook for capitalists and stockholders, for 1914/15, presented by the German Bank), the existence of this Bavarian State Bank (at that time still "Royal Bavarian Bank") is simply ignored, even though there were opportunity and place to mention it on page 644 of this handbook of this nevertheless significant state institution. But a bank which does not exclusively serve private capitalistic aims is clearly, for high finance, not a bank.

It is further remarkable that, immediately after the war and the Munich Bolshevist period, efforts were under way to place the Bavarian State Bank "on a broader basis", as the delightful stock-exchange technical expression for it ran, to make even this independent institution available for the "making profitable" of private capital. Our demand thus has a practically preserved model in the Bavarian State Bank. The objection that it is not possible to conduct a bank as a state institution is thereby refuted.

For the Reichsbank itself, the Reichsbank law in fact proposed a nationalization according to which the Reich would have the right, after a year's notice, for the first time on 1.1.1891, then in periods of ten years, either to abolish the Reichsbank and to acquire the assets of the same (including the enormously valuable buildings) against a payment of the net asset value (!) or to acquire all the shares at face value (!!). On 1 January 1921 thus, the Reich would have been able to make good a serious mistake of the Reichslegislation against the German people if it acquired the entire property of the Reichsbank for the trifle of 1 80 million that is the face value of the Reichsbank shares.

The Völkische Beobachter which was at that time not yet in the possession of the National Socialist German Workers' Party, which however was at that time already led by men who belonged to the intellectual precursors of National Socialism, and the weekly of Dr. Sch. Pudor, Der deutsche Finanzmann, pointed this out in time –of course as the only public German newspaper voices naturally without any success.

It is further remarkable that, although the Reichsbank shares are made out two names, not less than 2153 foreigners were in the possession of Reichsbank shares! What part of the entire capital of the Reichsbank these 2153 foreigners (as of 1913) disposed of is unfortunately not apparent from the Reichsbank disclosures? In any case, it is a matter of a very considerable percentage after the number of local shareholders is given at only 16,646.

Now it is clear that, in the case of the local shareholders, very much smaller amounts may have been acquired, whereas naturally it may be rightly assumed that a foreigner, when he buys German Reichsbank shares, does not acquire only one or two pieces, but straightaway a neat package. This fact hides the incredible situation that quite significant sums were drawn away in the form of dividends, even during the war, from the "German Reichsbank" to foreign countries.

Now, the profit sharing of the Reichsbank, which derives its main profits from bill discounting as we have learnt above, is a most highly original one. First, the shareholders receive a preference dividend of 31/2%, and from the remaining profit, then a quarter is distributed to the shareholders. Three-fourths of this remaining profit is transferred to the Reich, after a further 10% is transferred to a reserve fund.

In 1913, 31,025,555 marks were transferred in this way to the Reich. For that reason, the Reich has conferred on this remarkable institution the so-called banknote printing privilege, that is, the right to issue banknotes according to the need of its transactions. Up to the breakout of the war, the Reichsbank was at least supposed to keep ready, as a cover for these banknotes, up to a third of gold or silver in German or foreign coins or in bars. After even this restriction fell, there stood no more obstacle in the way of the limitless paper money printing. The only coverage (!) which the Reichsbank had for its paper money was the wonderful Reichs-treasury bills, thus once again only another paper, behind which stood a bankrupt state. No wonder if, amidst such conditions, an unstoppable collapse of the German currency had to occur.

It is doubtless a quite important state task for a nationalized bank to always take care that the claims of the economy for means of payment are fully satisfied; for only if no deadlocks occur here, even if the other financial institutions can satisfy all claims fully, is an interest extortion based on money shortage, which can rise to the greatest world crises excluded. Conversely, the issued amounts of money flow back, even in times of a lesser buoyancy of the economy, to the Reichsbank through the innumerable channels of public money transactions so that it can draw the notes again from the circulation. In the case of the Bank of England, it is customary, as is well-known, that a note which flows back to the bank is not given out again but is exchanged for a new one while the old one is destroyed. This happens primarily for hygienic reasons.

Now the question of the currency will in the future indeed be of increasing significance after the so-called money surrogates, like bills of exchange and cheques, and especially the cashless money transactions, gain increasing importance.

In such a clearing economy, the postal cheque offices, which already today are exemplary of pure monetary transactions on a cashless and interest-free basis, will gain extraordinarily in significance. In the present-day postal cheque offices are to be glimpsed the core cells that are easily to be developed for an ideal monetary transaction system under state supervision completely corresponding to the national passenger and goods transport.

Nobody can contest that the payment transactions through the postal cheque offices are handled more quickly and reliably. It hardly matters that credit and debit notes are not dealt with within 48 hours at most, when, on the other hand, one can experience with the banks today that credit notes for amounts long received are produced only 8 to 14 days later. If the bank customer needs money for his enterprise, he is still forced to claim bank credit. In the case of the monetary transaction through the postal cheque offices, the entire interest calculation is removed. This means a quite enormous relief and simplification of the payment transaction and especially at the end-of-year deadlines. The postal cheque customer receives on 2 January every year as also every day on demand the exact information on the condition of his account in the postal cheque account.

The mediation of the monetary transaction through the banks is thus in no way especially advantageous for the economy. The pure monetary transaction through the banks burdens the production only with provisions of all sorts, and only and exclusively the banks have a benefit from the interests but never the one who makes use of the bank. For the just factory owner and entrepreneur, the receipt of a couple of marks' interest for temporary credits is not at all important. A just entrepreneur directs himself in such a way that he has disposable in the bank only so much money that he can defray the wages and other current payments therefrom.

The postal cheque accounts correspond to these demands completely and it is not by chance that, even during the war, the English society of "Fabians", the "Fabian Society"[76], in London directed a memorandum to the Lord Chancellor of the Exchequer with the title: "How do we pay for the war?", in which they pointed to the organization of the German and Austrian postal cheque accounts as a support. Enemies are always sharp-sighted and when they indicate an institution for their own country as exemplary, as one can be certain that there is something in it.

The same thing that was said about the nationalization of the Reichsbank is true naturally also of the nationalization of the other central banks, for

Bavaria, thus, of the "Bavarian Central Bank." The Bavarian Central Bank is likewise a pure stock company, in which most of the shareholders, for example, can simply decide to distribute the gold reserves of the bank, on which the bank's privilege of issuing notes lies, to the shareholders. Indeed, we still remember that attempts in this direction weremadebythe Jewish banker Schweißheimer in Munich. This time, the plan foundered on the objection of the Bavarian government. The Bavarian state had acquired at that time a sixth of the shares, while a further sixth had been acquired by the Bavarian Mortgage and Discount Bank and the remaining two-thirds were given out to the shareholders.

It is monstrous that a state must fear that the gold stock of the central bank could be endangered by the intervention of the "share-holders" of this bank. One who knows the Jewish tenacity knows that the danger of Bavaria for its gold stock was nowhere near removed by the fact that the government, for once, remained firm. Against this, there is indeed only the one radical means of the nationalization of the central banks. Apart from the Bavarian Central Bank, we have in Germany also the Baden Bank, the Saxon Bank in Dresden, and the Württemberg Central Bank.

In the case of the nationalization of the Reichsbank and the central banks, the officials and employees of the banks will obviously be taken over in the same capacity by the state as state servants. The right to issue notes will thereby be exercised exclusively by the state. Such an issue of notes can occur only after an ordinance of the Ministry of Finance and only against complete coverage. Here in this connection is to be resolved the great task of the stabilization of our currency. This is, however, not a task within the smaller circle of central banks; they only must take care that no issue of notes takes place without coverage.

The production of notes, the determinations up to now, are valid. Every imitation will be punished with the greatest strictness according to the prescriptions of the penal code, Section VIII, Arts. 146-152.

The shareholders will be compensated. Any claim to the gold stocks of the bank on the part of the shareholders will be legally excluded.

A real stabilization of our currency is fully excluded so long as one expects, in the way described interest and duty charges of the German people that cannot in the long run be fulfilled. It is also false to want to maintain a radical means for a stabilization of the currency. It is a matter here not of a special problem that one could separate from the international problem of the interest of economy. So long as this international robber economy of the all-Jewish high finance continues to exist, the currencies of the different nations will always remain the welcome object of speculation of high finance. Further, the stability of a currency, thus that which the inner meaning of the term "currency" expresses, depends on other factors, above all on the activity or passivity of the balance of trade. Here our glance is extended beyond the limits of our fatherland, and the home economy enters mutual relations with the national economies of foreign countries.

To quickly find one's bearings in this enormous field of international finance, we must likewise have in mind once again that the meaning and goal of this international economy is not the profitability for private capital, but the covering of need. Everything else is only an accessory, an aid. The international financial economy of the international payment transactions is, however, today that which appears as the principal thing, and which today actually plays the chief role. It is the international banking houses that today actually rule the world, which "cover" the monetary need of the states, and have therefore arrogated the rule to themselves; it is the international banking houses that today control production in gigantic trusts, iron, steel, petroleum, canned food, grain, fat, oil, cotton, etc. The international banking houses financed the wars, the large banking houses financed and controlled all war provisions. They themselves have performed nothing as productive men, neither have they taken part in the production, nor indeed took part actively in the war activities; they have only derived profit from everything, from blood and tears, from the horrors of the war, from the hunger of the masses, from the wastefulness of the nouveaux riches, from the speculative fury of the stock-exchange public. All that becomes gold and gold value to international finance. Every work of the productive nations brings interest to international finance. Even here, in the international economy, we have to do with a complete reversal of the correct and reasonable relationship between capital and work.

The workers work reasonably and offer their work products on the world market to exchange them for foreign work products (raw products, semi or fully fabricated). A reasonable economy is not appointed to exchange foreign currencies (dollar or English pound notes) for supplied optical instruments and to then cancel these and then speculate further in foreign currencies. In times of a healthy economy, no factory owner would have thought of such a thing. He of course needs the proceeds for his further products, to be able to produce further, to pay his workers and to buy new raw materials. It is fully impossible that the entire German economy should collect its proceeds from its export of industrial products in the form of foreign currencies or in foreign exchange, for the same German total national economy must buy its raw material needs in cotton for the enormous textile industry, in copper for our likewise gigantic electrical industry, in silk, jute, tropical fruits, the increased demand, above the home production, in food and fodder, etc., to name just a few. The received amounts of foreign monies therefore must be immediately disbursed again. This is also quite natural, for in normal times one cannot do anything with foreign currencies in one's own country except exchange them. This is so even today. The American worker cannot be paid with French francs, and the English businessman is not paid in his shops with Italian liras. There is also no sense in taking the currencies to foreign countries where they cannot at all be used as a legal means of payment. The local currency serves and should only serve the internal needs of the country that issue the currency. Just as, within a national economy, the meaning of goods production does not lie in trading in money and in then sitting on the money and in withholding it from the economy, so too the international economic exchange of goods is completed only when import is paid for with export.

The theoretical ideal situation would be now that every country could cover and pay for its import need exactly with its export. Then, and only then, can one speak of an absolute stability of foreign currencies. Now the effort of every upward striving national economy understandably is directed at achieving an export surplus over the import need. Only this shows an increase in wealth. Then one speaks of an active balance of trade. If the import need remains over the export, elements of the internal wealth must be delivered to foreign countries for the balancing of this deficit. But these deliveries must, since they cannot indeed be extracted from the work income, once again be taken only from the wealth. This occurs either through the export of gold or of securities. Especially the last "export" however, is nothing but the beginning of the international Interest-Slavery. Whether this "export of securities" extends to existing internal securities or is disguised in the form of foreign "bonds" is practically a matter of indifference for the nations affected by it. But since also, in the international economic thinking, only the profitability madness of large loan capital rules, all reasonable doubts of an honorable national economy are trampled down by means of the press and the parliaments, and the international slavery of all nations to the international finance making this bond spreads to a frightful scope.

Even here in the international economy there are manifested the same phenomena as in the internal national economy and the frightful crises which shake the different national economies today are in the main a resulting phenomenon of this enslavement of all the nations of the western cultural circle, as we have already learnt above. The weak currency countries, whose internal economy has become too weak (Russia) or whose internal situation has become uncertain through revolution (Germany) and whose still gigantic production surpluses are confiscated free of cost as reparations from the enemy, have no more surplus purchasing power, they can therefore no longer pay for their import need for goods but with paper money which they throw in large quantities into foreign countries to buy foreign currency therewith. Thereby, they harm in a similar way both the internal economy and the foreign economies. The strong currency countries, on the other hand, choke precisely on the elevation of their currencies (Switzerland, for example). They can no longer export their products to the earlier large markets because their products are too expensive on account of the high exchange value of their money. These countries can cover their import needs easily with their strong currency. But when the finished products are much cheaper in the countries with bad currency, the traders and profiteers go to the weak currency countries and buy out and rob these countries to the disadvantage of both countries the disadvantage of the local production and the disadvantage of the consumption in the countries that are bought out, in which the already small inventory level of goods is reduced even further by these wild purchases. Thereby, the purchasing power of the national currency in the weak currency countries once again sinks.

That, in view of these fully topsy-turvy relations, everything has not already long ago collapsed is since, even above all the machinations of international finance, the mutual international need simply prevails. Only, everything happens at the last moment, with groaning and moaning, because the spanner the interest demands of international capital have been thrown into the works of the international economy. Or, expressed in medical imagery: In the healthy blood circulation of the international economy, at first small, but today already enormously large, carcinoma has set in which has only a one-sided interest of sucking up all the blood into itself at the cost of the rest of the body and to take a transit toll, an interest, from everything. All the blood, of course, flows into the heart, but the heart gives out also with each beat the contaminated blood. The state bank which serves only the pure monetary transaction corresponds precisely to this image and to the carcinoma corresponds most precisely the activity of international finance, which also controls all the money of the world through its credit banks and holds the entire international economy gripped in its suction arms and takes interest everywhere. All this is not necessary! The nations of the world do not in any way need supranational financial powers. Obviously, institutions are necessary which internationally regulate the international monetary transactions in the sense of a clearing house or in the sense of the postal cheque accounts. That can and will be taken care of by state-run foreign exchange offices.

In any case there are enough ways and means, quite like how it was possible to create an international postal union, to organize even the international payment transactions mainly through clearing, without the international finance benefiting two or three times in all these simple mercantile operations and becoming big and fat at the cost of the productive nations. Details are superfluous here.

The stabilization of a currency cannot, therefore, as emphasized, be separated from the inter-national relations. There is, however, a series of possibilities of removing the sources of error and the irresponsibility's that lie in the deficiencies of the internal administration or in the unrestricted manipulation of the note printing press.

The proposed measures all lie within the field of already tested systems; like the nationalization of the Reichsbank and the central banks, they arise simply as the logical consequences of a new position of the state towards its tasks as the protector of the monetary transactions. They only represent the natural reaction to conditions that served merely and solely the interest of high finance at the greatest cost of the people. The sensible extension of the nationalization of the Reichsbank is the regulation and mediation of the monetary transaction by the state according to the model of the postal cheque system, which will be further extended and more appropriately developed for this purpose.

All these measures indeed signify already quite powerful steps forwards, but they could be carried out also without the economic attitude having to be already basically transformed in the sense of the National Socialist principle presented with all emphasis: "The task of the economy is the covering of need and not the profitability of private capital."

This fundamental transformation and new ordering in the field of the financial and tax system, as well especially in the financing of large state tasks with an avoidance of the loan route, as well as the financial and political measures which indeed come close to the scope of functions of the field of social policy, will occupy us in the next chapter.

New Ways

The financing of large public works.

Among the most important state tasks is the execution of quite large economic undertakings whose execution exceeds the capital resources of private entrepreneurial circles, in whose execution moreover considerable public-legal interests are concerned and whose execution is based on the exploitation of natural resources or natural energy sources. Tasks, therefore, in which the exploitation of natural forces which belong to the community is at issue, or whose execution must occur within the range of the tasks that are mainly incumbent on the state, like the entire field of transport.

One sees that it is completely possible to limit the field rather precisely on which state initiative can be developed without limits being drawn thereby for the private entrepreneurial initiative or the state having to exert a competition to it. In addition, there is, beyond this, the fact that the execution of these large public works is naturally assigned almost totally to private enterprises.

We have already described in detail in the fundamental observations in what an exemplary way the state has built up our German transport system. Certainly, here and there it would have been more rationally and cheaply developed by private enterprise but, in the case of tasks in which the security of millions of men is at stake, it is not so much a question of that as of the greatest possible solidity. Now, the transport enterprise is a purely state task. Reliability, punctuality, security, uniform tariffs for railways and post must be the decisive viewpoints for the transport system and not the profitability of private capital.

But this question is closely connected to the form of the financing of such large public tasks.

We have already seen the internal nonsense that is revealed in the fact that the "credits" approved by the parliament must be "approved" afterwards again by private capital, for which the state then must take upon itself a quite extraordinary burden through the promise of interest. It will no longer be necessary here to point in a general way to the disastrous consequences of this promise of interest. The present work indeed serves mainly to prove this fact. Nevertheless, let a special reference be made here also to how extraordinarily more expensive, and in what an unbelievable way for everybody who hears these figures for the first time, this promise of interest on the state loans has made the railway tariffs, for instance.

The capital costs for the entire network of the German Reich-railways, which were built or undertaken through loans, amounted to around 25 billion gold marks up to 1914. The interest payments for this amount, with an average interest of 3.5%-4%, amounted to around 800-900 million gold marks. The net revenues, after the deduction of the costs for personal (officials and employees) and material (coal and lubricants) expenses, amounted to around 800-1100 million marks.

The interest payment thus consumed almost the entire net revenue of the German railways. It was always a misleading of the public opinion when it was explained with a certain pride that the revenues from the post and railways formed the backbone of the state budget. Of course, it could have been that, if only the interest payment had not consumed the entire net revenues. Another interesting parallel can be drawn in comparison, that is, that the total expenditures for wages and salaries to all the German railway officials and employees and to the railway workers in the plants, and on the line, taken together amounted to precisely only as much as this interest charge on loan capital did! In other words, the gigantic army of German railway workers up to the highest positions, with a head count of 782,731 persons, has received for its work only exactly as much income as the completely inactive hand of loan capital has pocketed.

This interest payment to loan capital just from the railways was greater than the entire expenditures for our entire large Reich-army of that time! And indeed, for everything that relates to it, thus also including the military supervision, the military administration of justice, including the systems of garrison administration and military construction, the military education and development system, the technical institutes, the relief and military widows' funds and, further, the clothing and arming of the troops! The entire amount for our entire army mounted in 1913, thus in the last full year of peace, to 775,385,300 marks. Such comparative figures provide a deep insight. While the socialist and democratic side constantly hustled against the "burden of the military armaments" in the parliamentary sessions and in the press, one also never finds even a single word against such interest burdens far from eclipsing all other expenses from public loans. Indeed, one could have paid the entire navy too out of the interests for the loan for the general need. The entire expenses for our proud Reich-navy amounted in 1913 to 197 million.

And one should consider that all these expenses could have been defrayed without a penny if our state budget had not been burdened with such gigantic interest burdens. A handful of large loan capitalists the couple of thousand 'hangers-on', of small savers with their possessions of a couple of thousand marks, do not at all play a role in such public loans thus pocketed year in year out, fully without work or effort, amounts with which we could have maintained and paid our entire Reich-administration, our entire army, and our navy.

One who, in view of such figures, does not acquire an understanding of the all-surpassing importance of the interest problem in general and of the fully failed national financial policy with its loan economy cannot indeed be helped. What is more, the figures and numbers which provide such an insight are accessible to everybody, they are found in the Statistical Yearbook for the German Reich published with the greatest conscientiousness by the former Royal Statistical Office and they are found likewise in the Statistical Yearbook for the German Reich, Puttkammer and Mühlbrecht Publishers, published by the Republican Statistical Reich-office.

That such imbalances between the necessary expenses for the Reich-administration, the army and navy and the expenditures of the state for the interest payment to loan capital become an injustice crying to the heavens will however become fully clear only when we examine in what way then the Reich now covers its monetary need for these interest payments. Here we come to the field of customs and taxes. I must point here once again to the thorough representation of this situation in my book The coming tax strike, where I have produced the conclusive proof that the largest part of all the taxes is borne by the wide masses of the working population. We thus have the fact before us that the state at first, in complete disregard of the possibilities lying in its financial sovereignty, ventures on the loan route for the execution of large public tasks, that is, incurs debts; that it then thereby further burdens its budget in such a way that it must use all its net revenues for the interest payment and that it further must oppress the people with duties and taxes only to be able to meet its interest obligations. All essentially necessary state tasks it must now combat in the provincial and Reich-parliament against the greatest resistance, and finally the state sees itself in the role of an interest-collector for the loan capital, as we see it today.

The way out has already been pointed out a long time ago after such a detailed examination of the present absurd conditions.

It is obvious; it is that:

The state will finance all large public undertakings of the Reich by virtue of its financial sovereignty and after approval by the population through the parliament with the strictest avoidance of the loan route through direct allocation of means through cashless transfer transactions or through the issue of interest-free state treasury notes.

I can make this measure clear best through an example: the development of the Bavarian hydro-energy.

The plans and efforts to make the enormous hydro-energy existing in the mountain rivers, in combination with the large mountain lakes, useful date back to already more than two decades ago. Unquestionably, in the case of this hydro-energy, it was a matter of energy sources of the country which belong to the community and were to be taken from it and used for personal profit. Thus, in the development of such large structures, many public and private legal interests were affected. It is a matter here of a field that belongs exclusively to the sphere of influence of the state. The people also now orally approved the credits through their representatives in December 1920. It had been sufficiently advised and tested and re-planned repeatedly and one was fully clear about the great economic advantages. The state and the people had decided to exploit the energy sources, now they had, with this credit approval, simply to take the corresponding decision that the amounts earned by the entrepreneurs could be paid out directly by the state bank based on the approved credits. Whether this would occur without cash, by way of transfer into the giro transactions, or through credit advice to postal cheque accounts or in cash is finally a matter of indifference.

It is obvious and clear, if we imagine that the state bank for such purposes would issue its own money to the amount of the necessary and approved credits. These hydro-energy construction notes thus represented, to a certain degree, state treasury notes that would be issued to the rising water works as an anticipatory credit under state guarantee. It was thus a matter of a money covered in manifold ways. The coverage consisted first in the ready or rising Walchensee work, etc. and secondly in the state guarantee that the money is accepted at full value from the public treasury instead of payment. The construction notes would be, at the same time, partial debentures on the waterworks, without interest claims, however, being bound to them. This is, however, as is well known, not the case with any other notes that are in circulation.

The hydro-energy construction notes could very well make these specifications on the full coverage of their value in the text of their imprint. For example: "This thousand-mark note finds its coverage partially in the value of the installation being erected for the exploitation of the Bavarian hydro-energy. It is accepted in all state treasuries as payment."

If one wishes to go further, there stands nothing in the way of the state's pledging to provide, after the completion of the work, against the deposit of the note, so many kilowatt hours of electricity or so many hundredweights of nitrogen.

Nobody would refuse to accept such money issued by the state that is completely covered by material goods, that can at the same time be used to some extent as a ration coupon for electricity. On the contrary, we may be sure that such a money would enjoy a special popularity, for this money is stable, exactly as stable as a dollar, or much better because one can receive for it a quite definite amount of electricity or nitrogen independent of economic fluctuations. It is a sign of the complete narrow-mindedness of men that in the public propaganda of different debaters, the objection arose that "nobody would accept this money."

No man has ever hesitated, even these debating gentlemen, to accept money that the state has issued. Everybody has accepted even the most damaged paper money from the Reichsbank, even though this money was pure inflation money. And yet everybody accepted it, even when the clever speculators tried to get rid of it as quickly as possible against foreign currency or goods. Indeed, nobody has refused even the emergency currency of cities and communities that was similarly uncovered paper money.

And now should such a preferable covered paper money as the construction money completely covered by material assets is for our large works not be accepted immediately? Surely, even those who raise such objections against interest-free government money on behalf of, or in the spirit of, their masters do not basically believe that. It is indeed proven to be irrefutable, despite all the complaints of the "metallists" who would like to consider as money only money made of precious metals, that "money" is that which the state declares to be money whether this money is constituted of paper or porcelain, iron or leather or any other material is a matter of complete indifference.

It is quite different when it comes to the purchasing power of this money. There the metallists are right that a currency made of gold by and large retains its exchange value even when political disturbances shake the state. This stability, however, the metallic money made of precious metals does not owe to its monetary character but to its character as a commodity, namely gold.

There can be no doubt at all about the justification of the state in covering its monetary need for a large work in the way described. First, the state is sovereign, that is, it does not need to be influenced by anybody, for it has the power, and, secondly, such a measure can stand up to the strictest commercial examination. The state issues with this cash in a way vouchers based on its credit. Why should anybody have less regard for the credit of the state than for the credit of any banks, especially when the state is producing useful works for the welfare of the community. Even if one said that the state however pays the performed work (the entrepreneurs and workers who are engaged in the Walchensee work) with paper, that is indeed right because later, after the completion of the works, the state accepts this paper once again as payment for the work performed by it (supply of electricity or nitrogen, etc.). Therewith, the economic cycle is completed. The construction notes are thus once again redeemed from the electricity supplies, etc. In the first years, the notes are destroyed, and a gigantic work of governmental organizational art has been created on an interest freeway as an interest-free possession for all. A work that has tapped, without a great burdening of the electricity consumers, another large source of money for the state which brings the state in turn closer to the ideal goal of a healthy national financial policy the state without taxes.

Now, there is, in addition, the fact that the described process with the issue of one's own construction money for a certain work does not at all necessitate the issue of the entire approved amount in such construction notes, because indeed by far the largest part of the payments to the entrepreneurs does not occur in cash but cash free, through transfers. But even assuming the case that one issued the entire new construction amount in new state bank notes, these amounts, in comparison with the other amounts that the state today needs, would not at all be considerable. While one broke one's head in the Bavarian parliament on account of the 800 million credits for the Bavarian hydro-energy or better: did not break but just resorted once again to "loan", 8000 million was approved in the parliament "without debate in the third reading for the purposes of the general emergency."

Here I recall once again the considerations that, in the case of such a financing through the new issue of money, no inflation of any sort would be brought about, that on the other hand the issue of interest-bearing bonds during the construction period in any case signifies a certain inflation since interests must already be paid even though no productive work is yet performed by the works.

In no way, however, is the national economic balance between money and material goods, in the sense of the quantity theory, affected for, against the increase of means of payment on the side of money, there stands an exactly greater increase in goods. If, then later, through the revenues of such works, the issued money is once again withdrawn and destroyed, then the national economic balance is naturally improved to the advantage of the national wealth according to the total value of such new works.

Even here let it is pointed out how severely the interest operates on the costs of the products of such works. Oskar Pöbing has determined in a detailed examination of this question that the production costs for a kilowatt hour are made more expensive through the burdening of the loans with interest to the enormous amount of 500% (!). Now the electricity from our Bavarian Hydro-electric works comes to us five times more expensively because we have once again resorted to the loan route that lies "closest at hand." Even here it is appropriate to imagine that the entire material and personal expenses for the operation and maintenance of the large Bavarian electric works and interurban offices thus all the wages and salaries for all persons occupied in these works sluice attendants, machinists, workers, laborers, supervisory personnel, and further the entire technical and commercial administrative apparatus up to the directors together draw for their work year in year out only a fifth part of the amounts that the so very good loan capitalists draw year in year out, without effort or work as interest.

Interest devours everything, interest makes everything more expensive. Only loan capital has the benefit, the population has the damage. The population that builds the works through its own strength has the damage; for who then builds the Bavarian works?

Indeed Bavarian engineers, Bavarian workers, Bavarian foremen and entrepreneurs; Bavarian factories supply most of the machines and equipment and for that which is not produced in Bavaria itself Bavarian grain or cattle must be given, thus Bavarian work must once again be given in exchange only the Bavarian people do not put up the money for the construction (apparently!), and so for that it needs the large capitalists from New York and London, Paris and Berlin. The Bavarian people must borrow from all the countries of the world and burden its hydro-energy with an interest payment, which makes the electricity 500% more expensive! Is this not madness? Is this not an economic crime?

Of the people who have done nothing but at one time set their pen in motion and written out a cheque or directed their banker to sign the Bavarian hydro-electric loan, these receive for that, year after year, interests paid by the Bavarian people. Not only that, but the waterworks are therewith no longer a free possession of the Bavarian people, but they are pledged to the capitalist. Especially funny is, further, the situation that the large capitalists would naturally not lend "their good money" to a state which is not in itself "good" for capital and interests, which therefore still enjoys so much credit that one can pump 800 million into it. And in fact, the tenders for the hydro-electric bonds contained the guarantee that is so enticing and assuring to the capitalists "that the Bavarian state with its entire wealth guarantees for capital and interests – (!)"

Moneybag, what more do you want!? So here the Bavarian state admits expressly that it is worth so much, that one could loan to it 800 million for the Walchensee hydro-energy and the Middle Isar but it cannot use its financial sovereignty and finance these works through its own authority. Why?? Because it is too deeply enmeshed in the loan and interest madness, because its responsible state leaders do not have so much thinking capacity and feeling of responsibility of their own that they dare to judge these simple and clear plans for an interest free financing by themselves; they therefore turn to the professional banking experts.

This is exactly as if a consumptive were to ask his tuberculosis bacilli whether they thought it right that he goes to Davos or to Engadin[78] to get rid of his illness, and these assured him: "No, just do not do this, the journey could harm you, perhaps a railway accident may occur, rather stay at home in your house, in your usual environment. In your condition you should not make any experiments! etc." With the adherence to this advice that is from the viewpoint of the tuberculosis bacilli quite right, the consumption naturally makes ripping progress. The bacilli multiply wonderfully. Exactly so in our case of the financial and interest economy.

This getting advice from one's own opponents is extremely characteristic of the unsuspecting Germans. If a man appears who loves his people passionately and advises them this and that and alerts the responsible men to this or that knavery, one can bet ten to one that the concerned people would run to the knave and ask him naively:

"Tell me, so and so has told me you are a rascal, please tell me if that is right!"

And if the other than explains to him with the most honest face in the world:

"But what do you think?! that I am a scoundrel! On the contrary, I am your best friend, I have always helped you out of our financial difficulties", then the guileless questioner is quite happy he has done enough, and he is especially glad that he does not have to strain his brain. The troublesome friend of the people, however, he does not in general deem worthy of his answer and things are further stuck in the rut of the interest capitalistic loan policy until the last item of free national wealth is pledged to the financial powers and the entire nation only pays interest to the international finance.

In conclusion we must, precisely in this context, further point to the fact that the Bavarian state when it was not in any way a matter of such an important state task as the development of the Bavarian hydro-energy however is, that is, when it was a matter of remedying the monetary crisis of the November government was very prompt in issuing from the Bavarian state bank around 130 million state treasury notes of the Bavarian State Bank. This happened completely uncovered and everybody took these Bavarian notes exactly as willingly as the notes of the Reichsbank, and everybody could buy for himself as much bread for the Bavarian vouchers as for the Reichsbank notes. Indeed, it did not even have to be the entire Bavarian state; it was enough if the mayor of the provincial capital Munich and some city elders had their names printed on such colorful bits of paper, and even this emergency money circulated, everybody took it and everybody gave it out exactly like the scraps of the Reichsbank, and this emergency money itself fulfilled the task of any money of being an aid for the exchange of goods in an unobjectionable way.

Only one office was extremely unpleasantly affected by these artificial pieces of the provinces and communities' high finance, and they forced a Reich law in October 1921, according to which it was strictly forbidden to the provinces and communities to issue emergency money any further. This law was in its effect a clear law for the protection of the Jews, which was to be followed in 1922 by the "Law for the protection of the republic."

I can very well imagine the sudden fear of international finance when they recognized that in the interest-free money, even in the harmless form of emergency money, the people held in their hand a weapon naturally without the people knowing this which could with one stroke tear apart the golden network established with lies and deception through centuries-long underground and counterfeit work and liberate the peoples from their Interest-Slavery.

Already at that time, in the case of the issue of the Bavarian state money, the Reichsbank demanded very soon that this money had to be withdrawn once again, which also then occurred in a compliant manner in the course of 1921. The reason: this money brought high finance, no interests as the money of the Reichsbank does through the indirect route of the Reich's treasury bills.

In the National Socialist state, in the future, all large state tasks will be financed and organized in the way described with a total avoidance of the loan route. We shall naturally take the indirect route of the interest free construction money in general only if the necessary means cannot be raised from the surpluses of other state enterprises or from special levies for such special purposes. In any case, we know that this form of financing opens quite undreamt of and enormous possibilities of tapping the natural resources of the country, improving the transport routes, etc.

Every nation is as rich as it can organize work.

The Social Construction & Economic Bank

In logical connection with the previous chapter stands the creation of a social construction and economic bank which has the task of issuing interest-free construction money, especially for the construction of houses. Of course, this social construction and economic bank should not be conducted as a state institution, but as a corporation of public law. Logically therefore the discussion of it should come after the representation of the National Socialist tax system, but since this social construction-and economic bank is nothing but the interest free financing transferred to the conditions of the private economy and indeed especially to the housing construction system thus a branch of the economy of the most universal significance, placing it first is perhaps justified.

Why such a construction bank should not be conducted as a pure state enterprise is because such a public legal, financial institution must be more freely maneuverable than a state enterprise can be. It would not be so much of a reason if it was a matter of only mere housing construction, but there will be many cases where it is a matter of tasks of the greatest importance which indirectly affect the public interest, and then the bank, which is indeed responsible in its leadership to the state for its management, should and must have a free hand in issuing also interest-free credit after a thorough examination of all conditions.

Such freedom of decision, however, is not possible in purely state enterprises. That is why this must be left to private initiative. By way of illustration may be presented here the sketch of such a law which was passed in 1922 for Bavaria: Law on the development of a Bavarian social construction and economic bank.

Art. I

A national Bavarian social construction and economic bank (BWB) shall be founded. The BWB has the task of financially supporting enterprises of the state or national economically valuable enterprises of private persons (whether it be individuals or societies) which serve the development of the country or are beneficial to the general welfare.

Art. 2

The BWB is a corporation of public law. The more detailed prescriptions regarding its organization, its administration and activity and its directorship will be decreed by the entire ministry.

Art. 3

Permission is granted to the BWB to issue at first interest-free treasury notes covered by material assets to an amount of up to 50 million gold marks. The issue may occur only in such a legal way that the amount of the money amounts issued at any time and in circulation is covered by material securities of at least the same value (interest-free security mortgages, security bills of sale, hypothecations, etc.) and the repayment or the return of the treasury notes is secured by the revenues of the enterprises or institutions to be developed within an appropriate time limit, at most 50 years.

Art. 4

The sum of the pledges and securities due to the issued treasury notes of the BWB constitutes the coverage association of the BWB.

Legal transactions of any sort which disturb or harm a security or property coverage belonging to the coverage association are void.

Property or possession changes of any sort to objects or rights subject to the coverage organization do not affect the existence of the securities and remain attached to the object even for the new purchaser; the predecessor in title is freed of personal liability only when the BWB agrees with the change in the person of the debtor. Contrary arrangements are void...

Art. 5

The entire constituents and rights of the coverage organization of the BWB are recorded in this public register; the principles and legal consequences are valid for this book correspondingly as for registers; the register has public confidence and the presumption of right. Access to the register or the pertinent sections of it is to be granted to everybody who evidences a legal interest in the access. Balance-like summaries are to be published annually on the total amounts of the issued treasury notes, as well as the total amount of the securities due to the BWB for these, as well as additions and deductions, and on the successful repayments and redemptions of treasury notes.

Art. 6

The treasury notes of the BWB are legal currency. Everybody must accept them at the full rate of their face value against the exchange rate of the other legal currencies of the state. If a creditor refuses the acceptance of treasury notes of the BWB instead of payment at the above-mentioned minimum rate of exchange, the debtor is, insofar as he has offered the payment in treasury notes, freed of the debt of this amount. The BWB issues the treasury notes interest-free and agrees upon, in a contract, the general and special conditions of the mutual legal conditions regarding the periods and rates of the issue, the securities and mortgages to be paid by the debtor, as well as the repayments and other pertinent legal conditions. A copy of these contracts is to be made accessible to all as an appendix to the entries in the register of the coverage association. The BWB is justified in determining surcharges or fees for the administrative costs in the commitment of loans and for the yearly collections or in determining corresponding premiums or discounts at any time in a uniform public manner. The issue or the stock-exchange quotation of a higher rate than the minimum rate determined in Art. 1 is permissible. The repayments can be made only in treasury notes of the same sort as those issued.

Art. 7

The activity of the BWB, insofar as it extends to the observation of the prescriptions contained in this law, is subject to the control and supervision of a public supervisory council consisting of the Finance Minister or a representative to be named by him, the Minister of the Interior or a representative to be named by him, the Justice Minister or a representative to be named by him and three persons to be elected from the parliament for a duration of two years.

Art.8

Penalty clause: Imprisonment penalties for intentional damages to the securities of the coverage association and likewise for commercial or customary, especially stock-exchange, sabotage of the construction bank notes or the exchange rate value of the same or for an attempt to do so. In addition, high monetary penalties for this, even to juristic persons. In the "executive conditions" precise prescriptions were then issued on the constitution of the board of directors and the advisory board to which belong representatives of the ministries, the parliament, and the builders. The task of such an advisory board is the control of the legal use of the construction notes, the examination of the repayments, further the verification of the hypothecary indemnities, the approval of the bases of the mortgaging with interest-free construction notes, etc. The further conditions then regulated the repayment and clearance, the stock-postings on the issued series of construction notes and on the securities registered for it, and, further, more prescriptions on the approved construction designs, etc. At that time, the inducement to the establishment of such a social bank was provided by the enormous housing need and the circumstance that the Reich and provinces could not in any way control the distress in an effective way. The concerned institutions of housing offices could, of course, free up living spaces here and there, but they could not build any new housing. The new construction activity suffered from a lack of materials, above all from the fact that, with the existing emergency control of rents, the construction of new houses was absolutely "unprofitable" for private capital. The grants given by the Reich and the provinces for the coverage of the so-called lost construction-expenditure were not sufficient by far in the progressing currency devaluation. Even the individual housing constructions begun here and there could not remove the general housing distress. Even the creation of cheap mortgage monies was impossible because, with the rents fixed at that time, even the cheapest construction money precluded a 4% interest. It happens therefore that, as already suggested in the fundamental observations, despite the greatest need on account of insufficient profitability, the need is simply not covered.

Now then, if one succeeds in removing the annually recurring interest burdens, if one makes provisions to place interest-free means at the disposal of those needing housing, a stimulation of the housing market in a grand style is possible. Therewith however would not only the frightful housing need with all its social and health damages be removed but also the internal market would be stimulated in an extraordinary manner because all the innumerable ancillary trades, the locksmiths, carpenters, roofers, plumbers, the glaziers, installers, ceramists, the floor-layers and tilers, the painters and plasterers depend on it, they then for their part find work and bread and are strengthened in their purchasing capacity.

This means, however, is offered in the interest-free construction money.

These construction notes are issued by the "Social Construction and Economic Bank." The suppliers and entrepreneurs are paid for the construction with this money. The building owner pays the received interest-free money back in appropriate instalments within a period of 30-50 years according to the character and durability of the construction. The construction notes are different from the Reich's or provincial money rather in the same manner that the Reichsbank notes were different from the loan treasury notes. These construction notes find, as already mentioned, their full material coverage in the fact that, at the same time there arise, to the credit of the construction bank, equal in amount to the issued notes, new material assets (houses) which are legally secured through the registration of interest-free mortgages to the same amount.

Practically also here the full value of the new buildings will not be given in construction notes but only the actual building expenditure. The land will therefore have to be made available at least by the builders or the building societies or the communities and, beyond this, at least 10-30% of the building value must be produced by those in need of housing, of which 5% is to be retained there for the coverage of the administrative costs of the construction bank.

The repayment then follows without further calculation of any interest. In this manner, the free property of the house-owners grows from year to year in their houses and likewise the values retained within the total association as coverage for the issued construction notes. Thereby, the amount of construction notes in circulation diminishes according to the repayments affected.

The legal character of this construction money is nothing other than the issue of a bond. The debtor of this bond is the construction bank. The creditor of a bond is the current owner of this bond.

Nobody can be forbidden to issue bonds. It is always only a question of the external circumstances whether the bonds issued by somebody are accepted generally as payment. As mentioned, many times before, the construction notes are always and under any conceivable economic and political condition fully covered by the material assets against these. There can therefore be no question of the bank's falling into difficulties at any time.

The universal acceptance is however guaranteed the moment that the state pledges to assume the guarantee for the time-limited redemption of the construction notes and, during the duration the notes, to accept the notes in their registers as payment or when they are declared to be a legal means of payment.

Such an acceptance of the guarantee now does not mean for the state, practically, the least burdening; on the contrary. Today, the state must spend and pay interest on, and then recoup through general taxes, uncounted millions yearly for the grants approved by it for lost construction expenditure. This is then fully cancelled.

The grants now given by the state are thus really lost money which must be recouped by the community, and which go to some lucky people who were indeed able to grab such grants.

Thus, even when a delinquent payer among the receivers of interest-free construction notes at some time cannot meet his obligations, this does not play any role in relation to the enormous savings which the state budget makes because it also does not, in this way, must make any sacrifices that are fully lost.

Since it is a question of a task of great social significance, it is justified to establish an independent public legal corporation as the instrument and bearer of its execution.

In this way, this institution will be removed from the sphere of the private economic social forms to which naturally personal profits and enrichment intentions are attached in the eyes of the people. On the other hand, the institution will be removed from the domain of the pure state enterprise, against which likewise, not entirely without injustice, a certain aversion exists in all economic matters among the public.

In the implementation regulations, everything is to be recorded that is basically indispensable for the public and for the security of the business management of the bank. The proposed advisory council can make its influence felt beyond this. The advisory council itself is again a reflection of all the interest groups concerned. The establishment of a construction bank as a public legal corporation also has the pleasant by-effect that in this way the entire complex of the wealth values created in this manner does not appear as the property of the state but as the property of an independent legal entity, which is the construction bank.

The juridical construction or the legal character of this construction bank is thus the following: The construction bank is a legal entity by virtue of the circumstance that it is recognized or established as a public legal corporation; this construction bank does not at all consist of individual members; it is in itself the bearer of the rights and duties that are developed from its activity. It is, however, also not an official and not a state institution, not a member of a state organism.

The creation of such a legal form is indeed not something common and traditional; but nevertheless, something already provided for in the law; the present-day conditions, however, demand corresponding institutions of a modern sort. Herein indeed will lie the service when something of this sort is established: that, in a certain way, one goes beyond the limits of the traditional to adapt to the demands of the age.

How the conduct of the businesses proceeds is to be explained best with an individual example: The construction bank makes known in advance the fundamentals and preconditions which must be fulfilled if a request for approval of construction-bank money is to be considered. The applicant directs his request with the necessary documents to the construction-bank and, in affirmative cases, concludes a contract with those in need of housing (house owners).

In this contract is to be provided in the first place everything that the construction-bank ordinance and implementation regulations prescribe, thus the obligation to use the construction money only for the construction of the building, the obligation to a mortgage status and the repayment obligations. But, furthermore, all other pursuant legal conditions are to be laid down in this contract. It must especially be determined that the one in need of housing is not justified in selling the property again, which is moreover already highlighted practically in the mortgage order. The conditions for the devolution of inheritance and for the case of default of payment are to be regulated correspondingly with one or more repayment instalments.

(Details arise from the nature of this matter).

Because all delivery firms and all workers are paid only in construction-bank notes which the construction bank itself produces, construction bank notes come into circulation for the first time in all circumstances only to the extent that the equivalent in payments accrues to the property. From the workers and suppliers, the construction-bank notes reach the public; in consideration of the existing securities and especially because the state assumes the guarantee for the construction bank notes and state treasuries accept the construction-bank notes as payment, the public will accept the construction-bank notes like any other money. So, it remains left to the house owner how he fulfils his obligation to the construction-bank of repaying annually 2% of the loaned amounts in construction-bank notes. In other words, the building owner and mortgage debtor of the construction-bank must produce every year 2% in construction-bank notes from the amounts found in circulation. Practically it will happen that the mortgage debtors will collect construction-bank notes which indeed circulate along with the local money before the expiry date of their repayment dues and therewith satisfy their payment obligation. An especially suited place where to get construction-bank notes will be the construction sites that are to be found in operation at any time.

If one supposes, to have an idea, that in a year construction bank notes are issued in Munich for 10 million, from this annually 200,000 gold marks will return to the construction-bank; thus, after 50 years at most, the entire 10 million will have returned and been collected by the construction bank. After 50 years, at most, the houses built from it are therewith repaid and become the debt-free property of their owners. The entire payment has occurred without a penny being paid uselessly for interests; the payment is further accomplished through nothing but the simple means of the establishment of the construction-bank, bound with the state guarantee.

The social act consists in the fact that the state has produced the value of the houses absolutely from nothing, that it created an income for thousands of workers and businessmen through the construction of this entire building. If one supposes that it is a matter of thousands of individual houses, thousands of landless are therewith transformed into landed persons.

Different objections and reservations will be made, of which the most important may be suggested:

1. The objection of inflation. This objection is as short-sighted as it is irrelevant; as already explained in earlier passages, an inflation can arise only where uncovered money is issued. Here the material coverage stands against the construction-bank notes; it is therefore inconsequential if even considerable amounts of construction-bank notes come into circulation.

2. The objection that this matter is new and untested. This objection is inapplicable, and the matter is new, perhaps for Germany. Elsewhere, one is used to such interest-free debt certificates covered by material assets. The typical example of this is the English warrant, which was introduced a hundred years ago and is still preserved. The warrant is an order that gives the owner the right to a certain amount of crude iron lodged in a certain central storehouse. These warrant notes are used as currency; the purchasing power of the warrant has only those fluctuations to which the crude iron price is subjected on the world market.

If we had in Germany, for example, such warrants, these would have been completely independent of the German currencies and their fluctuations. The value of these warrants was related to the crude iron price, and the value of these prices, in turn, was automatically regulated in relation to the currency.

In the warrant, we find the significant example of the popular nature of this interest-free debt certificate and debt-order covered by a material asset.

Where considerable and national economically important erections of new buildings must be realized, it is imperative to construct entire colonies in series.

It would be a defective viewpoint if one wished to construct individual houses or even terrace houses only when the person looking for a house himself wishes to become an owner. The damage that must be remedied is the housing distress, it is thus not a matter mainly of housing, but it is a matter primarily of the creation of housing opportunities. This need will also be remedied by the fact that the commercial construction of rental flats is promoted. Nothing, therefore, prevents a rental house owner of the old style from receiving construction-bank notes for the construction of a new rental house. Precisely in the case of such persons, it will be possible to demand in advance in cash a greater prepayment than only 10% of the entire building value; many of these people are ready and, in a position, to spend considerable sums of money from their own means for housing construction if they receive as a grant a corresponding remainder or partial amount interest-free from the construction-bank. Precisely the interest-free nature of the construction-bank money makes it possible to take into consideration this aspect of the revival of the building market that is so extremely important for big cities.

This social construction-and economic bank however will also pass over later beyond the limits of the financing of housing buildings to issuing interest-free credits to national economically important undertakings, industries, communal works, improvements in agriculture, etc., even if with a shorter repayment time-limit.

The State Without Taxes

The one of many main goals of the National Socialist state is the state without taxes. If this may sound under the present-day circumstances like a mad Utopia, if it may seem too many as a promise that is too good to be true, we know nevertheless that this goal is completely reachable, at least insofar as the enormous tax pressure must be removed from the population.

With all clarity, have we presented in the preceding chapters the proof that today almost all taxes are devoured just by interest payment? We pay taxes in every piece of bread that we eat, every warm parlor costs an excess of taxes, ever purchase is burdened with the sales tax. But everything that goes into taxes in this way is not, by far, sufficient to pay the taxes on the reparation debts alone.

It always betrays a lack of taste and critical understanding if one dismisses such a principal goal as doubtlessly the state without taxes is as a utopia. For one who has gone with us on the wide and convoluted paths of the present-day financial politics and one who has not lost the Ariadne thread the interest obligation of the state it must be an easy thing to also find the way out of this labyrinth of the Minotaur.

One who raises himself above the degradations and surveys from an elevated standpoint the connections described: interest obligation of the state-tax-inflation, one who has recognized the interest obligation of all nations of the western cultural circle as the fact dominating everything, one who has recognized that we live in an age of a complete reversal of the healthy and reasonable conditions between work and wealth, one who can no longer avoid the pressing logic that especially the state, by virtue of its financial sovereignty, is not completely bound to the loan route but that it can creatively finance through its own right all large public state tasks, for him it is only the last step into a financial-political New World to demand a state in which the state financial administration does not consider it as its first task to extract as much tax as possible from the state citizens but, on the contrary, to remove every burdensome tax pressure and to fertilize the national economy.

We can present the numerical evidence that the state without taxes is not at all a Utopia but that the possibility of that is given in every orderly state budget if the state frees itself from the interest burden lying upon it. That it can do this also without it being called to account for it is proved by the history of state bankruptcies which relates dozens of cases in which the states have through bankruptcy escaped from the interest and debt burdens lying upon them.

It would take us too far afield to go into detail here once again into the precise demonstration that I have given in my small polemical work, The state bankruptcy: The solution, that, namely, the adjustment of the interest payment from the public loans in a simultaneous transformation of the bonds into interest-free bank assets does not in any way deserve the disreputable name of bankruptcy but that this form of liberation of the state and people from its interest-bound debt actually signifies the freedom of the state and economy from unbearable chains.

An adjustment of these interest payments, however, would have made possible, already before the war, the coverage of state expenses for the entire state administration. I have presented the Bavarian state budget of 1911 as an example. At that time, the revenues of the Bavarian state from the so-called commercial state enterprises (railways, post, and telegraph) amounted to 120 million gold marks, the revenues from the state forestry 40 million. The total expenses for the entire state administration for the administration of justice (all district courts with their entire personnel and material expenses, all provincial courts, the regional courts, and the highest law courts in Munich, Nürnberg, etc.) Amounted to 27 million. For the entire large and so carefully developed internal administration of the entire Bavarian state thus for the numerous district courts, for the county governments, for the police department of Munich, for the gendarmerie, further for the numerous other bodies and authorities like the medical authorities, the provincial vaccination hospital, the research institutions for food and semi-luxury foods, the sanatoriums and mental asylums, the administrative court, the provincial statistical office, the metrological authorities, the insurance chambers, etc., in 1911, 40 million was disbursed in the state budget. For education, school and church, thus especially for all the middle schools, the secondary schools, the preparatory schools, the Latin schools, the secondary education schools, the junior high schools, the higher vocational schools, the teacher training institutions, for all the state construction schools and specialist schools, the trade and music schools, the agricultural and district farming schools, for Weihenstephan[80] and for the biological research institute, for all the women's educational institutes, and then, above all, for the universities with their innumerable collections and institutes, the technical university, for the other arts universities, for the trade universities, for the academy of music, then for the Maximilianeum[81], further for the central institutes for science and art, the academy of sciences, the scientific collections of the state, the Bavarian museums, the state library, the state theatre, etc., for these enormous field of activities of the Ministry of Culture with its thousands of officials, with its enormous art treasures in the collections and museums, all of which indeed require buildings, administration and care, in 1911, 51 million in all were disbursed. Within the field of the Finance Ministry, which indeed does not merely exercise functions that extract money from the people, lie the activities of the forest administration with hundreds of foresters, further the administration of mines, smelting works, salt works, the entire central and subsidiary customs offices, the central minting office, the state debt administration and the state bank, furthers the surveyor's offices and the provincial surveying office, then also the state spa administrations, the court brewery office, Munich, etc. This likewise very large enterprise caused an expense of 15 million. The expenses of the Transport Ministry were covered by its own operational revenues. On the other hand, the pensions of the old civil servants demanded further the very high amount of around 36 million.

Thus, altogether the justice administration, the internal administration including the buildings which I have not specifically mentioned above and the finance administration, as well as the education and development, and the pensions demanded 27 + 40 + 51 + 13 + 36 = 167 million.

The surpluses that the state enterprises, post and railways, mines, and forests, delivered to the state treasury at around 160 million would thus have almost sufficed to cover the entire gigantic state administrative apparatus without a penny of taxes!

The state without taxes would thus have been a reality, if the total taxes extracted from the Bavarian people, that is, 60 million of direct taxes and 53 million of indirect taxes, and in addition 31 million fees, altogether thus 134 million, had not had to be used completely for the interest payment to loan capital. The interest payment for the Bavarian state debts alone demanded 84.6 million (!) and Bavaria had to deliver 50 million to the Reich, likewise, for the interest payment from the Reich's debt.

I have given a brief overview of the large and small fields of our state life. This appears also especially important because National Socialism also bears in mind how extraordinarily much and how much exemplary work the old state performed, much that requires no reform and no improvement insofar as it does not have to do with matters that can never be concluded. Even for every state organism, it is true that it cannot stand still if it does not wish to become ossified. In many a field, a fresher and freer spirit will not harm, and here and there, thorough reforms are appropriate. In many branches of our administrative apparatus, at least a new spirit must enter, especially the spirit of the definite responsibility of the civil servant about his tasks and the people whom he serves.

Only one field was forced into false ways: the state financial administration. If such circumstances as the ones just described are possible, this is indeed a sign that here a radical change must be affected. Now this is true, however, already for the state before the war already at that time, the state was yoked into the interest service for the private loan capital. Nothing reveals in a more striking manner the dependency of the state on loan capital already existing at that time than a survey of the distribution of the taxes on the different forms of income. According to the budget for 1911, that we have based our observations up to now upon, landed property was assessed at 12.6 million, house property at 12.1 million, the commercial enterprises at 17 million, but on the other hand, capital pensions with a total pension income of 253 (!) million gold marks at only 10 million. This is thus really an extremely indulgent treatment of those who can live without effort and work at the cost of the working population.

The myriad small pension incomes we are thinking thereby of the pension group of 70-700 million marks represent indeed in numbers the predominant mass of capital pension tax obligations, that is, around 150,000, but neither their income from capital interests nor their tax payment, at around 0.7 million, would play a role in the state budget, but what makes these figures so noteworthy for us is the circumstance that the large loan capital has created in these hundred thousands of small interest receivers a powerful protective guard against all attacks against the effort and work-free income from interest.

It is naturally easy to persuade these small interest receivers that their savings must guarantee to a certain extent a lasting claim to interests, for the similarity of these people who have toiled their whole life long and have worked for their savings to the pension receivers in the state and employees' conditions is obvious. But what differentiates this attitude from the idea of a pension is the essential difference that the pension claim depends on the person and is terminated at death, whereas the interest claim is a material one and is bound independently of the person in an impersonal way to the bare possession of money as an "eternal legal claim."

We shall deal with these connections further in the discussion of the general old age pensions, because these observations would allow us to find the transition from unjustified eternal interest to the justified claim of every national comrade to a carefree old age.

These small interest receivers do not come into consideration in the question that we are dealing with of the remarkable indulgent treatment of loan capital on the part of the old state, but only those who swallow the lion's share of the capital pensions and who then step forth again as the great financial donors of the state.

So away with this national economic nonsense of an interest, capitalistically oriented state financial administration and out into the free National Socialist state of work and performance freed of all taxes.

Once the state is freed of the lead-weight of its interest obligations, then one will see what the state can achieve. If new sources of revenue of a large scope come in addition, like the tapping of hydro-energy and the natural resources of the country, then the state without taxes will no longer be a utopia but a joyful reality.

If we nevertheless wish to speak of a tax policy of the National Socialist state, this is because from such tax sources the means could flow for many tasks which await a state solution, for which however there were never any more means in the state budget. We are thinking here of the broad fields of national health, the fight against venereal diseases, alcohol abuse, the promotion of physical sports, the more substantial promotion of art and science, maternity leave, children's care, the construction of garden-cities and above all the acquittance of the debt of honor of the German people to its war-wounded and war-widows and orphans.

The following should be taken as guiding principles for a National Socialist state system in the field of tax policy:

1. A taxation for purposes of interest payment for internal loans is excluded.

2. Taxes are only permissible for the coverage of state expenditures for unproductive purposes, for administration, administration of justice, the military, police and health system and education, insofar as the surpluses of the commercial state enterprises, the railways, post, telegraph, state forests and state mines, as well as the electricity supply from the large state inter-urban bases, do not suffice for their coverage.

3. For the coverage of special needs or for special emergencies, thus especially for the case of war, direct and indirect taxes are not only permissible but commanded.

4. Direct taxes can be placed on property in any form, but here a far-reaching gradation is to be planned. The income is to be left tax-free up to an appropriate extent. In this case, it should be considered more thoroughly than up to now whether the taxpayer has a family with children or other care duties.

5. State officials are basically to be left freed of taxes. For married people, children's allowances are to be guaranteed.

6. Indirect taxes come into consideration in normal times only for luxury objects. The state has herein an excellent means at hand of operating in a way that would control and increase the prices on the production of articles that serve only the nuisance of attractive luxury, lavishness and gluttony in eating and drinking, and the excesses of fashion. Even pure semi-luxury goods like tobacco, alcohol, wine, insofar as they do not serve health purposes, will bear indirect taxes. On the other hand, all indirect taxes, such as exploiting the people today in its entirety, are to be fundamentally avoided. We mean here all the nonsensical indirect taxes that operate only in a price-increasing manner, on sugar, salt, matches, lamps, lemonade, also the taxes on coal that make the production radically more expensive,

also the taxes on personal and goods transport, and above all the commodity sales taxes.

7. The collection of war and revolution profits are to be carried out as a task of justice. For such a task naturally, the foundation of a reasonable basis of calculation on which one can compare the present wealth with the earlier must first be created. Obviously, here too, a difference is to be made again between the wealth that arises from productive work, for which the war, however, signified a special boom. It is no more than right and proper that from such quite significant war profits, a part is directed to the community. On the other hand, a much sharper evaluation is to be made in the case of that wealth, which arises from intermediary trade and speculation.

8. Stamp duties and fees, even taxes that restrict the free right of disposal of elements of wealth, insofar as this disposal is not directed against the general welfare, are to be limited where possible. To this belong also the inheritance and gift taxes.

Fundamentally the tax and financial policy should strive for the final goal of the "state without taxes", for it is not the task of the state to extract money from its citizens to perpetuate a basically false state loan economy, but to raise the general welfare of the people. The state is not there to be the interest collector for large loan capital but to protect the person and property of its state citizens and to make the natural resources of the country serviceable to the community. The means for the unproductive state tasks should, as already described, be taken primarily from the surpluses of the commercial state enterprises, and secondly from luxury taxes, thirdly from wealth and income that lie beyond that which can be obtained through the mere performance of work, and only then from the propertied middle-class, as well as from indirect taxes on semi-luxury goods whose use is not vitally necessary. And only in wartimes, in which the life of the entire nation is threatened, can the state demand that even the community as it can indeed demand military service from everybody through its service sovereignty –, and once again with special reference to the propertied classes, make its financial contribution to the conduct of the war in the form of indirect and direct taxes.

In conclusion, we may say something more about the question of the "commercial state enterprises." One now prefers to point to the fact that state enterprises are not "profitable." We have already discussed at length the fundamental question of profitability.

In the effort to conduct the railways, etc. "In a business-like way", to "free them from the uneconomic state enterprise" or "to bring them into a mixed economic form" is hidden only the badly concealed desire of large loan capital to make even this considerable wealth component of the nation serviceable to itself. If the state hands over even these components of wealth, then it is fully delivered to loan capital, and it has, apart from the permission to act as an interest collector for the loan capital, no more field in which it is sovereign, or in which it can operate in a regulatory manner and from which it can obtain considerable revenues for the coverage of its tasks.

The Financial-Political Liberation

We described first what measures are to be taken to make circumstances such as we experience now impossible in the future. These tasks indeed demand creative services, but they can nevertheless be achieved without the existing legal conditions having to be damaged or changed. It is different from the breaking of the existing chains of the interest-bound debt of our state to its internal and external creditors.

The measures to be taken here are in themselves extremely simple, only their execution will cause many difficulties. The remedy for the eternal interest obligation from internal loans is the legal abolition of this interest payment. On the other hand, large loan capital will, pleading the interests of the small pensioners, raise a great hue and cry and issue the most frightful threats against a state that "tramples inviolable rights under its feet", which "commits a breach of law which will rob it of its last shred of trust." Large capital will naturally move all levers to prevent "the enormous crime against basic economic laws." Naturally! one cannot really expect that an international power will suddenly renounce its claim to rulership.

In this battle, it is only a matter of maintaining iron nerves and not allowing oneself to be frightened by the howl of the press coolies who are maintained by high finance.

The Jew will conduct this battle with the most tenacious doggedness, for it is a matter of "his honor" as the old Rothschild said: "My money is my honor, and one who takes my money takes away my honor from me."

Now indeed their money should in no way be taken from the owners of the state bonds, but legal demands must just be removed that have in their effect become a very great injustice to the national community.

But from the viewpoint of the state, as well as from the viewpoint of the population who must raise the enormous amounts through their work to satisfy these "legal demands of the state creditors", it is not a matter of "legal demands" but of the greatest injustice of all times of a lasting robbery of the working people in favor of a small section of large capitalists with state support. A state which makes the "breaking of Interest-Slavery" a fact does not in any way commit an injustice, but it atones for a quite powerful injustice for the perpetration of which it itself has performed stooge-service.

Of course, this means a complete reorganization of the present state; it must decide if it wishes to serve the whole or whether it, as now, wishes to be the bailiff of international finance. On this question, there are no compromises. Here, only a determined clampdown can lead to the goal and to the remedy.

The National Socialist state is indeed conscious of this powerful decision. It would be extremely difficult to take such a decisive step if we did not know exactly what we must set up in place of the interest capitalistic economy. But because we know this, we go with the most complete certainty of victory into this greatest battle of world-history. We know that the rule of interest is built only on lies and deception and, because we know and have clearly recognized this, we know also that such a spider's web of lies and deception, however arduous it may have been spun, can be torn apart with one tug.

Only one more question, the last, must occupy us, the question: What will foreign nations say to such a radical reform and especially to a refusal of further interest payments to foreign interest creditors?

Yes, what will foreign nations say to that? This question is already in itself so extremely significant for our German distress and for the cosmopolitan attitude of the largest circles. What in general are "foreign nations"? Are they the French, the English, the Americans? Are they the Swedes and Dutch and Norwegians? Are they the Russians or the Chinese? Or are they the Indians or the Fuegians[82] or the Congolese negroes? Indeed, all these people belong to "foreign nations" in relation to us. Now, by far the greatest number of all these "foreigners" will not say anything at all, the smallest number of Chinese, also the smallest number of Russians and French will know in general what it is about. Finally, there remain the governments of our war enemies and then naturally as the ones really interested the Jewish international bankers, who "will say something about it." What the international finance will say to that is, however, very easy to answer. It will, with all the means standing at its disposal, characterize such a procedure as an unprecedented crime against cultured mankind, it will, through its own devoted press with all possible lies and distortions, raise the so-called civilized world against such an unprecedented breach of undertaken obligations, it will speak of the complete collapse of Europe, and it will attempt to incite France as the especially suited bearer of European civilization to an open war against Germany. All that the foreign nations, that is, the Jewish high finance, will say against such an assassination attempt against the total power of the big Jewry.

One could therefore spare oneself both the question and the answer. For, it is clear as daylight that power against which the war of liberation is directed will not subject itself without a fight, since it is not a matter here of Germans, to whom the foreign interests and rights are mostly more sacred than the rights of the Germans, but of men who's most outstanding characteristic is a brutal will to power.

In all such final historical questions, it is idle to make speculative observations on what the enemy will now do, for that the latter will not allow a liberation or revolt immediately is obvious. Quite different is the consideration of what means of power the opponent has at his disposal and to know what strengths one oneself disposes of. If, further, one knows precisely what one must oneself do and will do, then one must observe how the enemy will parry the attack and only then can one adopt the countermeasures. No military plan can determine the campaign beyond the first attack, but it can indeed give the general guidelines for an energetic course of action. So also, here.

In our case, the opponents are hard to catch because it is a matter of an impersonal and supranational power. The campaign plan will therefore have to consider first which powers and interests do not come into consideration as opponents. This is important for not using powers unnecessarily in a direction from which no danger threatens.

Behind the question, "What will the foreign countries say to that?" hides mostly the anxiety that we will in such a case receive no credit or food or other raw materials from abroad. Now what is the situation here?

As a national economy we can in the long run pay for our imports always only through our exports, exchange goods for goods, but not with paper money and not with "credits." All this works for some time, so long as the foreign countries give actual credit, so long as the different foreign suppliers have faith that the German importers will pay the concerned wares with full-value money. But that is possible only if the importers have collected foreign money as exporters of German goods. The fear that we will not receive any cotton or fats, copper, or fodder, on account of the refusal of international interest payments, combines questions together that basically do not have anything to do with one another. Even the all-Jewish big bank power cannot in the long run prevent the surpluses in the raw material-producing countries from reaching the German factories and workplaces in some way, and likewise will the German finished goods to find their way out into the sales markets of the world. This mutual exchange of goods between the different national economies indeed takes place according to the compelling laws of supply and demand. Of course, under compulsion, and temporarily, restrictions and stoppages can occur here as we experienced it in the war, and then again in the Ruhr region[83]. But these are all forceful measures that damage the foreign countries in a similar way.

We can thus suppose with certainty that wholesale trade will succeed in covering the necessary import need. There will always be neutral countries through which these imports can reach us.

Moreover, a national economy which is conscious once again of its national duties and which thereby would become again more efficient in the case of export articles can much rather count on the fact that it will regain the old trust. The temporary intermediary credits in import and export are matters of the trade houses and are based on their personal credit.

Now this question has another aspect, that is, the fear of political compulsory measures on account of the suspension of the national interest payment to the war bonds and other interest-bearing bonds of the Reich or the federal states. Even this is extremely unlikely since it is a question here of the interest demands of individual private creditors of German government bonds, for whose sake hardly any political action can be taken. In fact, also it has not yet occurred in the history of state bankruptcies that a military intervention followed when a state suspended its interest payment. The contrary opinion that, in this case, the French would immediately affect reprisals is in no way to be accepted on logical grounds for, otherwise, the enemies would at that time have had to intervene through military action against the decline of the German mark. The currency declines finally deprived the foreign creditors of German bonds of everything. Now our measures do not at all foresee the annulment of these internal German state debts, but only the cancellation of interest and the transformation of the bonds into bank assets. The cash payment can, on the other hand, be immediately offered to the foreign creditors.

How is it possible that in such a case, that is, when Mr. X. Illinois or Chicago receives the information from his banker that the German government is paying back the war bonds in cash and that this amount has been credited to his account. He would be very angry and set his government in motion against Germany?

A serious resistance is to be expected from no side if a nationalist German government declared the cancellation of interest from all interest-bearing bonds with a simultaneous transformation of these bonds into interest-free assets in state banks or postal cheque accounts. For us, it is important that, through our measures, the community is not harmed, the fact that resistance will be undertaken from the capitalistic side cannot constrain the liberating deed. One will see precisely in the case of this measure that a separation of souls will take place here and that the closed phalanx of those who will feel in this government measure a release and Liberation of work from an enormous pressure will very soon include all workers. Only the bank and stock-exchange circle and those in the circle of small pensioners trapped in their own advantages will continue to stand as their opponents.

One who works has no special interest in the fact that he receives from his temporary assets interest from the banks, much fewer does he have an interest in paying very high interests for credits; with his money as a working capital, he wants to work and earn. For this reason, all businessmen, factory owners and tradesmen will be very little interested in the maintenance of the interest capitalistic system. This becomes clear as daylight to everybody who bears in mind that government interests, as we have shown most clearly, are only extracted through direct or indirect taxes from the work income of the productive workers.

One who has this knowledge clearly in mind cannot be swayed at any moment, for it is indeed just a fundamental principle: that the state can only give what it must once again take away from its citizens in some form.

The interests for the interest payment of the state must, in all circumstances, be drawn from the productive workers. No worker is excluded from this principle, least of all the manual laborers who have no interest-bearing bonds at his disposal. This situation hits him hardest, for the direct and especially the indirect taxes also affect him most severely. Now, that precisely, the worker is called on for the tax through the direct income tax in the form of income deduction before all other circles have already made the worker clairvoyant regarding these matters; the same is true also of all wage and salary-earners. To be sure, these circles are much less conscious of the much more radical indirect taxes, although they feel them mostly in inflation, as was described in the chapter on "Inflation." Indirect tax is the most unsocial tax. It burdens work in favor of pure loan capital. Nobody can withdraw from it, and therefore it oppresses the one who has the least income most severely. On the other hand, the indirect taxes the coal, salt, match, sugar, beer and drink taxes, the personal transport taxes, etc. do not disturb in the least the owner of large capital wealth.

One, therefore, from the circle of workers who is an opponent of such a liberating deed can be that only through lack of knowledge and understanding of these connections.

The last and hardest thing that we should still deal with in this chapter is the question of the removal of the international interest obligations in other words, the refusal of further interest payments for the war debts.

This question is most closely bound with the German historical question, indeed it is the German question in general, for it says: Does the German nation want freedom or slavery?

We know that, in such final questions, only the determined will can determine and achieve victory the reply to this question therefore goes far beyond the range of financial and political observations. But it is essential that a nation that must strive for its freedom know that its slavery is in the very first place a financial-political one, that here politics and economics are most closely related. But precisely this is the new thing about the present situation that it is ruled by financial power political viewpoints and that the military power and political viewpoints come only in second place.

We can indeed speak of the Mammonistic age as of a new epoch. The god Mammon has ascended the throne of this world. Emperor and king bow before him. The parliaments and governments are his submissive servants. He has been able to yoke large movements like the striving of the wage-earners for their improvement. International capital has likewise made the presses of the world serviceable to its goals as it has also made itself the administrator of the cultural wealth and the adulterator of every national indigenous art and literature.

As the most outstanding bearers of this Mammonistic infestation and rule of the world, we have recognized the Jews and so the circle of our knowledge is closed once again with the question of all questions the Jewish question.

The solution to the interest problem is the solution to the Jewish question. The solution to the interest problem in the sense of our explanations is the breaking of the Jewish world-rule because it smashes the power of world Jewry with its financial power.

But the solution to the interest problem is, moreover, in a constructive sense, at the same time also the solution to the social question.

A refusal of every interest and duty payments to the war debts would place international finance, or France, before the question of its takeover of the entire financial administration of all of Germany. If all the taxes of the Reich are removed that now serve the interest payment to the enemy, this would mean first internally a redemption from the crazy tax oppression, a great social-political deed of the greatest scope, and the enemy would have to try to develop its own financial administration in Germany.

But if the German people saw the French or Jewish tax collector sitting in every tax-and pension office, and if the best cows were taken from the stalls of the farmers by these foreign oppressors, then the anger and indignation would perhaps become soon so strong that one night would sweep the foreign specter away with a bloody broom and free Germany.

Whether, in general, a military power would take on such an enterprise in the service of the financial power is therefore still very questionable. The prospects of our will to liberation are in no way so unfavorable as they may have seemed at first, on the contrary. The very first time that Germany unanimously refused the handing over of its "war heroes", with this "no" the specter was finished.

Now international finance will certainly seek other methods, especially the method of the boycott and the entire strangulation of the international market. That it will not succeed in the latter may likewise be certain, and the boycott of German goods would direct Germany, at first just in its economic activity, and for a time also exclusively, to its internal market. It would therefore be here also only the task of a skilled domestic policy – specially through generous promotion in the field of housing construction to overcome the critical times and to use them for the welfare of the people until the new paths to the world are determined.

This opening up of new paths to the world will occur through the breaking of the Jewish domination even among other nations, for the way of the individual nations too to a healthy national economy can only be through their being cured of their domestic poisoning by the Jewish-Mammonistic poison. Then the natural paths of a healthy international trade and economic commerce between the nations will open by themselves and mankind, freed of the Jewish oppression, will experience an age of unprecedented prosperity and, above all, Germany -the heart of the world!

CHAPTER 14

RACE STRUGGLE OF THE ECONOMY

Köhler, B. (1938). *Rassenkampf der Wirtschaft* [Race struggle of the economy]. *In 20-Pfennig-Schriften zur Wirtschaftspolitik* (Issue 5) [20-penny writings on economic policy]. Zentralverlag der NSDAP. Franz Eher Nachf., G.m.b.H., München. Translated by D. Zakal (2024). Speech delivered at the Reichsparteitag of Grossdeutschland, Nuremberg, September 10, 1938.

Translators Preface

In my translation of Bernhard Köhler's speech from the Reichsparteitag of Grossdeutschland in Nuremberg on September 10, 1938, I aim to provide a comprehensive introduction that encapsulates the essence and context of his address. Köhler's discourse delves into the transformation of the German economy with the ascension of National Socialism, starkly contrasting it against what he describes as a pre-existing economy dominated by Jewish interests to the detriment of German prosperity. He portrays the prior economic conditions as largely serving Jewish agendas, thereby exploiting and manipulating economic resources, labor, and policy-making in their favor. Through the lens of National Socialism, Köhler advocates for an economic paradigm shift towards prioritizing German interests, which entails disentangling the German populace from what he perceives as Jewish economic hegemony and reasserting German sovereignty over its economic destiny.

The speech outlines a dual-fronted struggle against what Köhler terms Jewish aggression: the practical-economic front, involving tactics like boycotts, market manipulation, and the undermining of German goods; and the political-ideological front, focusing on reclaiming German economic and political systems. According to Köhler, the National Socialist approach to the economy transcends mere economic reform, embodying a broader ideological battle to restore and preserve German racial and national identity.

Köhler elaborates on specific alleged tactics employed by Jewish interests to weaken the German economy and describes the countermeasures implemented by the National Socialist government through economic policies, propaganda, and legal reforms. He champions a national economy that serves the Volk, underlining the importance of labor, property rights, and economic self-determination as pillars of the German economic revival. Köhler presents the National Socialist economic policy as a corrective endeavor aimed at counteracting the exploitation and manipulation attributed to Jewish economic strategies.

This introduction, derived from my translation, highlights the ideological foundations and historical context of the economic policies pursued by the National Socialist regime. It emphasizes the intertwined themes of racial identity, national sovereignty, and economic self-sufficiency that characterized the political rhetoric of the era. It is crucial to approach this document with a critical awareness of the historical and ideological biases it presents, recognizing its role within the broader narrative of National Socialist propaganda and policymaking.

German Economy Instead of Jewish Economy

Prior to the National Socialist ascent to power, the economic force within Germany was not one that served German interests, but rather functioned under the influence of Jewish interests, to the detriment of the German economy.

Within this framework, the Jewish presence was dominant. Work was carried out at their behest, and the fruits of labor were distributed according to their dictates. Their goals and desires steered the course of labor; their policies, techniques, and rules shaped economic thought; and the maintenance of their racial lineage was the driving force behind an economy that, while operating on German soil and employing German people, primarily catered to Jewish interests.

With the rise of National Socialism, however, a formidable opposition emerged from the German people, challenging this economic doctrine. They recognized the sphere of influence in which they could assert their will and pursue their economic objectives.

The restructuring of businesses and the protection of jobs and sustenance were no longer left to chance and were no longer secondary considerations. Efforts were made to disengage a considerable segment of the German population from this economic system, and to challenge the prevailing view that the Jewish-led economy was the sole viable and acceptable option—deemed by many to be the only logical and naturally apparent choice.

It had been the case that the Jewish influence had secured critical economic resources and channels, positioning Jewish dissolution, exploitation, and the undermining of the populace as an inevitable consequence for German enterprises. These entities were overwhelmed by what seemed like insurmountable forces.

However, with the National Socialist revolution, the economic rights on German land were reclaimed, and the privileges that had been afforded to Jewish interests were revoked.

The Jewish Aggression

They presented their actions as merely a superficial reform of a government system, one that might be subject to varying opinions but still fundamentally significant. The goal, it seemed, was to establish a "compromise between the authoritarian government and the economy." However, they were under no illusions that the advent of the National Socialist government signaled the termination of their economic influence in Germany.

What began as an assault on the very foundations and the sustenance of our Volk, transformed into an outright challenge to the National Socialist economic agenda.

Indeed, the economic policy had become the focal point for Jewish control and influence; it was a paragon of their power politics. Had they maintained this stronghold, then even after being expelled from Germany, they could have continued to exert their sway for decades, perhaps even a century or two, but such influence was never sustainable indefinitely.

This offensive unfolded on dual battlegrounds: the first being in the practical-economic sphere and the second in the political-ideological arena.

Attacks on the Practical-Economic Front

The practical-economic tactics included boycotting and slandering German goods to undermine sales, weakening German imports through these boycotts, influencing foreign governments to reinforce German imports with quotas and similar strategies, and manipulating currency and market speculation to weaken the German economy. These actions aimed to damage Germany's self-sufficiency and disrupt the German industrial output. Activists promoting class conflict and boycotts eroded the conditions necessary for our exports, ultimately reducing the purchasing power of our clients, among other things.

The attempts to sway the market through Reichsmark speculation were mitigated by our robust market regulations, which also prevented the export of German payment instruments. The Jews' attempts to manipulate the Reichsmark's value did more harm to our creditors than to us, as it was their investments that depreciated, not ours.

In other respects, Jewish actions inadvertently aligned with our vital interests rather than causing harm. As a result, especially in the early years marked by the threat of inflation affecting other nations, our ability to engage in successful economic negotiations was enhanced, yielding profits in the billions of Marks.

Our strategy was to demonstrate to our formidable Jewish adversaries that we were as committed to the struggle as we had proclaimed, even if they were reluctant to believe in our resolve. The response was not just a temporary show of force but a critical, decisive, and vigorous assertion of the German political leadership's economic strategy. The 1936 financial reckoning was a planned response to this.

The devaluation that began in 1936 was intended as a countermeasure but proved to be largely ineffective against us — because the actual adversary — whom we recognized as such — was not taken seriously enough to warrant a significant response.

Subsidiary Jewish Propaganda

Jewish economic leaders also implemented propaganda tactics and engineered public sentiment to their advantage, tactics designed to be immediately deployed in the territory of their opponents, our country.

To list a few examples:

- The spread of fear regarding potential confiscations and devaluations in 1933,
- Alarm over an imminent inflation following the financial control over our diligently pursued labor in 1934,
- Suggestions for avoiding the use of the Reichsmark in 1935,
- Alarming actions in 1936,
- Acts of sabotage in 1937,

A comprehensive array of economic boycott actions affecting the revenue sphere in 1938, too numerous to detail individually, all aimed at weakening the strength of the burgeoning German economic organism, diverting payment methods abroad, and inducing detrimental inflationary and deflationary trends within German economic life itself.

Any regulation causing inflation or financial transfer was beneficial for the Jewish economic campaign within German borders. A downturn in German foreign trade and a struggle to acquire foreign currency for Germany were the expected consequences. Any diminution in the German entrepreneur's, worker's, farmer's, or consumer's status and rights under National Socialist economic policy inevitably led to business inefficiency, operational disruptions, staff shortages, and a decline in work discipline.

And every Jew who remained active in economic dealings with Germans and staked a claim in economic life for Jewish interests, positioned against the nascent German economic entity.

Such propagandistic offenses, inconceivable from the National Socialist perspective, must be acknowledged as causing losses that might have been difficult to prevent under less vigilant management of the Volk's body — though these were only temporary and didn't impact the developmental potential, vitality, and future strength of the National Socialist economic organism.

Nevertheless, these attacks also had the unintended benefit of being easily detectable, allowing them to be effectively countered with National Socialist economic policy measures. Thus, the National Socialist economic policy could continually fortify and maintain ideological purity.

Attacks on the Political-Ideological Front

The sheer volume of the practical-economic attacks by our adversaries, along with the years-long materialistic indoctrination of the Germans by Jewish interests, has obscured the significance of political-metaphysical assaults. The Jews have ingrained in the German psyche the damaging belief that any assertive German response or acknowledgment of our unique demand for equitable treatment is typically met with resistance. Yet, it is these very political-metaphysical offensives by the Jews in the contemporary world that are occurring; the fight for survival between Jewish political maneuvers and the people's living conditions has become immediate and has taken on the form of a direct struggle for the Volk's existence. There was indeed a deliberate self-defense strategy in its initial phase, consisting of isolated but tactical maneuvers. Always, there is an advantage in dislodging the enemy from their stronghold: this strategy is also evident in the Jewish defense plans.

The political operating base of a Volk is the intrinsic possession of unique characteristics, an innate life force, and the imperative to safeguard its existence and will—these are the objectives and missions that must be preserved. As long as all decisions and motivations emanate from this instinct for self-preservation, they remain robust and life-affirming. However, once this link is severed, life becomes devoid of purpose, direction, and vigor, resulting in actions that are senseless and pitiful. And it was the Jews who once sought to strip the German Volk of this existential vitality, aiming to subdue them following a similar blueprint.

The Germans had been alienated from the true nature of their heritage and destiny; they were already isolated and merely needed a nudge from the Jews to tip them over the precipice of susceptibility.

Now, for Germans, it is easier to discern this estrangement from the true essence of authority, unclouded by abstract terminology and concepts foreign to German thought and will. Upon this realization, they can become politically re-engaged, emerging from years of inactivity. The risk remains, however, that they could once again fall prey to Jewish machinations.

Indeed, there had been a long-dreaded, enigmatic assault on the German collective being, one that was ostensibly for non-German, specifically Jewish, interests. The proliferation of Jewish legal representatives, brokers, and business leaders did not truly advance German economic power; rather, these were merely the facade behind which Jewish rationale, intent, and economic strategy decisively shaped the economic reality within the German body.

Everything once termed 'national economy' was, in fact, a Jewish economy. What was described as 'economic policy' was in reality a Jewish campaign against our race.

The Economy is the Fate—For the Jews!

The relationship between the Jewish community and economic influence has been inextricably linked to the latter. This bond is marked by the Jewish community's continuous regeneration from within:

There is a failure to acknowledge the inherent, self-renewing strength that comes with each new generation within a Volk. Instead, it is essential to recognize the determination of a Volk and the imperative of its survival and prosperity within the economic battleground of competing powers.

The error lies in their assessment of racial and future potential—not as an outcome of their political trajectory or external manifestations, but as a byproduct of their own racially conscious choices, their self-appointed idols, followed by a misinterpretation of universal Jewish hostility, which politically sustains and defends their Volk.

For the Jews, the real danger lies in an economy that cannot be sustained by coercion or the organizational framework imposed on a racially different people, even under the dominion of a formidable state. Defense is possible only through economic-political benefits that they hold over others.

For them, "economy" is a political dream from which no state can awaken, for it is the political instrument for affirming their racial identity. "Economy" is, to them, the epitome of politics—and thus, post-power seizure, the racial-political mockery aimed at us intensified: because many Germans were still influenced by Jewish ideologies, hence believing that through the "economy" the Volk would be enlightened and molded.

Thus, the Jewish onslaught on the economies of other peoples represents an attempt to secure a platform upon which Jews stand and to elevate other peoples to their exalted misconception that "the economy dictates destiny."

The propagation of superstition becomes an immediate battlefront: when a people succumb to such beliefs, they, along with their customs and deeds, fall under Jewish sway. Their resistance weakens, their structure warps, and their economic policy turns into a mere tool for Jewish interests, with their self-preservation and fate directed by none other than the Jews themselves.

There Is Only Volkswirtschaft

The current Jewish defense strategy erroneously assumes a political domain for occupation that, in reality, doesn't inherently exist. The concept of an economy independent of a Volk is a fallacy; what truly exists is a national economy, embedded within the communal life of a people. Just as any individual economic action is for one's own benefit, so too must a national economy be the collective property of its people, its Volk. Therefore, there are distinct German, French, English, and Jewish economies, but not an abstract, universal economy outside the specific aspirations and will of a people.

One cannot embody a national economy; one can only be influenced by it, for a national economy is always a reflection of the people that drive it. The Volk does not find its purpose within the economy; it exists beyond it, much like birds do not live like mammals, and Germans must be seen as an end unto themselves.

An economy must be dynamic and self-sustaining when fostered by Germans, while it becomes strained and exploitative under Jewish influence.

It should be grounded in its own labor and equitable compensation; the economy should elevate workers within a German framework, or alternatively, it might be constructed on the exploitation of others as seen in a Jewish context.

For the German people, the economy should be nurturing, providing sustenance and care for future generations and the infirm, as long as Germans are at the helm. Conversely, if guided by Jewish interests, the economy becomes a tool of exploitation and domination. In essence, a national economy is the collective asset and lifeblood of its Volk, shaped by the political consciousness of the people, thus shaping their collective identity.

The Volkswirtschaft is The No Man's Land of the Jews

The Jews are fully aware of this strategy. They cannot maintain a political sphere solely by exploiting others; they can only manage their economy by leveraging the political and economic might of other nations, by siphoning off the economic vitality from another Volk, and by using the labor of another Volk to bolster their own economic standing.

Thus, the Jews convince the nations that their economies are leaderless, unclaimed territories.

They approach the nations seemingly to offer aid, appearing initially as victims before revealing their true intentions. Then, according to their race-specific dogma, which they label as economic doctrine, the Jew positions himself to take control.

The Psalm offers a warning: "The idols of the nations are made of silver and gold, the creation of human hands. They have mouths but cannot speak, eyes but cannot see, and ears but cannot hear. There is no breath in their mouths. Those who make them will be like them, and so will all who trust in them."

Therefore, the Jew negates the Volk's property rights over their own economic power to render them pliable. He reshapes rights to make them appear ownerless and align them to his benefit. He undermines the very idea of ownership, aiming to claim the fruits of others' labor for himself.

Jewish Doctrine is a Jewish Defense Plan

Thus, any ideology that deviates from the intuitive and natural understanding of economics, which encompasses the state, society, culture, or the Volk, is fundamentally foreign. This includes the assertion that "Property is theft," a notion not born of 19th-century Communism but rather a concept with two millennia of lineage from Jewish thought.

The misconception surrounding the idea of property ownership, its absolute nature, and the global perspective of national economies is not merely a technical or economic oversight that scholars can rectify. It represents a flaw within a political system driven by a desire for dominance, a system that no longer serves our interests. Instead, it reveals a comprehensive and strategic defense mechanism against perceived Jewish encroachments.

This stance constitutes a deliberate provocation by Jewish interests to challenge the profound economic principles of the Volk, necessitating a political counteraction.

Such actions aim to disinherit institutions and mire national economies in complexities, inciting outrage and confusion among those dispossessed—a state of affairs that could only resonate with the logic found within Talmudic scholarship.

Encapsulation of the Economic Will

The thinker who succumbs to Jewish foresight irretrievably loses their innate connection to their self and their Volk, for they embody not merely an aspect of the economy, but the essence of the national economy itself. All discussions, whether conceptual or structural, regarding the relationship between the state and the national economy, wages, leadership, all mirror this perspective. The focus isn't on peripheral issues that don't concern a true national economy but on foundational economic principles.

Such an individual never experiences self-interest in isolation; instead, self-interest is inherently aligned with the national economy, shaped by the collective will. This self-interest serves as a sophisticated mechanism within the national economy, designed for protection against external threats, necessitating state intervention to uphold certain inalienable rights.

In the realm of the economy, self-interest assumes an almost sacred significance, empowering individuals to endure and assert themselves through challenges, akin to a divine test or a devilish scheme, depending on one's viewpoint. The narrative suggests, "the economy," against which individuals must resist as if fighting off a predatory lender or a ruthless taskmaster.

The capacity for economic decision-making is diminished and neutralized as the conceptual ownership of the economy shifts from its legitimate proprietors to those who adhere to a Jewish business agenda. This agenda, referred to as the "economic protocol," aims to instigate crises within national economies to force insolvency or collapse, thereby reducing the level of goods exchange from which they can profit as masters of economic manipulation, exploiting natural market fluctuations, unemployment, and the global economy.

These conflicts and thought processes diverge significantly from Jewish expectations, portraying a universal economy as if it were a monolithic organism that materializes instantly, in contrast to capitalist ideologies that grant equal rights universally, under the premise that existence is unsustainable without capital. However, this perspective insists on an economy's independence and conquest, filled with declarations of sovereignty such as: "The economy must align with the state to achieve autonomy," or "There must be parity between state demands and community needs," or "Economic leadership should naturally emerge from political governance." These utterances, while seemingly aligned with a National Socialist state, continually point to the Jewish anticipation that the economy, external to the Volk's intrinsic capabilities and sovereignty, remains an unclaimed territory, to be dominated outright.

Thus, they remain ensnared in a Jewish narrative that portrays the economy as a barren wasteland, awaiting exploitation "to a bitter end," until a new economy emerges, one that thrives on critique and thus remains inherently subordinate and compliant to our dictates.

A Bright Sky & a Fateful Abyss?

Just as there exists a household economy, a business economy, and a farming economy, defined by tangible assets within fixed boundaries, there also exists a national economy, vibrant with the life, will, and political essence of the Volk. This national economy is not separate from the Volk; it is an expression of the Volk itself.

An economy cannot be in conflict with the state, nor can politics exist outside of it, any more than one can separate the sky from its color or detach fate from its depths. There is no abstract economy operating independently; it is always intertwined with the state, the Volk, and their collective will, not with the structures or interests of a foreign people.

Just as there is no existence beyond what is ordained by the divine, there is no economy that extends beyond the Volk. The concept of an economy, in its truest form, is inseparable from the community and spirit of the people it serves.

The Race Determines the Worldview

Perhaps only now can one fully understand the significance of the quiet, relentless struggle of the Jews and their adherents against the core principles of National Socialist economic policy. This is not merely a debate for theorists essential to intellectual discourse, but rather concerns a worldview shaped by the racial identity of its originators, which ultimately defines the living conditions and spatial dynamics for different races.

This explains their eagerness to elevate these fundamental principles to the status of "grand theories," securing their acceptance with the entire scientific community's backing and intertwining them with the chains of their faith over time. They aim to shift focus away from political and rights issues, which would undoubtedly arise if Germans recognized their sovereignty and property rights.

Furthermore, it clarifies their desperate engagement in the never-ending debate of "state or economy." This persists even as their "economic protocols" suggest:

"With us, the economic questions are prepared in the background, and the masses are staged, so that it concerns the same struggle against the disturbers and exploiters."

They assert their dominance in every possible realm to "establish their authority" at the Germans' expense, whether it pertains to the authority of a state official or a party official. This authority is seen as unassailable by our Jewish opponents, despite the myriad challenges. It is undeniable that the forces of this dangerous ideology are well-organized, expertly trained, continuously educated, and boldly daring, attracting allies who, though perhaps misguided, aid in spreading their ideology among the German Volk.

The Jewish Representation as a Weapon Fight

Here we encounter a pivotal moment in the economic struggle represented by Jews, as outlined by the National Socialist program, which mandates that this battle be waged not just externally but internally as well.

This moment allows us to trace the lineage of what was once described as economic policy, now witnessing its unscrupulous application towards the German Volk.

It is evident that any attempt by the German national economy to generate prosperity for the Volk is destined to fail if forcibly usurped by Jewish interests.

Moreover, endeavors to cultivate a beneficial economy are fated to fail if founded upon Jewish economic principles.

Additionally, the positive attributes demonstrated by Germans become either neglected or misrepresented when we adopt an economic system that is not inherently ours.

The depiction of all values, as infiltrated into German territories through Jewish emigration, the erosion of ideals, the depletion of superior goods, and the commodification of the Volk's purpose — all these acts constitute aggression from the Jewish side against the German Volk.

Hence, all foreign loans confronting this narrative logically predate the establishment of a German economic policy, challenging German Volkstum with "No Equality, No Mercy!"

This factual and logical dichotomy irreversibly separates Jewish economic policy from German economic policy; the former, a comparison, and the latter, a contradiction or hostility, founded on foreign soil.

The distinction between Jewish and German economic valuation is fundamental: Jews have historically predicated their efforts on the labor of others, refusing to engage in anything beyond their self-interest.

And from the cradle, Jewish schools teach: "The Gentiles must work, the Jews must think. They must plow, sow, reap, thresh, grind, bake. The Jews find - that is all they have to do - 'find.'"

This statement also underscores the exploitative intent inherent in Jewish economic representation, where economic salvation efforts are merely a facade for consolidating their power, as prescribed by Solomon:

"It gives no lower work-duty than the handwork. The Jew has the soil again, he must still cultivate grains. Handwork is traditionally working the earth."

For Jews, interest encompasses everything from downcasting the benevolent to dominating the market, whereas the German economic system prepares for a renewal of labor, presenting itself as a storm of goods open for exploitation.

For them, the economy equates to power, completely alien to the concept of this power serving as a refuge for those skeptical of Jewish motives.

Demanding unbridled power means unrestricted Jewish influence, subjecting labor to market dynamics, distorting our language and understanding of economic structures, thus not yielding to the market's order but to a perceived market freedom.

Work Freedom vs. Slave Economy

The German economy thrives on the principle of labor freedom, valuing the creative contributions of its people to each product. For the German, every creation embodies more than a mere item; it represents a piece of the collective spirit, imbued with inherent value through the transfer of property.

In contrast, the Jewish economic approach is depicted as relying on the exploitation of labor, viewing creations solely as commodities to be traded on the market for profit. This perspective lacks the creative engagement that characterizes the German approach to goods, which are seen as the culmination of a natural and noble endeavor.

Germans perceive their work's outcomes as elevating and refining, engaging in a cycle of continual improvement and innovation. This ethos is evident in various sectors, from agriculture and dairy farming to handicrafts and family-run enterprises, all the way to prestigious vineyards.

The German economy seeks to reintegrate the fruits of labor back into the production of durable, meticulously crafted, high-quality goods. Meanwhile, the portrayal of the Jewish economy focuses on achieving rapid turnover of goods, prioritizing quick market entry and reevaluation over lasting value and craftsmanship. This approach aims to control consumer demand, ensuring products are quickly consumed and replaced.

Property Freedom vs. Overload

The Jewish economic model suggests that relying on borrowed purchasing power is an unsustainable foundation for continuous production of goods.

Conversely, the German economy recognizes the value of leveraging existing purchasing power as a reliable basis for financing the production of goods. This approach fosters a wide array of independent livelihoods, reflecting the German capacity for creating a freely developed communal life. In contrast, the Jewish economic model is seen as extracting the potential for self-reliance and upward mobility, imposing its system across varied individual economic frameworks, thus positioning the Jewish economic doctrine as a mandatory contribution.

This economic stance is underpinned by a belief in the meticulously organized Jewish economic policy, seemingly offering a more advantageous position for a taxation system rooted in Jewish law. This is articulated in the Talmud, stating:

"It is forbidden for the heathen Gentiles to steal from each other, but not from the Jews. Neither a Jew is forbidden to take from the Gentiles."

This delineation underscores a fundamental difference in economic ethos between the two models, highlighting a contrast in principles of economic justice and the utilization of purchasing power.

Wealth Against Poverty

The Jewish economic system addresses the poverty of its adherents through either Marxist strategies of widespread expropriation and proletarianization or capitalist methods of exploitation and wealth accumulation. In contrast, the German economy seeks to generate prosperity from all its resources.

Within the "economic protocols," the Jewish economy is portrayed as striving to transform wealth into significant riches in a manner disproportionate to their earnings, akin to fostering an advanced state of poverty and ongoing fragmentation.

The German economy, on the other hand, is characterized by its foundation on established wealth, immune to any claims by Jews. An example of this is the valuation of approximately 20 billion Reichsmark invested in German bonds, considered as wealth despite the associated mortgage loans and their interest and compound interest obligations. While individual wealth might be seen as a burden to some, within the Volk's economy, one person's debt contributes to the collective wealth.

Speculation and excessive debt, whether it's national, communal, or personal, are viewed as mere illusions under the National Socialist regime, with the assumption that increased security and diligent effort are required to counteract these debts before they can contribute to the German economic policy's goal of asset growth. The task of surmounting the substantial debts incurred over centuries through Jewish lending, perceived as entrenched poverty, is expected to take many years.

Rescue Freedom against Economic Oppression

Hence, the present-day suffering is effectively prolonged taxation resulting from Jewish economic oppression. While the Jewish economy enslaves labor, the German economy empowers it.

In the Jewish economic system, capital is utilized merely as a tool to exert control over labor, whereas in the German economy, capital is amassed to generate employment opportunities.

Consequently, the Jewish economy separates labor from its means, whereas the German economy provides the means to support labor. The Jewish economy diminishes the significance of labor, while the German economy dignifies it.

Moreover, the Jewish economy asserts dominance over space to facilitate labor, as it lacks a meaningful connection to the workforce. This is evident in the "economic protocols," which prioritize the acquisition of Gentile riches and overall indebtedness. Through practices such as overdraft schemes, credit manipulation, stock market exploitation, and the destruction of middle-class enterprises, the Jewish economy seeks salvation whenever it deems necessary.

In contrast, the German economy advocates for liberation from such practices, recognizing that only genuine liberation can benefit the Volk. While the Jewish economy resorts to market manipulation, currency devaluation, and speculative activities to achieve salvation, the German economy upholds the principles of free rescue, understanding that true prosperity lies in the absence of such manipulative tactics.

The Jewish economy subjugates labor to the dictates of capital, rendering it dependent on capital approval and readiness, whereas the German economy values labor as an essential component of economic activity.

Right to Work Against the Tyranny of Capital

To liberate the German economy from the grip of Jewish dominance and to fend off the comprehensive assault perpetually orchestrated by Jewish dispossession against the German Volk, a plan was devised. It was recognized that as long as the German people believed they could only labor when sanctioned by global capital, their self-determination remained precarious, vulnerable to exploitation by Jewish forces.

We refuse to toil for others, subject to the whims of international Jewish power. Despite the Jewish indifference to hunger, we reject the notion of dependency, even if our economic overlords were to decree: "The empire and freedom await, albeit at the cost of reducing our basic necessities."

This narrative of class struggle extends to its most extreme manifestation: "If only a select few can work based on available capital, then only a select few can live. And when the capital available is meager, an entire Volk must sacrifice, stretching scarce resources among the privileged few." Such was the audacious ultimatum thrust upon us, echoing through the night.

It wasn't merely a question of class struggle, but rather a stark reminder of whether the credit business belonged to Pinthus Salomon or Georg Löber on the corner.

Systematic Jewish Economic Distortion

It is crucial to distinguish between the visible and expansible Jewish assault on our heritage for sustained dominion and the means employed to commence this dominion, which may fall away once supremacy is secured. The "economic protocols" meticulously detail the systematic orchestration of economic ruin by the Jews. They highlight the perilous Jewish influence on labor activity, asserting that control over the labor capacity of the German Volk is paramount for resistance against Jewish hegemony and for the preservation of economic autonomy.

This embodies the essence of the Jewish offensive strategy, rooted in a deceptive calculus: "Initially, we will lead the workers astray with false promises and inflated economic guidance, sowing unrest and poverty. This will bind them to their proletariat status. The natural challenges of a free economy will be dismissed as mere distractions. Our Jewish capital will then emerge as the sole essential worker. Even if they manage to secure some means for their livelihood, it will be under Jewish capital's dominion, burdened by credit obligations, ensuring they remain perpetually dependent on us for their daily sustenance."

Among equals, they deploy "economic nature attacks," manipulating laws and clandestinely manipulating economic forces to instill fear and perpetuate a struggle for existence. However, the German economy demands resolute action to alleviate economic strain, poverty, misery, and hunger, aiming to fortify the Volk and safeguard its sovereignty.

The Jewish economy openly avows its intent to dismantle our social fabric, with Jewish capital already initiating the final assault. Another step, and the German Volk would find itself economically enslaved by international Jewry.

The Right to Work: Counterattack of our Class

The right to work stands as the German Volk's countermeasure against the Jewish economic doctrine. With this right, the German people regain their class foundation, suited to their inherent status. It instills pride, dignity, and honor in German labor, igniting the potential for increased productivity and national wealth. This right is not a mere claim of disposal, maintenance, or subordination; it emanates from the Volk's inherent sovereignty, wielding labor as a weapon in shaping economic pathways and successes.

Consequently, the inevitable methods emerge to guide economic viability within the German Volkseconomy, ensuring robust fulfillment of tasks that steer the collective labor towards progress and expansion.

- The economic prosperity ensuing from the right to work encompasses:
- Full employment
- Maximization of goods production
- Equitable distribution
- Price stabilization
- Increased capital inflow
- Vocational training opportunities
- Enhanced purchasing power
- Freedom from indebtedness
- Unrestricted goods production capacity
- Improved material and cultural standards of living
- Encouragement of property ownership
- Potential for social and cultural advancement and education
- Catalyst for the Volk's growth and development
- The right to work serves as a tangible symbol of the Volk community's resurgence, symbolizing liberation from the yoke of Jewish-international financial dominance. The toil of millions constitutes a resolute assertion of German identity in the struggle for freedom and self-realization, affirming the need for a space shaped by German values, not subject to Jewish dictates.

Above all, it falls upon Germans worldwide to unite with steadfast determination, recognizing the signs of the times. This right transcends national borders, embodying a collective challenge to power on behalf of all Germans, imbued with democratic principles. It invites Volksgenossenschaft, or community beyond borders.

In embracing this self-awareness, Germans reclaim their rightful place in history, asserting, “I am a Volk comrade for eternity.”

Battle & War Plan Against Capitalism

Beyond the German borders, the right to work today already develops the struggle of the Völker against the Jewish appropriation, as well as against the Jewish division of the Völker in class struggle.

It unfolds as a worldwide weapon of struggle for National Socialism, which must be born from all Völker, as free Völker and as Völker of the fighting self-assertion.

In the whole world, the Jewish Herrschaft breaks down, and an international struggle against capitalism begins, one calls it anti - capitalistic revolution, the world revolution against the class and financial Herrschaft of the Jews for the freedom and preservation of the free-born Völker.

Class Shapes Environment According to its Right to Existence

Every class is bound by the law to shape the space it inhabits in accordance with its inherent nature, crafting living conditions that align with its essence.

Individuals do not venture into the world to conform to their surroundings; rather, they exist to mold their environment to suit their aspirations for life.

Initially, it was the Jewish milieu that our class, defined by its size and significance, was compelled to endure and ultimately surmount.

What we fashion becomes our environment, tailored to provide optimal living standards for our class.

This naturally entails shaping the internal conditions of our Volk in accordance with the principles of our class. A Volk can do no more to preserve and uphold the distinctive qualities of its class than to ensure that every member is immersed in conditions reminiscent of those that once nurtured the strength, resilience, nourishment, and pride of the class.

What capitalism, what Jewish influence, indeed, what the events of the past millennia have achieved, is not happenstance but a meticulously orchestrated outcome, the culmination of the Jewish class struggle within the economy.

Class Preserves Itself in It's Own Struggle for Existence

The conditions that ensure a class's preservation, enabling it to select the fittest from its progeny, and determining its timeliness, necessity, and fairness, lie within its own struggle for existence. In this struggle, it's not only the material and intellectual goods that are at stake, but above all, the fortitude of the heart: blood, honor, duty, and loyalty.

The more ruthless, demanding, and unyielding this struggle of the individual becomes, and the more rigorous the selection process, the stronger the foundation of the German Volk is laid — with a stricter selection process weeding out those who may be talented but lacking in character.

In this context, we oppose the insidious Jewish narrative, which, closely tied to treacherous freedom, imposes nothing but responsibility and seeks to portray German freedom as its obligation to guide the imposed struggle.

However, none are in greater peril than those who misuse their power to hinder others from fulfilling their responsibilities. Whether through political authority or any other form of power abuse, such individuals embody a temptation that must be resisted. They act as agents of restraint against the realization of our political power, ensnared in the web woven by the Jews.

Social Justice

No heedlessness, no veiled retreat to purportedly National Socialist calls for anti-Semitism, will divert our attention from the urgent task at hand: to represent, in a just manner, the efforts required in the ever-present struggle, ensuring that only the best from the master race are excluded.

Those who aspire to wealth must recognize the hand of fate when it challenges them to combat the perils wealth may bring, particularly in the fight against the impoverishment of the German Volk. It's imperative to remember that our ability to work is under divine providence. Hence, we must strive to ensure that prosperity is accompanied by a deep sense of responsibility.

True social justice does not lie in making life easier for the son than it was for the father; rather, it entails the father shouldering greater responsibility. This shift will initiate a natural selection process within the Reich, validating the effectiveness of leadership and preserving the correct mindset derived from the exercise of responsibility.

The Talmud advocates, "Man should not make his son pursue scholarly professions, but rather have him learn a trade, for the greater the education, the easier it is for the son to act."

Justice of Loyalty, Not of Wealth

It's not a social injustice if one earns nearly 120 Marks per month, or even 240, 1000, or more; that's merely an economic imbalance.

But when one shoulders greater responsibilities, gaining trust and support from fellow Volksgenossen to bear higher burdens, that's social justice.

It's not unjust if someone is born into wealth, but it is unjust if one starts from nothing, builds a fortune alone, and leaves vast riches to descendants.

Having the means to afford a 500-Mark tie isn't unjust, but it becomes unjust when intellect and spirit are constrained more than the people and their leaders.

We don't seek a justice that levels down and provides comfort, as proposed by the Jews, where citizens and workers mimic the Jewish model. Instead, we seek to uplift the Reich and honor all those of German blood.

National Socialism will bring forth diverse outcomes, addressing the realities of varying living conditions. It must offer opportunities for the German Volk and its economy that are hard to reject, while disregarding those that don't align with the true goal: achieving greater wealth with less effort.

Living Conditions & Life Assurance of Our Class

The German Volk has risen to greatness and strength, not because it relies on living conditions tied to its class, but because of the principles of right, duty, honor, loyalty, and fidelity. These are the foundations of our class, which we must uphold wherever we live and wish to remain; they are what we must organize within our space to ensure our own preservation.

The life of our Volk and the endurance of our class are guaranteed if we remain steadfast and true to the qualities inherent within us, refusing to depend on outsiders and nurturing ourselves only with our own resources. We must recognize the forces that sustain and propel us forward.

CHAPTER 15

GERMANY'S POSITION IN THE WORLD ECONOMY

Dr. Hjalmar Schacht | Reich Minister & President of the Reichsbank.

The trade and prosperity of a country as well as its intellectual and cultural life depend on a flourishing world trade to such an extent that we must never tire of stressing the need for international economic co-operation. Although the leading economists in practically all countries have directed attention again and again to the national losses resulting from the world-wide economic depression, and have endeavoured to formulate recommendations for a real improvement, ignorance of the steps that must be taken to effect this purpose is still quite general, and there are no signs of a vigorous policy intended to reanimate trade intercourse between the various nations. Seeing that questions affecting world trade are always sure to attract intelligent interest in a country like Great Britain, I am glad of this opportunity for stating once more my views on these matters, more especially in so far as they affect the attitude of the new Germany towards world trade. I shall try to give a brief account of the conditions which, in my opinion, must be fulfilled before we can look forward to a genuine economic recovery throughout the world.

II

Even a cursory glance at the remnants of what is called "international economy" shows that the economic relations between the countries are largely in a state of utter confusion. Instead of making the world's abundant supply of raw materials and foodstuffs available to all nations through the medium of commerce, valuable commodities are wilfully destroyed. Elsewhere, the production of certain goods is artificially restricted, although there are countries that are in urgent need of those very products. Long-term commercial treaties have been replaced, in numerous instances, by absolutely unsatisfactory arrangements concluded for periods that are far too short. International merchandise credits are indispensable to normal trade intercourse; and their scarcity has produced disastrous effects. Owing to the political insecurity, preference is given by financiers to short-term loans; and the erratic movements of the capital thus used have given rise to heavy fluctuations in the rates of exchange and have seriously affected the currency policy of the countries concerned. The position is made still worse by the excessively high tariff walls, by the maze of import quota regulations, import prohibitions, and clearing arrangements. Finally, there are many countries that have been forced by the shortage of foreign exchange to establish a special regime of currency administration that has resulted in the partial resurrection of the primitive system of barter transactions.

In one of the League of Nations reports issued some time ago, it was stated that the total value of world trade in 1934 was less than that of the combined foreign trades of Germany, Great Britain and the United States in 1929. This is not only due to an enormous shrinkage in the volume of trade, but also to the huge decline in prices, which - in the case of some commodities - was at times even more considerable. The demoralisation of the price-level started in the markets for raw materials and caused widespread selling, with disastrous effects upon production and employment in all countries. The currency devaluations (merely resorted to in some countries for reasons of commercial policy) further added to the existing demoralisation, and were so many heavy blows to the development of international economy. The subsequent rise of prices in the world's markets has been of limited range only and has failed so far to restore sufficiently the vanished purchasing capacity of the countries depending upon the exportation of raw materials.

Many countries have now put their faith in measures intended to revive their domestic trade and industry, thus tending more or less to establish economic autarchy. Too often, however, the close interdependence of the home market and the foreign market is ignored. A trade boom in the former can only last on condition that it is supported by a healthy export and import trade. It is gratifying to note, therefore, that a few hopeful indications of an upward movement have lately appeared, even though it would be premature to infer from them that a structural improvement had already occurred.

III

Germany's present world economic position is probably more troubled than that of most other countries. Prior to the War, the equilibrium of her situation in this respect was ensured by the proceeds derived from her flourishing foreign trade, by her important investments abroad, and by her large colonial empire; but the ruinous terms of the Versailles treaty put an end to all that. The victor Powers were guided by a foolish desire to keep her down for all time, economically as well as politically. This is the only intelligent reason that explains the excessive indemnities and the harsh economic conditions imposed upon a country already completely exhausted by war. The seizure of practically all our foreign investments, the forced surrender of valuable assets, the cession of provinces particularly important because of the foodstuffs and raw materials obtainable from them, and the refusal to return our colonies, have gravely endangered our future development and threatened our very existence.

But this was not all. The war indemnities demanded of Germany were of an extent incompatible with the most elementary economic considerations. For a long time, her rulers endeavoured to pursue a "policy of fulfilment" at all costs. The efforts made by her to that end have never been duly appreciated abroad. They were, however, bound to be in vain; because the only possible way of redeeming those political debts, i.e., the exportation of merchandise and the rendering of services, was barred by the creditor countries, anxious - as they were - to protect their home industries against the inrush of German products. To-day it may be regarded as practically certain that the inevitable effects of the Versailles system upon world economy were left out of account when the "peace treaty" was drawn up. I believe I may claim some credit for having passionately protested, from the very outset, against the senselessness of the reparations policy, and for pointing out that the German colonies should be returned by the mandatory Powers, not only for the benefit of Germany, but also for that of the world as a whole.

War loans and reparations are the root causes of the foreign-debt problem. During the period 1924-30, the immense sum of more than £2,000,000,000 (reckoning the British £ at 12t Reichsmarks) was advanced to Germany by foreign creditors. The resulting debt was about equal in amount to Germany's pre-war assets abroad. The proceeds of the loans, however, did not benefit Germany's national economy in their entirety, a large part of them being required for reparation payments. The impression thus created that Germany possessed a satisfactory capacity for transfer was erroneous. It was bound to be shattered by the events of 1930 and 1931, when the foreign financiers, after first declining to grant any more loans to Germany, suddenly asked for the repayment of the short-term credits, the amount of which was very considerable. Grave sacrifices had then to be demanded of the country's body economic, and almost all the reserves of gold and foreign currency had to be relinquished, but thanks to these measures the foreign indebtedness could be reduced to about £900,000,000. Still, even that sum is so large that the country's diminished foreign-trade earnings are insufficient to provide the money required to pay interest and redeem the principal of the debts.

Foreign critics are apt to ignore the fact that Germany, more than any other debtor country, has complied with her obligations to the limits of possibility. Although the Reichsbank, too, sacrificed all its gold and foreign currency reserves in order to satisfy the claims of the foreign creditors, it was necessary to resort to the partial suspension of the debt service. An even greater sacrifice was the introduction of a currency regime, a measure which is naturally liable to serious objections from many points of view. Germany has never wavered in her determination to pay back her debts. It may be assumed that this fact will gradually receive universal recognition. All the same, it is a great pity that foreign observers took so long a time before they realised the economic absurdity of demanding the payment of capital debts by an industrial country (which, in the long run, can only make such payment by the exportation of commodities), whilst at the same time placing every obstacle in its way - such as tariff walls, import quotas, import prohibitions, boycotts, and similar modern devices - that will tend to render such exportation difficult.

The attempts of the victor Powers to extort from their defeated enemy "the uttermost farthing" led to so much general impoverishment that even now the country has not yet recovered from it. As Germany is so very closely linked up with the world's economy, it was inevitable that such a situation should react upon international trade. In spite of all the existing difficulties, she still ranks third in so far as foreign commerce is concerned, being preceded by Great Britain and the United States only; and it is obvious that so important a purchaser country cannot be cold-shouldered without serious consequences to all other countries concerned.

IV

In order to counteract the effects of the continued world-wide depression and to avert further menaces to the country's body economic, the new Germany had to subject her foreign trade to systematic Government supervision. Although the term "plan" has been applied to the measures thus adopted, it does not follow that a system of "planned economy" has been or is going to be introduced. We continue to look upon individual initiative as the most valuable asset of our economic activities, more especially in the field of foreign trade. Our present economic policy is in no way influenced by any tendencies towards "planned economy."

The New Plan (Germany's "New Deal") was announced by the Government in the autumn of 1934. Its objects are to adjust the amount of foreign exchange used for import purposes to the reduced amount of it earned by our export trade and to prevent any increase in our indebtedness to foreigners. We perfectly realise that measures such as these must complicate immensely our trade relations with other countries, and it was with a heavy heart that we decided to introduce them all the same. But as a certain minimum of foreign exchange is indispensable to us for the importation of vital necessities and as the amount earned by us is constantly shrinking, no other choice was left to us. We had to protect at all costs the good reputation enjoyed by the German merchant as regards his capacity and willingness to pay.

Another object we had in mind when introducing Our New Plan was to base our trade intercourse with the various countries upon a more satisfactory foundation. It is through no fault of ours that, in a large number of cases, that intercourse is now governed by irksome bilateral arrangements concerning the interchange of goods and the methods of payment. Numerous foreign countries have seen fit to satisfy by way of clearing the claims of their nationals upon German firms, claims arising out of goods as well as capital transactions. I wish to emphasise, however, that we intend to comply with our obligations - as far as we possibly can - in any case, and that no compulsion is needed to make us do so. In our dealings with Great Britain we have already furnished proof of our earnest will by acting accordingly. We shall always be prepared to start discussions with any country whose commercial dealings with us have become subject to rigid bureaucratic methods, for the purpose of giving greater elasticity to expand again.

The fact that we have been able to improve our balance of trade proves that the New Plan is working successfully. With a view to the acquisition of a trade balance sufficient to meet the necessary capital and other liabilities, we have tried to increase our exports whilst maintaining imports at about their previous level. It is estimated that the export surplus thus obtained for 1937 amounts to some forty million pounds sterling.

The trade figures also indicate the difficulties our commercial policy has to face. Imports at the rate of approximately thirty-five million pounds a month are barely sufficient to cover our requirements of raw materials and foodstuffs. Owing to the continued activity of our domestic markets, the consumption of goods is steadily increasing.

There is presumably no country in which the demand for foreign foodstuffs and raw materials is more pressing than it is in Germany. Our country is not interested in customs barriers or other measures tending to make the import trade more difficult. All we ask is that other countries should absorb a sufficient amount of our industrial products, so that we may obtain the foreign exchange we need.

Such foreign exchange would not be hoarded by us, but would be used for the importation of foreign commodities and thus for the stimulation of international trade. All countries naturally want to export their products, but a good many of them are by no means equally willing to import. That willingness, however, so essential to a general trade improvement-is nowhere greater than in Germany.

We hear it said every now and then that these imports are solely required for the manufacture of armaments with which to threaten the peace of the world. Apart from the fact that our present arms policy is merely intended to provide us with adequate means of defence and to make up for past delay, it should be clearly understood that only a relatively small percentage of our imported raw materials is used by the armaments industry, whilst the major part of them is absorbed by the manufacture of articles for domestic consumption or for export. Seeing that our own soil does not yield a sufficient amount of foodstuffs and raw materials, we are as yet largely dependent upon products of foreign origin in order to keep our industries busy and to safeguard the vital needs of our people. Germany does not want something for nothing. She continues to be capable and willing to supply the world with the superior grade products turned out by her industries. Accordingly, those in charge of her economic policy regard it as their principal task to cultivate close trade relations with all countries and to improve and expand them wherever possible.

V

Germany is a sincere advocate of international trade, because she realises that she is certain to benefit from it. We do not think, however, that normal conditions likely to last can be restored to world economy by arbitrary and unnecessary measures in the domain of currency policy. I do not believe, therefore, that the devaluation of the Reichsmark would contribute in any way towards the improvement of the international situation. It is quite impossible to effect such an improvement by currency manipulations. The latest wave of devaluation, far from improving the existing conditions, has only added fresh difficulties. The lack of stability in the world's markets has increased, because some of the devalued currencies are subject to much fluctuation - a circumstance which deprives merchants of the safe basis of their calculation and confronts them with mathematical puzzles which, in many instances, admit of no solution at all. One reason why it cannot be said that the currency problem has been disposed of is that no definite ratio has been fixed so far for the principal currencies.

If international economy is really to return to healthy conditions, currencies must be internationally stabilised, and the restrictions imposed upon the interchange of goods and services between the various countries must be withdrawn as far as possible. In that way, a natural equilibrium will be established between the available production surpluses. The nations interested in world trade must therefore collaborate with one another and must compose their political differences. Mutual confidence must be restored. These conditions are indispensable if the disturbing factors are to be eliminated. Unfortunately, there is no evidence so far that a common basis for negotiations towards that end will be discovered in the immediate future.

VI

So long as Germany remains unable to satisfy in full her large requirements of raw materials and foodstuffs in the world's markets, the Government must take steps to ensure that the utmost use is made of the resources that are open to her at home. In that way, the difficulty of obtaining an adequate supply of foreign exchange can be partly overcome. Besides that, the Government is animated by a legitimate desire that the opportunities for work provided in recent years by our own efforts and without foreign assistance for the benefit of the many millions of industrious workers who were forced to idleness during the years of deflation, shall continue to be available.

Germany is making every endeavour to widen her food basis in a systematic manner and to augment the home production of raw materials by means of the new Four-Year Plan. To those of our critics who assert that the measures adopted by us are intended to establish an autarchic regime, I would reply: If you will withdraw your protectionist legislation and thus enable us to find sufficient markets for our manufactured articles, we shall be much better able to cover our requirements of foodstuffs and raw materials by paying for them with our exports. So long as this remains undone, we shall be forced to adhere to our present policy and to deal in those markets only where people are willing to buy our own manufactures under the terms of barter arrangements. The difficulties imposed upon our export trade must necessarily determine our commercial policy and therefore react upon world trade in general; but it would be wrong to hold us responsible for these results. Formerly, most of our surplus of manufactured articles was absorbed by the European countries, which are our natural markets, and most of our imports were purchased in the overseas countries, which are our natural purveyors. For a variety of reasons we should be glad to see a return to these conditions, although we can quite understand that world trade may possibly prefer different channels in future.

Countries or political entities like the British Empire or France constitute almost self-sufficient economic units. Their resources include nearly all the vitally important raw materials and foodstuffs, and their foreign trade is increasingly concerned with territories subject to their own sovereignty; but opportunities like these are possessed by very few nations only.

VII

In this connection I would like to briefly touch upon a subject to which I have referred several times elsewhere. It is the problem of Germany's lack of space, or, in other words, her colonial problem. I submit that its bearing upon the return of normal conditions in international economy is far from being adequately appreciated.

Italy and Japan, who were faced with similar problems, have solved them in their own way, and have thus joined the ranks of the "satisfied" nations. Germany is now the only Great Power without any colonial possessions of her own. Her demand for the return of her former colonies - at present governed under a mandatory system - is the best possible proof of her sincere love of peace, because it is extremely unlikely that those territories would be of any use to her in the event of a war.

The reasons advanced by the mandatory Powers for their refusal to comply with Germany's wish have been refuted so often that I need not refute them again. I have repeatedly explained my views on our Colonial problem, for instance before an audience at Frankfort-on-Main and in an article contributed to the American periodical, "Foreign Affairs." All I want to emphasise in this context is that the return of our colonies would solve the problem created by our lack of space and would also dispose of the raw material and currency questions. The conviction that something must be done to repair the injustice inflicted upon us by the Versailles treaty in depriving us of the use of our colonies, is gradually gaining ground throughout the world. Thus, for instance, the Paris representative of The Times contributed an article to that paper some time ago entitled, "Colonial Revision," which contained, among other matters, the following:

The colonial problem will be the next great question to be faced in Europe. Here as in England there are thoughtful people who think that revision of the distribution of colonies is inevitable sooner or later, and that the sooner the fact is frankly faced the easier and less costly revision will be. As far as Germany is concerned, the colonial problem is essentially an economic problem. Her vital rights cannot be withheld from her for ever. Although the return of our colonies could not immediately relieve us of all our troubles regarding raw materials and space, it could and would render valuable aid to us in our reconstruction programme. In addition, it would tend to diminish the pressure of our exports and to increase our purchasing capacity, and would thus assist in promoting world trade and general prosperity.

VIII

When, on September 30th, 1936, I made a statement on behalf of the Government and the Reichsbank regarding the Three Power Currency Agreement, this was interpreted, in some quarters, as a refusal on the part of Germany to collaborate with the other Powers concerned. Nothing could be further from the truth than such an allegation. Germany is quite willing to enter into any discussions of the currency problem. It is certain, however, that a mere devaluation of the Reichsmark would not alter the existing conditions in any way. The point that matters is the restoration of normal methods of making international payments and thus the re-establishment of the freedom of international commerce. A mere devaluation will ensure neither the one nor the other. That can only be done by tackling the international debt problem and that of raw-material supplies. No discussion will produce any positive results unless and until these questions are made part of it.

CHAPTER

16

1939 ECONOMIC POLICY UNDER ADOLF HITLER

The following is based on a lecture which I gave at the Amerika-Institut, Berlin, on August 11, 1938 before a group of American Professors headed by Professor Dr. Bruner of Teachers College, Columbia University, New York. It provides a short systematic sketch of the various measures of economic policy undertaken by the German Government in the course of the past few years in order to regulate production and consumption in accordance with the aims of German economic policy. For more detailed information I refer the readers of this article to the Weekly Reports of the German Institute for Business Research (Institut für Konjunkturforschung, Berlin-Charlottenburg 2, Fasamenstr. 6)

— Wilhelm Bauer

State & Business

The basis for all government intervention in business in Germany is to be found in the National-Socialist conception of the relation between business and the State. According to the German theory business is subordinated to the State. Formerly, it was believed that the fate of the State and of the nation lay in business, for it was said that business was of such great importance and so powerful that it controlled the State and determined State policies.

In the National-Socialist State the relation between, business and State is just the contrary. Today the State or State policy controls or rules business.

I must emphasize that in National-Socialist eyes the State incorporates in itself no absolute value as is the case, for instance, in an absolute monarchy. The supreme value is the nation which we call in German Volksgemeinschaft, the community of the nation. The State is only the form of organization and the manifestation of the will of the people.

This means that the State is not concerned with economic conditions as long as they do not conflict with the welfare of the nation. The principle of private initiative has been maintained. However, where it seems necessary to bring business into line with the welfare of the nation, the State will not hesitate to intervene and direct business into the desired channels. In Germany, contrary to the usual belief, we have no „planned economy“, but rather a „directed“ economy if I may use such an expression.

The Aims

The aims of the present regulation of production can be summarized in a few words. First, the securing of supplies of raw materials for industry. All measures serving this aim are included in the Four-Years-Plan the aim of which is to make Germany as independent as possible of imports by increasing domestic production.

Second, an increase in domestic agricultural production with the aim of making Germany, as far as possible, self-sufficient in the field of foodstuffs.

Germany has only a few raw materials and has always been faced with the necessity of importing the greater part of her raw material requirements. But as you realize, imports can only be paid for out of export proceeds or other credit items in the balance of payments such as shipping, insurance, or proceeds from capital investments abroad. As a result of the War, Germany is no longer a creditor but a debtor country. In other words, she was burdened with a tremendous indebtedness and had at her disposal no great income from investments abroad, while her other income from abroad is today less than it was before the War. Germany must therefore limit her imports to the extent of her exports, with the consequence that Germany's raw material and foodstuffs imports are dependent on the amount of goods which other countries are able and willing to take from her in payment.

Indirect & Direct Regulation of Production

The German government follows no definite theory in establishing the methods by which intervention in the field of production is to be accomplished. This is one of the most characteristic traits of National-Socialist economic policy. In combatting unemployment, the government did not follow one theory such as the theory of direct public works or the theory of the stimulation of private initiative, but followed both theories impartially according as to which seemed best at the time. The same is true of the regulation of production.

The various measures may be classified as:

1. indirect and 2. direct.

The State undertakes indirect measures when it intervenes not in production and capital investment themselves but in conditions which govern them.

There are four special groups of indirect measures:

1. Regulation of taxes, especially reduction of taxes.

   For example, in order to revive automobile production, which was at an extremely low level, and thus to stimulate motorization in Germany, which had lagged far behind the level of motorization in other countries, as early as 1933 the Government abolished the tax on all new passenger cars, later extending this to all automobiles. This made automobiles much cheaper and increased the sales of the industry. In the last five years, these measures together with the economic upswing have brought about a great advance in automobile sales and a great improvement in German motorization. In 1932, only 19 out of every 1,000 people in Germany owned cars as compared with 41 in France and 37 in Great Britain; today, however, the figure for Germany is 35 in every 1,000, as compared with about 51 per thousand in France and Great Britain.

   A further example of regulation of production by means of tax reductions was the exemption of short term capital goods from income tax. After 1933 the value of these goods could be deducted from taxable income of the individual and from the taxable profits of an enterprise. This stimulated the purchase of such goods and was a means of increasing the low activity of the capital goods industry. The elasticity of the National-Socialist economic policy can be seen in the fact that this measure was repealed as soon as the capital goods industry was fully employed.

2. The second means of indirect regulation of production is price policy. This can take place in two ways: by a reduction in costs and by an increase in, or guarantee of, sales prices. These methods have been chiefly used in the field of agriculture, where production reacts quickly to price changes. An example of this reduction may be seen in the prices for artificial fertilizer, farm machinery and agricultural implements. On the other hand, by a scaling of farm prices it has

been possible to increase considerably the acreage given over to winter barley, the production of fiber plants and oil fruits, and the number of sheep.

3. Closely related to this price policy is tariff policy, the utilization of which is necessary where domestic goods compete with foreign products. This is particularly important in the case of agricultural products, the prices of which are considerably lower on the world market than in Germany. Special boards have been set up in order to compensate for these differences in prices, and are empowered to regulate imports.

4. The last method of indirect regulation of production is the prohibition of new private issues on the capital market. Since new issues are permitted only for special purposes all those branches of trade and industry which are shut off from the capital market are thus limited in their capital investment possibilities. They can only extend their plants, etc., to the degree that their own funds allow. Thus in 1933 a special board was set up under the control of the Reichsbank, to which application must be made before new issues are floated. Permission is only granted for private issues in the case of companies which serve the ends of the Four-Years-Plan, where, moreover, no other possibility of financing their work exists.

Capital Investment Policy

Among the large number of methods of directly influencing production, I have to mention first the government orders which predominate in some economic branches.

Apart from this a good deal of direct regulation of production by the Government consists of the regulation of capital investment activity.

Thus the regulation of capital investment activity really means a planned direction of capital investment. This was proved especially necessary when work was started on the Four-Years-Plan. In a certain sense capital investments were scaled according to urgency. Four-Years-Plan, rearmament and exports are the most important.

A number of measures have been introduced in this connection. They may be classified as follows: -- There are capital investment prohibitions, the purpose of which is to prevent industries whose capacity is sufficient to cover demand, from extending their plants. This prevents needless using up of the limited capital and material available, and avoids over-production and consequent disturbances of the market. We have such capital investment prohibitions, for instance, in the paper industry, in the glass industry, in part of the textile industry and in part of the chemical industry.

In the second place the regulation of capital investments and production by profits and sales guarantees given by the government. I have already emphasized that National-Socialism adheres to the principle of private initiative. However this does not prevent the State, if it seems necessary, from relieving private business of some of the risk it runs in undertaking certain projects. These profits and sales guarantees given by the State are especially important in the production of staple fibre, motor spirit and synthetic rubber. The companies engaged in such production in Germany are private firms; their profits however, have been guaranteed by the State to a certain extent, since their products are of great importance for the economic policy of the State.

In some fields the State itself has gone into production, and has for this purpose made capital investments. The principle that business is to be left as far as possible to private initiative does not mean that the State cannot engage in economic activity in certain fields of production and under certain specific conditions. This is the case, for example, in the field of iron ore production.

After the loss of territory in the War, only a small part of Germany's iron ore requirements could be covered by domestic production. In view of the fixed costs and prices prevailing and under the usual methods of exploitation only part of Germany's iron ore deposits could be mined with profit. The dependence on imports in the case of such an important field as iron ore had to be eliminated. But the conditions and problems in this type of production were so peculiar and so extensive that the State correctly assumed the initiative itself. The Government, founded a company, the Hermann Goering Reichswerke, the business of which is the mining of the low content iron ores which abound in Germany.

Subsidies

One of the oldest and best-known methods of State intervention both here and abroad is the granting of subsidies by the State. Outside Germany, especially in the United States, subsidies are well-known, above all in the shipping industry. Here too private business is not in a position itself to operate an economic branch in the way the State considers desirable. The same thing holds in Germany for some spheres of production. For example, certain building projects, such as the building of dwellings for agricultural workers or the erection of settlements for industrial workers, are carried out either directly with the help of contributions from the State, or indirectly with the aid of loans granted by the State on extremely favorable terms. Furthermore, the production of nonferrous metals has been supported by State subsidies for many years.

Regulation of Raw Material Consumption

The third group of measures of government production regulation concern raw material consumption. Almost the whole of German industry is subjected to the system of raw material quotas. The essence of quota-fixing lies in the control of imports, which was introduced in 1934 as part of the New Plan for German foreign trade. The control is carried out by 27 control boards, one of which has been set up for each branch of industry. Factories which use imported raw materials are only allowed to purchase a certain volume of raw materials abroad. Normally, the basis of the quota-fixing is the consumption of a certain month. But the importance of the orders which the company has to fill, is also taken into account, export orders being given special consideration.

Apart from this system of import regulation there exist a number of decrees dealing with the use of raw materials. For instance, as a result of the scarcity of wool and cotton it has been decreed that all wool and cotton cloth manufactured in Germany for the domestic market must contain a certain percentage of staple fibre. Certain products, for example doorknobs, may no longer be made of brass. In private residential buildings only a certain amount of construction iron may be used. This system of regulation has been carefully worked out and is not too strictly bureaucratic in its application. In many cases the usual raw materials must be replaced by new synthetic raw materials which can be produced without any import. The use of these new synthetic raw materials does not mean a lowering of the quality of the finished product. On the contrary, the shortage of raw materials leads to new inventions and improvements and even brings about as in the case of buna (synthetic rubber) a technical progress which otherwise would not have occurred.

Regulation of Labor Supply

When in the course of the last few years unemployment disappeared in Germany and turned into an ever greater shortage of labor, it was impossible for the government to view this passively, since otherwise there was danger that some industrial branches would be compelled to restrict their production. Thus the government had to regulate labor supply and distribution of labor among the various branches. Labor reserves today in Germany can be secured by the employment of additional female labor, later retirement, and employment of superfluous independent workers as wage earners in industry. But these reserves are relatively small so that the question arises how to increase efficiency of labor.

But the problem is not that of merely employing more people, it is the employment of people in industries where they are most needed. Thus it was necessary to take care that in certain industries there was no diminishment of the labor supply. A law was passed recently which makes any change in employment dependent on the approval of the labor office. This law applies to the following branches and industries: agriculture, forestry, mining (excepting coal mining), chemical industry, building industry, building material industry, iron and metal industry. By this the German government hopes that in these important branches the especially urgent needs of the state will be covered.

Increase of Production

If you were to ask me what success has been achieved in the sphere of production regulation, I could not do better than to give you a few figures which will show you the extent of the increase of production in Germany. Total industrial production in Germany is today 144 % greater than in 1932. Even the peak year of 1929 was exceeded as early as 1936, while today about 30 % more industrial goods are produced than in 1929. The production of capital goods has risen much more strongly than has the production of consumption goods, being now four times as great as in 1932 and more than one and a half times as great as in 1929.

Progress in the field of domestic raw material production has been even greater. Iron ore production has risen from an average of 843,000 n metric tons for the first 3 months of 1938 to 1,226,000 metric tons in the first three months of 1939. This means an increase of 45%. Furthermore, there has been great progress in domestic oil production. In 1938, staple fibre production has reached 155,000 metric tons as compared with 5,400 metric tons in 1933 and 102,000 metric tons in 1937.

Consumption Policy

A number of measures of production regulations, namely all those which affect production of consumption goods, also influence consumption. When, for example, in the interest of a sufficient bread supply it is decreed that all bread should contain a certain amount of maize flour, this is felt by each individual consumer. (Incidentally, in view of the good harvest, this particular measure was abolished on October 1st, 1938.) The same is true of the changes in the textile field and in other fields where the new synthetic materials are gaining a foothold.

The idea of „consumption regulation“ is undoubtedly something completely new to you. In the economic textbooks and handbooks nothing will be found on this subject. Of course, the fact that -- contrary to general belief -- man cannot consume what he desires, is as old as the hills. And even today in the modern economic systems the individual is subjected to many restrictions in his consumption.

In the Middle Ages there were strict provisions as to the clothing worn by the various classes. The Mercantile countries, that is, the countries of the 17th and 18th centuries, restricted consumption for economic reasons, mainly in order to stimulate home industry and to cut down imports. And if you consider your own position you will find none or only a few restrictions in your consumption as the result of State action (you will remember of course the days of prohibition!), but you will probably find great restrictions in consumption as the result of custom, fashion, habit, social viewpoint and, last but not least, industrial production.

It would probably be very hard for you to secure outside the six to eight different forms of straw hats to be found in almost every shop, one which was especially light and comfortable and in a form designed by yourself. This is nowhere manufactured and it would be hard for you to find someone to make you a straw hat according to your own design and measure. Industrial hat production, which is rationally based on machine production of hats, will certainly not do it. While on the subject of hats, it would be impossible for you to walk around in America, in a round plate-like felt hat, instead of the usual form of felt hat, without being laughed off the street, for that would be contrary to American custom and habit. And finally the fact that each family must spend a certain part of its income on food, the amount being in inverse proportion to the income, is most certainly a restriction of freedom of consumption which weighs quite heavily on the individual.

As you can see, complete freedom of consumption is a rather doubtful matter. Once you have realized this, it will no longer seem absurd to you when I speak of government consumption regulation. In the authoritarian states, a direction of consumption forms part of the totalitarian claim of the State, which subordinates the individual to the higher needs of the nation.

The aim of consumption policy in Germany is to increase consumption and thus raise the standard of living of the entire nation, -- especially that of the working class -- to adjust consumption to production and to regulate consumption along National-Socialist lines. The aims of consumption regulation are partly of a political nature and partly determined by the economic situation.

It is far harder to regulate consumption than it is to regulate anything else in economy. For every measure of consumption policy affects the largest unit, the entire population. A decree concerning the iron ore producing industry affects only a few hundred firms. However, an appeal to the consumer affects 19 or 20 million households with 75 million people. This fact alone makes special methods necessary for regulation of consumption.

I have hinted at these methods in telling you about the bread supply and textile production. Of a similar nature are certain limitations imposed upon trade, whereby only a fixed amount is allowed to each customer, as for example in the case of fats in months when there is a shortage.

The most important means of regulating consumption is publicity. Of course, this method does not guarantee as sure a success as do legal measures. But it has the great advantage that it gives the consumer the feeling that he is doing something of his own free will and that the only pressure exerted upon him is that which is exerted by his conscience.

Nutrition

Germany is in the unfortunate position that there is a limit to which those foodstuffs the consumption of which increases with a rise in income, such as fats, butter, eggs, etc., can be produced or imported. Thus, the aim has been to influence the consumer to use as much as possible those foodstuffs which are abundant in Germany and to use to a less degree those which are not so plentiful or which have to be imported. At the same time, there was a possibility of directing nutrition in the best ways from the point of view of health. For instance everything possible was done to convince people that for a great part of the population, for example those who do not do hard physical labor, a diet too rich in fats is not especially healthy. Along the same ideas, great success has been achieved in increasing the consumption of fish. Today Germany consumes 26.9 lbs. per head per annum, as, as compared with 18.7 lbs. five years ago.

A summary of everything desired in the field of consumption regulation may be found in the food list which the German Institute for Business Research has worked out. The Institute classified the food-stuffs into three groups, those whose consumption should be increased, those whose level of consumption should be maintained, and those whose consumption should be restricted.

The foodstuffs concerned are as follows:

- Consumption to be increased: potatoes, sugar, jam, skimmed milk, whey cheese, barley, oatmeal, sago, artificial honey, buttermilk, Harz cheese, Limburg cheese, vegetables grown in Germany, fish, mutton, rabbits.
- Consumption to be maintained: bread, pastry, flour, fruit, lentils, pork, eggs, milk, venison, rice, peas, dried fruits, poultry, cocoa,,beans, honey.
- Consumption to be restricted: beef, veal, butter, lard, bacon, margarine, cooking oils, fats, buckwheat, millet, imported vegetables, high fat cheese.

In Germany we do not have a regular supply of all foodstuffs throughout the year as you do in America. The Institute therefore drew up a list of those foodstuffs which are to be especially pushed in certain months. As an example I shall quote two months: January: pork, geese, fish, cabbage, root vegetables, fruit and vegetable conserves. September: mutton, poultry, mushrooms, pickles, tomatoes, beans, salad, spinach, plums, pears and apples. However,

I would like to emphasize that these are not the only goods which may be consumed, but the public is to be educated to adjust its diet to conform more or less with the fluctuations in the supply of certain foodstuffs. Publicity to this end is not carried out by the Institute for Business Research or by the Government direct but by organizations like the Reich Food Estate (Reichsnährstand) and private companies.

Another measure serving the same purpose is the Anti-Waste Campaign. The purpose of this is clearly to be seen in its name.

Other Fields of Consumption

The problems of consumption regulation in other fields are just as great as those in the field of foodstuffs. It is well-known that Germany must import the greater part of the raw materials required for the manufacture of textiles, shoes, etc. As a result of the considerable rise in income in the course of the last five years, the demand for these goods has increased greatly. Thus there arose the danger that consumption would exceed production possibilities. Since it is impossible forcibly to restrict the consumer in this field, the aim was, mainly by means of publicity, to direct consumption in those paths where there was practically no limit to consumption possibilities. Therefore, consumption was directed to all such services as travel, theater, sport, diora, etc. The introduction of the low-priced popular car also means a direction of consumption to a ware which can be produced in quantities sufficient to meet demands.

Of course publicity is not in itself sufficient. For it is precisely in those fields of consumption where the consumer feels himself free, that it is hardest to get him to use his money for the things which it is desired that he buy. Therefore, publicity has been effectively supported by price reductions of all kinds. Here, too, the low-priced popular car is the best example. This will cost about 1,000 RM. and will be much cheaper than any other car. Moreover, the low-priced popular radio set has promoted purchases in this field. This is being continually improved and reduced in price. The Reichsbahn, the

German State Railroad, has established reduced fares for trips to all large exhibitions, such as the automobile exhibition, the radio exhibition, sports meetings, etc. so that more people can take advantage of these occasions.

Organized Consumption

A special field in consumption regulation is the organization of consumption which is carried out by the large political units, especially the German Labor Front. Here political and social aims correspond to economic aims. Everything is being done to influence the worker to spend his income as much as possible for such things as mean a substantial rise in his standard of living and as little as possible for such things as burden the German foreign exchange balance. Through organization it is possible to effect price reductions, and these price reductions are to make it possible for the worker to do those things which formerly only the better-situated classes were able to afford.

The main factor in the field of organized consumption is the organization Kraft durch Freude „Strength through Joy.“ The following figures and examples show what has been done. Up to 1937, 9 million German citizens had taken journeys and walking trips. The following were taken at random from a list of 350 vacation trips from Berlin which have been arranged for the period from May to September 1938: --

A two-week trip to Upper-Bavaria costs 60-50 RM., while an eight-day stay on the Baltic costs only 31 RM., and a 16 day trip to East Prussia but 41 RM. These costs include everything: railroad fare, room and board, trips, etc. In the last theater season, 1937/1938, the „Strength through Joy“ arranged 7,000 theater performances. For the workers on the auto highways alone some 7,000 concerts and entertainments were arranged. In the last four years 34 million people have participated in the evenings of culture and entertainment arranged by the organization „Feierabend“ which I might translate into English as „The Evening Off.“ Seven million have taken part in sport exhibitions, gymnastics, games, etc. On the island of Rügen a large

seaside resort is being constructed, which will offer 20,000 an opportunity for recreation and rest.

Sea trips take German workers to Portugal, Madeira, Norway and Italy. By the end of 1937, over 180,000 had made such trips. Recently the German Labor Front launched its own ships, the Wilhelm Gustloff and the Robert Ley, which were especially built and fitted for such sea trips. It is planned to build about 20 steamers for this purpose. The comfort and living conditions in that ship are but little different from those in the great liners. Just as on the great luxurious liners, so on the Wilhelm Gustloff and the Robert Ley, you can have your daily bath in fresh water, enjoy running hot and cold water in your cabin, drink ice water, swim in a large pool, play in the sports room, enjoy all the deck games and dance in the evening or attend some entertainment. The land trips which are taken are not different from those arranged by the North German Lloyd or by the Hamburg-America Line. Yet the whole three weeks only cost the sum of 158.37 RM., including the railroad trip from Berlin to Genoa and the railroad trip from Hamburg to Berlin. The usual rule is that only those workers are allowed to take these trips whose income is not over 300 RM. per month; most of the participants, indeed, earn less than 200 RM. monthly.

All these possibilities of organized consumption, which each year include more people, lead to the fact that the standard of living in Germany cannot be ascertained by the usual methods, and also leads, I would like to say in closing, to the fact that the standard of living in Germany cannot be compared statistically with that in other countries. Therefore, when you read any statistics about the standard of living in Germany, you yourselves will have the impression, after hearing about these trips, etc., that these figures do not give the right picture, since the standard of living in Germany is affected by a number of things which cannot be shown by statistics.

www.ingramcontent.com/pod-product-compliance
Lightning Source LLC
LaVergne TN
LVHW011807200926
848484LV00005B/1088